Translating English-Language Theatre into Spanish (1939–2019)

New Trends in Translation Studies

Volume 42

PETER LANG

Oxford · Berlin · Bruxelles · Chennai · Lausanne · New York

Translating English-Language Theatre into Spanish (1939–2019)

Olaia Andaluz-Pinedo

PETER LANG
Oxford · Berlin · Bruxelles · Chennai · Lausanne · New York

Bibliographic information published by the Deutsche Nationalbibliothek.
The German National Library lists this publication in the German National Bibliography; detailed bibliographic data is available on the Internet at http://dnb.d-nb.de.

A catalogue record for this book is available from the British Library.

Library of Congress Cataloging-in-Publication Data

Names: Andaluz-Pinedo, Olaia author
Title: Translating English-Language Theatre into Spanish (1939-2019) / Olaia Andaluz-Pinedo.
Description: Oxford ; New York : Peter Lang, 2025. | Series: New Trends in Translation Studies, 1664-249X ; volume no. 42 | Includes bibliographical references and index.
Identifiers: LCCN 2025008205 (print) | LCCN 2025008206 (ebook) | ISBN 9781800799639 paperback | ISBN 9781800799646 ebook | ISBN 9781800799653 epub
Subjects: LCSH: American drama--Translations into Spanish--History and criticism | American drama--Censorship--Spain | English drama--Translations into Spanish--History and criticism | English drama--Censorship--Spain | Censorship--Spain--History--20th century | LCGFT: Literary criticism
Classification: LCC PS161.S7 A53 2025 (print) | LCC PS161.S7 (ebook) | DDC 822.001/4--dc23/eng/20250508
LC record available at https://lccn.loc.gov/2025008205
LC ebook record available at https://lccn.loc.gov/2025008206

Cover design by Peter Lang Group AG

ISSN 1664-249X
ISBN 978-1-80079-963-9 (Print)
ISBN 978-1-80079-964-6 (ePDF)
ISBN 978-1-80079-965-3 (ePub)
DOI 10.3726/b20046

Published by Peter Lang Ltd, Oxford (United Kingdom)
info@peterlang.com – www.peterlang.com

This publication has been peer reviewed.

To my mum, for all her light

Contents

Figures

Tables

Acknowledgements

I would like to express my gratitude to everyone whose help and support have contributed to the publication of this book.

My thanks go first of all to Jorge Díaz Cintas for his encouraging comments and useful feedback, which have been fundamental to the development of the book, and also to the editors at Peter Lang for their assistance along the way.

I am very grateful to the supervisors of my doctoral thesis on which this book is based, Raquel Merino Álvarez and María Pérez López de Heredia, and would like to thank them for believing in me, as well as for their advice and suggestions.

I am extremely fortunate to have had the chance to spend time with, and learn from, exceptional academics at the University of the Basque Country, the University of León, the University of Cantabria and the University Jaume I. I would like to thank everybody, especially the members of the TRALIMA, TRACE, LEAL and TRAMA research groups, for their support on a professional as well as a personal level.

I would also like to thank Rocío Baños, Catherine Boyle, Geraldine Brodie, Ramón Espejo, Berta Muñoz and José Miguel Santamaría for their insightful comments made at different times during this research and to Blanca Arias for guiding me through the initial steps necessary for the publication of this book.

My thanks go also to the theatre professionals who have been kind enough to provide material for my research and to reply to my questions: Nacho Aldeguer, Eduardo Galán, Susana Gómez and Juan Vicente Martínez Luciano.

I would also like to acknowledge the financial support received from the Margarita Salas postdoctoral grants (*Grants for the Requalification of the Spanish University System 2021–2023 of the University of the Basque Country UPV/EHU, European Union-Next Generation EU*).

Finally, my special thanks go to my parents, brother, grandparents and friends. I am deeply grateful for all that we have shared.

CHAPTER 1

Introduction

During the period of Francoist dictatorship and censorship in Spain (1939–1978), many works for the theatre originally written in English were translated and censored.[1] As Merino-Álvarez (2009) observes, far from being performed only at that time, a fair number of these plays are still in circulation today. The fact that they have lasted over time, as censored translations and as retranslations, poses a series of questions that lie at the heart of the present study.

This research focuses on theatre translation and represents a continuation of the TRACE-theatre studies (TRAducciones CEnsuradas de teatro / TRAnslations CEnsored of theatre), which centred on theatrical works translated during the period of Francoist censorship (Merino-Álvarez 2000; Pérez L. de Heredia 2004; Bandín 2007). The study in these pages draws on a corpus of translations and retranslations of plays originally written in English, introduced in Spain during the years of the dictatorship and which continue to be enjoyed in the twenty-first century, either as stage productions or in published form.

The longevity of the translations of plays produced during the censorship period, together with their retranslations up to and including the beginning of the twenty-first century, is an area that has not received much scholarly attention. Although a significant amount of research has been carried out on plays that were introduced during the Francoist regime (Merino-Álvarez 2003, 2010; Pérez L. de Heredia 2004; Espejo 2017), no analysis has yet addressed the survival of these works into the twenty-first century, either as

1 Although censorship in Spain officially ended in 1978, documents registered in a similar manner as during the period of censorship can also be found until 1985 in the censorship files held at the Archivo General de la Administración (Merino-Álvarez 2017a).

censored translations or as retranslations. Consequently, an exploration of the extent to which translations from the censorship period are still being used in contemporary Spain seems to be in order. The retranslations are also a potentially interesting area of study as pointed out by Chaume (2018: 24–25):

> From a translatological standpoint, investigating retranslation can certainly foster descriptive translation studies. Besides the ever-important analysis of the preliminary norms informing retranslation as a professional practice, new avenues of inquiry have been opening up for researchers. They may include exploring operational norms at the microtextual level, which may question translational rules from a diachronic perspective and within the same culture.

This study broadens current research on theatre translation, adding pieces to the 'mosaic' (Merino-Álvarez 2000: 122) of translated theatre in the twentieth and twenty-first centuries in Spain. It particularly seeks to shed light on the following questions:

1) Which authors, plays and target texts (TTs) from the censorship period have persisted into the twenty-first century (2000–2019)?
2) What translation strategies characterize the TTs included in the corpus?
3) How have the sensitive topics subjected to self-censorship in the TTs from the censorship period evolved in subsequent TTs?

The compilation and analysis of the TEATRAD catalogue (TEAtro TRADucido / translated theatre) helps to provide an overview of the playwrights, plays and translations that have survived into the twenty-first century; these are also used to shortlist a handful of plays for a detailed scrutiny.

The study of the TEATRAD corpus will be approached from two perspectives. The first offers a general characterization of the TTs, based on whether they lean towards the source text (ST) culture (i.e. adequacy) or the TT (i.e. acceptability), two productive concepts borrowed from the Descriptive Translation Studies (DTS) framework (Merino-Álvarez 1994b). This type of analysis aims to achieve a better understanding of the translations of plays that have survived in Spain from the twentieth into the twenty-first century.

The second approach focuses on the evolution of some of the topics that were censored or self-censored during the Francoist regime, namely sexual morality, politics, religion and foul language. Researchers such as Gómez Castro (2009), Cornellà-Detrell (2015) and Gutiérrez Lanza (2015) have pointed out the need to examine the way in which these topics have been treated in the translations and retranslations that have continued to circulate in Spain after the censorship restrictions were lifted.

The current investigation is closely related to the previous TRACE-theatre studies and expands on them by charting the works that have lasted from the censorship period up to, and including, the first two decades of the twenty-first century and by focusing on the translation of topics deemed to be sensitive by Francoist censors.

The methodological framework draws on DTS (Toury 2012), the TRACE protocol (Gutiérrez-Lanza 2005b; Merino-Álvarez 2017a) and corpus linguistics (McEnery and Hardie 2012). Thus, the approach is empirical, target-oriented and concentrates on the detection of recurrent patterns in the translations. The TEATRAD catalogue was compiled and explored from this perspective. A corpus was then built and analysed using TAligner (<http://hdl.handle.net/10810/42445>), a piece of software adapted to suit the structural peculiarities of plays and their translations.

In a nutshell, the main objective of this research is to describe and compare a corpus of plays, first translated during the period of Francoist censorship in Spain, which are still in circulation today. A general characterization of a corpus of TTs will therefore be included, together with an exploration of the translation techniques adopted when dealing with the following topics: sexual morality, politics, religion and foul language. The hypothesis is that the TTs display differences depending on their orientation (whether they are to be performed or read) and on the period in which they were translated (during or after the years of censorship). The following steps structure this enquiry:

1) Reviewing relevant literature regarding the specificity of theatre translation and the works that were introduced in Spain during the Francoist regime.
2) Defining the fundamental concepts of the methodological framework, based on DTS, the TRACE protocol and corpus linguistics.
3) Compiling a catalogue of plays that were first translated during the censorship period and are still performed or published in the first two decades of the twenty-first century (TEATRAD catalogue).

4) Exploring which authors, plays and TTs registered during the censorship period have survived into the twenty-first century.
5) Building a parallel corpus of plays and their TTs from the censorship period up to, and including, the twenty-first century (TEATRAD corpus).
6) Characterizing the TTs in the corpus, based on their translation strategies, in terms of their inclination towards adequacy or acceptability.
7) Examining the topics that were (self-)censored in the TTs during the censorship period and their evolution in subsequent translations: sexual morality, politics, religion and foul language.

This book is divided into seven chapters. Chapter 1, the current introduction, presents the object of the study, the research questions, the methodological framework, the general objective, the main hypothesis and the organization of the study itself.

Chapter 2 offers a review of some of the key works on theatre translation that are especially useful for this study. Two fundamental aspects of theatre translation are discussed: the duality of theatre as performance and literature, and the particular mode of discourse found in theatre texts which is written to be spoken. There is, then, an examination of contributions from the TRACE-theatre studies: the TRACEti catalogue (TRAducciones CEnsuradas de teatro inglés / TRAnslations CEnsored of English theatre), the identification of (self-)censorship as a recurrent theme under Franco's dictatorship and the issue of the continued circulation in the twenty-first century of plays introduced during the period of Francoist censorship.

Chapter 3 describes the articulation of the methodological framework around concepts from DTS, the TRACE protocol and corpus linguistics. It explains the stages for creating and analysing the TEATRAD catalogue, including its design, the sources employed for the documentation and the procedure for the detection of regularities. The steps undertaken for building the TEATRAD corpus in the TAligner tool, as well as for the collection and classification of data, are then specified. The chapter concludes with a discussion of the process to identify recurrent characteristics of the TTs and the diachronic translation of (self-)censored topics.

Chapter 4 focuses on the TEATRAD catalogue and reports on the authors and plays that have survived over the years. The analysis also brings to the fore the translations of these plays that have been distributed in the twenty-first century. This comprehensive overview is pivotal for making a well-informed decision regarding the selection of the corpus used in this study. The TEATRAD corpus is made up of TTs and STs of *The Glass Menagerie* by Tennessee Williams, *The Crucible* by Arthur Miller, *Happy Days* by Samuel Beckett and *The Lover* by Harold Pinter.

Chapter 5 presents the results of the corpus analysis in terms of the global translation strategies applied. It includes an examination of whether the translations are adequate or acceptable in the light of the evidence gathered not only during a preliminary contextualization, but also (and mainly) through macrotextual and microtextual comparisons.

Chapter 6 examines the evolution of the translation of certain topics which the Francoist regime deemed to be problematic (sexual morality, politics, religion and foul language) and analyses the manner in which they have been dealt with in the subsequent TTs of the same originals.

Chapter 7 concludes with the main findings and contributions of the research and suggests potential avenues for further investigation.

CHAPTER 2

Translated theatre in Spain (1939–2019)

The situation has improved significantly since Santoyo (1995: 20, my translation) described research on theatre translation in Spain as 'moorland with sparse and fragile vegetation', although some areas still require further development. In this chapter, the focus is on the special nature of theatre translation and particular attention is paid to the contributions to research centred on the translation into Spanish of plays between 1939 and 1985 made by the TRACE-theatre studies.

2.1. Theatre translation

In her significant work on theatre translation, Merino-Álvarez (1994b) offers a framework for understanding the nature of plays and their translation, which has been particularly useful in the analysis of the TEATRAD catalogue and corpus.[1] She considers theatre to be part of the dramatic field,[2] underlines the duality of theatre as performance and literature and stresses the fact that plays are written to be spoken:

1 The specific nature of theatre translation was the object of interest in some early works (Corrigan 1961; Levý 1968; Meyer 1974; Bassnett 1978, 1985, 1998; Zuber-Skerritt 1980, 1984; Wellwarth 1981; Griffiths 1985; Van den Broeck 1986; Newmark 1988; Pavis 1989; Santoyo 1989; Mateo 1995a; Törnqvist 2002).

2 Similarly, the present study conceptualizes theatre as part of the 'dramatic field' (Esslin 1990), which also includes cinema and television. Despite the fact that each medium has its own characteristics, and as such, they are often studied separately, we should also be aware of their points of convergence.

> When we speak about theatre, we inevitably refer to two aspects that define the dramatic genre and that are indissolubly linked: theatre as literature and theatre as performance; in other words, what is known as printed text (page) and performance (stage). We tend to think that a play has been, or can be, performed and that its author conceived it for the stage. (*ibid.*: 10, my translation)

The inherent duality of theatre texts as performance and as literature has received considerable attention from the perspective of Translation Studies (Santoyo 1989; Bassnett 1991a; Merino-Álvarez 1994b; Mateo 1995a, 1995b; Aaltonen 1996, 2000; Espasa 2000; Törnqvist 2002; Pérez L. de Heredia 2004; Braga Riera 2006, 2024; Bandín 2007; Ezpeleta Piorno 2007; Ramos Pinto 2008; Carrero Martín and L. Lapeña 2020). These studies generally concur on the importance of taking into account whether the translations of plays are performance-oriented or reader-oriented.

In order to understand the performance or reader orientation of translations, their position within the theatrical or literary systems can be illuminating. In this regard, drawing on Even-Zohar's (1990) polysystem theory, Aaltonen (2000: 33) argues that if a text is performance-oriented, it is part of the theatrical system, and if it is reader-oriented, it is part of the literary system, although fluctuations between the two are also possible:

> The two systems in which dramatic texts mainly function and which therefore set up the parameters for their creation, circulation and reception are the theatrical and literary systems, housed within the larger cultural, social and economic systems [...]. Texts may belong to both or only one of the systems, and they can move in and out of them as well as from one into the other.

The scholar highlights two fundamental aspects of both systems. On the one hand, the dynamic nature of the two systems means that, although a translation may have been created for its inclusion in one of the systems, it might be used in the other. Indeed, as Merino-Álvarez (1994b) notices, some translations intended for performance are also published, while other translations that have been originally published with readers in mind may end up on stage. Aaltonen (2000) and Merino-Álvarez (1994b) suggest studying theatre translations in relation to the system for which they were originally produced. In the present book, the term *performance-oriented target text* (or *performance-oriented translation*) refers to a translation intended for use in a theatrical production, whereas *reader-oriented target text* (or *reader-oriented translation*) includes those with publication in mind.[3]

As Aaltonen (2000: 33) also notes in the above quotation, theatrical and literary systems have their own characteristics, which affect the creation, circulation and reception of texts. In a later work, Aaltonen (2003: 144) underlines the challenges of conducting research in theatre translation, claiming that 'theatre translation is a problematic and complex research site, which is, at least partly, to blame for the lack of academic interest in objects in this environment.' Some of the differences between the theatrical and literary systems are reviewed in the next paragraphs, following the tripartite process alluded to by Aaltonen (2000), that is, creation, circulation and reception of theatre translations.

Firstly, the creation of a theatrical work as performance or as literature involves the participation of different agents. In the case of theatrical productions, a substantial number of professionals take part in them in addition to the target authors,[4] including producers, directors, actors, sound and light technicians, stage designers and, under the Francoist regime in Spain, also censors whose authorization was necessary before a play could be staged. Aaltonen (2000: 29) refers to all these agents as 'tenants' who add meaning through their particular interpretation of a play: 'Readers are tenants who move into texts and occupy them for a while. In the theatre there are many tenants, and just as many meanings to be taken of texts.' In contrast to this multiplicity of agents, in reader-oriented translations, framed as they are within the literary system, only target translators, revisors and editors are typically involved. Under Franco's dictatorship, publications also had to undergo a process of censorship, and the boards of censors were different from those used for theatrical productions.

Target authors show differences depending on whether they operate in the theatrical or the literary system. In the case of Spain, Merino-Álvarez

3 Similar distinctions may be found in the literature, although terminology varies. For example, Aaltonen (2000: 33) uses the term 'drama translation' to include 'translation work for both the literary and theatrical system', and 'theatre translation' to refer to that 'confined to the theatrical system alone'.

4 In this study, as in Merino-Álvarez's (2000), the term *target author* is used to refer to those responsible for the actual target texts, since they include different profiles.

(1995) registers the presence of three main target author profiles in performance-oriented translations: theatre professionals (directors, actors, producers), playwrights or writers specializing in other genres and professional translators, although, as Brodie and Cole (2017) note, a target author can belong to more than one of these categories. Merino-Álvarez (1994b) also observes collaborations between practitioners with links to translation and to theatre, such as playwrights, actors or directors. In her study of three plays translated for the stage from English into Italian and German in the twentieth century, Perteghella (2004) identifies different collaborations: (1) between an academic, who is also a specialist translator, and a novelist; (2) between the original playwright as a self-translator and a specialist translator; and (3) between two directors who are also translators. Drawing on interviews with different agents who collaborated on productions staged in London in 2004, Brodie (2017) offers a very interesting view of target authors and their ways of cooperating, including language specialists familiar with the theatrical sphere, who are in charge of literal translations, playwrights who derive indirect translations from literal ones and translators who carry out direct translations. Of course, as Aaltonen (2000: 32) notes, the profiles and collaborations of target authors can adopt different forms in different theatrical systems:

> Theatrical systems and subsystems may vary in their choice of professionals who will be responsible for the rewriting or translation of the foreign texts. Some may employ two categories of translators, that is, those who produce the 'literals' […] and those who write the stage versions on the basis of these literals […]. Often for commercial reasons, some systems may employ surrogate translators who contribute primarily their name and status to the translation, but who may also take part in writing the stage versions.

The issue of fame and power in the selection of target authors, together with their socio-cultural visibility, seems to play an important role in different theatrical systems, including the Spanish (Merino-Álvarez 1994b; Aaltonen 2000; Brodie 2017). As Brodie (2017: 1) argues, 'identity and position feature largely in the projection of performance.' On the other hand, reader-oriented translations are usually signed by professional translators (Merino-Álvarez 1993a).

Secondly, the circulation of works clearly differs in the theatrical and literary systems. (Translated) plays can reach spectators or readers either through performances or from the sale of books (Merino-Álvarez 1994b), and both avenues are also possible in the new digital environments, through recorded performances as well as electronic and audio books. In addition, within each system, subsystems are found relating to different theatre venues and publishers targeting audiences with dissimilar tastes and expectations. As Aaltonen (2000: 31) puts it, the theatrical system 'is in itself a complex network of subsystems, mainstream and fringe theatres, as well as various producer and consumer subsystems, who all have their expectations and preferences *vis-à-vis* the discourse of theatre texts'. In this respect, Brodie (2017: 15) notes the potential influence in performance-oriented translations of the venue in which works are staged: 'site participates in the concretization of a translation through performance [...]. And not only site. The organization which inhabits that site has its own ethos, which impinges on the development of a translated play'. For instance, Merino-Álvarez (2000) emphasizes the fact that during the Francoist period in Spain there was a key distinction between commercial and non-commercial theatres, the latter including the so called *Teatros de cámara y ensayo* [chamber theatres], which normally received a lower number of patrons than commercial ones and in which more avant-garde and risqué plays were staged. Regarding the literary system, some Spanish publishers specialize in the publication of reader-oriented translations, for example, Cátedra, while others focus on the publication of translations linked to theatrical productions, such as Escelicer (Merino-Álvarez 1994b).

Finally, the reception of translations varies significantly between the theatrical and the literary systems. In the former, the work is received through the acoustic and visual channels, by means of multiple semiotic systems. Kowzan (1975) differentiates five categories – spoken text, bodily expression, actor's external appearance, playing space and non-spoken sound – while Fischer-Lichte (1999) lists fourteen – sounds, music, linguistic signs, paralinguistic signs, mimic signs, gestural signs, proxemic signs, mask, hair, costume, stage conception, stage decoration, props and lighting. In this respect, Delabastita (1989) alludes to the similarity between theatre and cinema in their use of some of these codes, and Chaume's (2004a) typology of channels and signifying codes in audiovisual programmes also shows some points of contact. For instance, in theatre, as in audiovisual productions, linguistic, paralinguistic, musical and special effects codes are conveyed through the acoustic channel, whereas iconographic and mobility codes are transmitted through the visual channel.

Bassnett (1985: 101–102) believes that the target author of a performance-oriented translation should be aware of the multiple codes at play, without forgetting the importance of the written text for the translation process: 'The written text, *troué* though it may be, is the raw material on which the translator has to work.' As noted by Merino-Álvarez (1994a: 130), play texts are made up of two components: 'frame (stage directions, name of the character, etc.) and dialogue (the speech to be uttered on the stage)'. In performance, the frame is generally transformed into different codes that are transmitted through the acoustic and visual channels – such as paralinguistic and mobility codes – while the dialogue is linguistically coded and received through the acoustic channel. In the case of theatre as literature, translations are perceived through the visual channel in the form of a written text.

Other reception factors hinge on this difference between theatre as performance and theatre as literature. According to Törnqvist (2002), some of these aspects are common to theatre, cinema, television and radio productions, while others are exclusive to the theatre. Regarding the common factors, Törnqvist (*ibid.*) observes that productions are linear and subject to time constraints,[5] making it especially important for translations to be easily understood. On the other hand, in theatre as literature, readers can go back and forth in the text and the physical page allows for the addition of translator's notes if necessary. Furthermore, stage productions are closed in the sense that the text is accessed through a series of decisions, such as the type of mise-en-scène, and simultaneous, since several characters and actions may be perceived on stage at the same time. By contrast, in literary texts, nonverbal aspects are open to the reader's imagination, and the reading evolves in a consecutive rather than a simultaneous way. When compared with cinema, television and radio performances, Törnqvist (*ibid.*) suggests that the characteristics of theatrical productions derive from in-person communication, such as direct feedback from the audience in the form of their reactions to what happens on stage, the uniqueness of each performance, the spatial conditions of the mise-en-scène due to the shape and size of the stage or the location of the audience and the importance of proxemics.

5 Although they are generally conceived for linear viewing, recorded audiovisual productions allow viewers to fast forward, rewind and pause at their convenience.

2.1.1. *Translation strategies in performance- and reader-oriented texts*

Aaltonen (2000: 36) argues that the difference between performance- and reader-oriented translations lies not in textual characteristics but in their function within the theatrical or literary system: 'only the function [...] rather than any intrinsic properties defines both a dramatic text and a theatre text.' In other words, performance or reader orientation is an extratextual consideration. Yet, these two systems show differences in terms of the translation strategies that are commonly implemented.

Aaltonen (*ibid.*: 41) observes that systemic preferences regarding global translation strategies are often made explicit through the comments of practitioners: 'In theatre translation the attributes "academic", "scholarly" or "literary" are used to describe one pole and "adaptation" the other, and a systemic prioritization of one strategy over the other is often made plain.' In her opinion, translation behaviour involving a high degree of alteration of the original is found more often in the theatrical than in the literary system, an observation shared in studies written by such scholars as Merino-Álvarez (1994b), Kruger (2004a, 2004b), Pérez L. de Heredia (2004) Ramos Pinto (2008, 2012), Mateo (2010a) and Cebrián (2015). Aaltonen (2000: 41) notes that target authors claim that this is due to the particular needs required by staging a work or by notions such as *performability*,[6] while in the literary system faithfulness to the original seems to be prioritized:

> In the theatre, orality, immediacy and communality unavoidably introduce a new dimension to the translation of texts, and, while in literary translation contemporary Anglo-American discourse emphasises the translator's invisibility and the faithfulness of the translation (Venuti, 1995a: 1), theatre translation actively rewrites, or adapts, many aspects of the source text, justifying this strategy with references to the 'requirements of the stage' and criteria such as 'playability' and 'speakability'.

6 As in the case of the concepts of *playability* and *speakability* (Bassnett 1991b; Aaltonen 1996; Schultze 1998), that of *performability*, which appears in a number of studies in relation to performance-oriented translation (Sanderson 2002; Johnston 2004), lacks a clear definition to make it useful in this context. For a thorough revision of these concepts, see Espasa (2000, 2009).

Research conducted by Merino-Álvarez (1994b) at a macrotextual level on a hundred theatre translations shows a myriad of translational approaches in which a tendency to acceptability can be detected in performance-oriented translations, exemplified in the numerous cases of omissions and additions of characters' utterances. The tendency in the case of reader-oriented translations is towards adequacy, thus pointing to different conventions in the theatrical and literary systems. The four performance-oriented TTs analysed at a microtextual level in her study reflect diverse approaches in relation to the STs, whereas the reader-oriented translations show a greater proximity to the ST. More specifically, Merino-Álvarez (*ibid.*) observes that the performance-oriented TT of *Busybody* (Jack Popplewell, 1965, transl. 1967), signed by Vicente Balart as the translator, was adapted specifically to suit the actress Isabel Garcés. In the case of *Mulatto* (Langston Hughes, 1935, transl. 1964), signed by Alfonso Sastre, a new play was created with the introduction of numerous additions to a previous Argentinian translation. Similarly, the TT of *A View from the Bridge* (Arthur Miller, 1955, transl. 1980), signed by the director José Luis Alonso, was an adapted copy of an Argentinian translation. On the other hand, the performance-oriented translation of *Passion* (Edward Bond, 1971, transl. 1989), by Carla Matteini, can be said to be adequate just like the reader-oriented translation of *A View from the Bridge* by Jacobo Muchnik and Juan Ángel Cotta, published in 1956.

In her study of theatre translations in Finland, Aaltonen (2003) puts forward the idea that the different ways of approaching the (re)translations of plays in the theatrical and literary systems are influenced by the precision with which different aspects of their reception are defined, such as the part played by the audience, the time and place of the staging and the expected life span of the text. For the author, 'translation strategies in targeted retranslation can be many. [...] The texts, although they may exceed the life span of a production, are mainly seen as material for a particular production' (*ibid.*: 147), whereas 'loosely targeted (re)translations are not likely to highlight any particular thematic reading of their source text but rather encourage the perception of it as an open text. Their expected life span is long' (*ibid.*: 155–156). When discussing the variety of performance-oriented translations, Aaltonen (*ibid.*: 141) argues that retranslation 'is an inherent part of text production in the Western text-based theatre, where texts are constantly being rewritten for new performances', and goes on to indicate some of the reasons for retranslation:

> One of the most common motivations for commissioning a retranslation is the need to update the language, which is done at regular intervals [...]. Another motivation may be a director's wish to highlight a particular reading of the play or even a particular translation strategy. Practical considerations may also give rise to a retranslation. (*ibid.*: 154)

Kruger (2004a) compares the presence of a number of prototypical conversational traits (contractions, discourse markers, first and second person pronouns, time and place adverbs and the like) in two translations of *The Merchant of Venice* (William Shakespeare, 1598, transl. 1949 and 1991) into Afrikaans: a performance-oriented and a reader-oriented version. She finds that the former includes a higher number of conversational traits; a difference that is statistically significant. In another work, Kruger (2004b: 323) offers an in-depth examination of discourse markers and claims that the stage translator 'has ingeniously applied a variety of discourse markers to bridge the gap between real conversation and the fabricated, "tidied up speech" (Herman 1998: 24) usually found in dramatic dialogue'.

Pérez L. de Heredia (2004) focuses on the period that goes from 1939 to 1963 in Spain and identifies cases of self-censorship in several performance-oriented TTs of *A Streetcar Named Desire* (Tennessee Williams, 1947, transl. 1951 and 1956), *Cat on a Hot Tin Roof* (Tennessee Williams, 1955, transl. 1958 and 1959), *Sweet Bird of Youth* (Tennessee Williams, 1959, transl. 1962) and *Desire Under the Elms* (Eugene O'Neill, 1924, transl. 1953 and 1961), which illustrate the domestication of problematic moral discourse. The tendency towards acceptability found in these translations contrasts with the adequacy of the reader-oriented TTs of Tennessee Williams's *A Streetcar Named Desire* (transl. 1961 and 1966) published in Argentina.

Ramos Pinto (2008) explores several translations of *Pygmalion* (George Bernard Shaw, 1912, transl. 1945, 1962, 1972, 1974 and 1987) within the context of twentieth century Portugal. Focusing on linguistic variation, she puts forward the idea that performance-oriented translations are closer to the target culture, leaning towards acceptability, while reader-oriented translations make repeated use of footnotes and, as such, lean towards adequacy. She also observes that reader-oriented translations tend to standardize the dialogue, bringing it closer to written discourse than to speech, and therefore prioritize adequate solutions. In a later publication, Ramos Pinto (2012) reiterates that reader-oriented translations seem to be closer to their STs, whereas performance-oriented ones reveal specific interpretations of a text in line with the objectives of a particular theatrical production, a commonly accepted approach in the field.

Focusing on the treatment of humour in the Spanish translations of the plays *An Ideal Husband* (Oscar Wilde, 1895, transl. 1918) and *A Woman of No Importance* (Oscar Wilde, 1893, transl. 1911), Mateo (2010a) observes that in the performance-oriented translations references to the source culture are deleted, implying a greater degree of domestication than in reader-oriented translations. She further argues that, when translating humour, the solutions may be related to some of the characteristics of the performance such as 'the immediacy and the need for complicity between the spectators and the text that is heard on stage' (*ibid.*: 331, my translation).

Cebrián (2015) compares the translation into Spanish of cases of deixis found in the first two acts of a performance- and a reader-oriented translation of *Cat on a Hot Tin Roof* (Tennessee Williams, 1955, transl. 1966 and 2000), and concludes that the latter includes fewer deictic markers than the performance-oriented translation. Commenting on her findings, she states that 'working with a text that *a priori* is not going to be performed might lead to the avoidance – consciously or unconsciously – of mechanisms that can boost the theatrical potential of the text, such as the deixis' (*ibid.*: 190, my translation).

A bias towards acceptability is also found in other studies that focus exclusively on performance-oriented translations (Aaltonen 1996; Brodie 2017; O'Leary 2018; Marinetti 2020). When discussing the various translational approaches to the ST followed in different theatrical systems, Boyle's (1992: 117) claim is especially interesting: 'if theatre is holding "as 'twere, the mirror up to nature" then the question is not what any given play reflects of its country of origin, but of the country in which it is being performed.' Similarly, Johnston (2012: 45) foregrounds the importance of making a connection with the sensibilities of the target audience in performance-oriented translation, when he claims that: 'Translation, and especially translation for the theatre, is a process that engineers movement – movement between the narratives, concepts and structures of life that are embodied in foreign-language texts and the perceptual and conceptual space of the spectator.'

Aaltonen (1996: 210) concludes that partial acculturation can be observed in the way in which cultural aspects are dealt with in the translations of Irish plays performed in Finland, noting that 'audiences have to be able to relate to an unfamiliar reality, and cultural specificity will therefore need to be manipulated in such a way that there will be enough common ground in the play for them to understand it.'

In her analysis of the translations used in the staging of eight productions of foreign plays in London in 2004, Brodie (2017) argues that most of the solutions lean towards acceptability. An example of this occurs in the political rewriting of *The House of Bernarda Alba* (Federico García Lorca, 1945, transl. 2005) by David Hare, a playwright with an openly political profile, who worked the final text on a literal translation by the actor and translator Simon Scardifield. This extreme target-oriented rewriting is referred to by Brodie (*ibid.*) as 'the Hare effect'.

On the topic of translating with a political agenda, O'Leary (2018: 59) examines Alfonso Sastre's transfer into Spanish of various plays by Sean O'Casey and concludes that, in the 1960s and 1970s in Spain, Sastre's 'decision to comment on politics and social transformation using texts in translation allowed him to discuss radical change indirectly', a point also raised by Merino-Álvarez (1994b) in the already mentioned Sastre's translation of the play *Mulatto*.

In her study of performance-oriented translations of the Italian playwright Carlo Goldoni in eighteenth century Britain, Marinetti (2020: 2) notes that 'the rewriting or domestication of a text is not just a matter of linguistic difference, but the manifestation of visible and invisible cultural forces which actively shape translations in the culture for which they are intended.' In particular, she highlights the role played by censorship following the *Licencing Act* of 1737, as well as the self-censorship undertaken by translators and the participation of actors in the creation of performance-oriented translations.

When discussing the translation strategies applied in various theatrical and literary systems, Aaltonen (2000: 45) argues that a label is needed to denote transfers in which significant changes are introduced to the ST: 'there is a need for a term to describe a translation strategy which does not translate the source text in its entirety but makes additions, omissions and changes to the general dramatic structure of its settings, plot and characters, thus suggesting new readings from it.' Research into the nomenclature associated with reader- and, particularly, performance-oriented TTs has highlighted a lack of consistency in the use of such terms (Merino-Álvarez 1992a; Aaltonen 2000; Braga Riera 2006, 2011; Perteghella 2008; Brodie 2017, 2018). According to Merino-Álvarez (1994b), the term *translation* was typically used in the second half of the twentieth century in Spain to refer to reader-oriented TTs, while *version* and *adaptation* were used more frequently for performance-oriented TTs, although *translation* was also employed and, more sporadically, other labels such as *free version* or *translation and adaptation*. This multiplicity of terms used in the theatrical system can be related to extratextual issues, such as the status of a given work within that system. For instance, in her discussion of the UK theatrical system, Brodie (2017: 159) suggests that '[t]he activity known as *translation* in the theatre is not perceived as sufficiently creative for celebrity billing, whereas the product known as the *adaptation* or *version* has a recognized existence alongside the original source text.' On this issue, Merino-Álvarez (1992a: 85, my translation) suggests that a textual analysis is needed to establish any potential connections among the various expressions used and the actual transfer carried out and makes the case for a 'descriptive study of what is actually hidden behind the label'.

To sum up, numerous authors have identified differences between the theatrical and literary systems, not only in terms of their extratextual traits, but also in relation to the translation strategies applied in each system. In order to elicit these strategies, an empirical study is essential.

2.1.2. The translation of prefabricated orality

Researchers specializing on theatre translation have commented on the nature of theatrical texts as written to be spoken and have also underlined this oral dimension as part of the specificity of original and translated plays (Merino-Álvarez 1994b; Mateo 1995b; Espasa 2001a; Ezpeleta Piorno 2007; Teruel *et al.* 2009; Carrero Martín and L. Lapeña 2020; Braga Riera 2024). Dramatic dialogue is characterized by a particular mode of discourse which has been termed *prefabricated orality* (Chaume 2004a; Baños 2009). This concept refers to 'an orality which may seem spontaneous and natural, but which is actually planned' (Baños and Chaume 2009: online). As Espasa (2001b: 60, my translation) points out: 'Dubbing and theatre share the paradoxical task of (re)creating credible texts, which seem to be oral although they are based on written texts or scripts, and what is ultimately provided for the actors/dubbing team comes in a written form.'

Following Gregory and Carroll's (1978: 42) classification of modes of discourse, dramatic texts correspond to 'non-spontaneous speech', which means that theatre texts, like audiovisual ones, can be described as texts that are written to be spoken as if they had not been written down. Given the dual nature of theatre as performance and as literature, House (1981) argues that plays can also be understood as written to be read as if they were speech. Performance-oriented TTs can therefore be defined as 'written to be spoken as if not written', while reader-oriented TTs would be 'written to be read as if heard'.

As Baños (2009) notes, non-spontaneous speech is located in an intermediate position on a scale between spoken and written discourse. Briz (2001) also sees the various instances of spoken language in writing and of written language in speaking as part of a continuum, observing that a formal or colloquial register may be used in both speech and writing or that either of these can be imitated. Plays evoke speech and, depending on the situation, they mirror different types of discourse and registers, among which we can find those that are typical of spoken language, notably conversation and colloquial register.

Pfister (1988) claims that there is a clear distinction between spontaneous interactions and theatre dialogue, since the latter hinges on two communication systems: an internal one (between characters) and an external one (between the author and the audience, be them spectators or readers). For the scholar, the degree of deviation of theatre dialogue from spontaneous speech is affected by historical and typological factors, arguing that there is less deviation in naturalistic plays and more in those written in verse. In this sense, Burton (2014) emphasizes the general view that modern theatre is essentially conversational and presents a study that links linguistic traits of (original) plays with those of conversation.

Research on prefabricated orality shows how the evocation of orality is realized through the use of linguistic traits that are specific to spontaneous speech (Chaume 2004a; Baños and Chaume 2009; Pavesi 2009; Baños 2014; Arias-Badia 2020). Those traits are *orality markers*, defined by

Baños (2014: 408–409) as 'features typifying spontaneous spoken register used in prefabricated dialogue to reinforce its orality and to convey a false sense of spontaneity', and key to the study of prefabricated orality in dramatic dialogue. Baños and Chaume (2009) and Baños (2009, 2024) propose an analytical framework for the study of orality markers in audiovisual texts based on works that outline detailed attributes of orality in Spanish and English (Vigara 1992; Briz 1996, 2001; Carter and McCarthy 1997; Biber *et al.* 1999) as well as of prefabricated orality (Chaume 2004a; Pavesi 2008; Romero-Fresco 2009a). This framework considers the phonetic-prosodic, morphological, syntactic and lexical-semantic levels, the latter two being the ones where most of these traits are concentrated. To date, this is the most extensive classification of orality markers in translated audiovisual texts for the linguistic transfer of English to Spanish.

The aforementioned distinction established by Pfister (1988) between the two communication systems in theatre, that is, the internal one between characters and the external one between the author and the audience, is useful to understand the relevance of orality markers in dramatic texts. In the former, orality markers have a similar function as those described in the literature on spontaneous spoken language (Biber *et al.* 1999; Briz 2001), with the difference that their use is planned. The role played by orality markers in the external communication system is different. For viewers/readers, these traits evoke spontaneous spoken discourse and are crucial for determining whether dialogue is credible and plausible (Baños and Chaume 2009; Romero-Fresco 2009a; Zabalbeascoa 2012; Arias-Badia 2020; Baños 2021). In this regard, Chaume (2007: 79) indicates that the credible representation of spontaneous spoken discourse is paramount for quality in dubbing: 'another cornerstone for good dubbing quality is that the target language sounds realistic, credible, and plausible; i.e. it does not take us away from the storyline.' Although it refers to dubbing, this observation can easily be applied to theatrical productions, given their similarities as dramatic texts. Some orality markers also carry information that is important for the understanding of the message, the situations and the characters, and, as such, can affect the audience's involvement and identification with the dramatic work (Zago 2015). In this respect, it is worth noting the close relationship between orality markers – such as terms of endearment or foul language – and characterization (Bednarek 2011). As Baños and Chaume

(2009: online) argue, it is essential to recognize the importance of dramatic dialogue, which contains orality markers, and its relevance for translation: 'Bearing in mind the critical role that fictional dialogues play in audiovisual texts and their translations, it is worth delving into the study of the resources available to recreate spontaneous dialogue on the screen.'

According to Baños and Chaume (*ibid.*), the translation of orality markers requires the selection of linguistic resources that would be recognized by the target audience as being characteristic of spontaneous spoken discourse, since '[t]he challenge does not lie so much in trying to imitate spontaneous conversations, but in selecting specific features of this mode of discourse that are widely accepted and recognized as such by the audience.' This requires a command of resources in the target language that produce a similar effect but may not correspond to those used in the source language. As Baños (2014: 409) observes: 'the translator takes the role of the scriptwriter, and should thus master the linguistic features available in the target language to imitate spontaneous conversation – which might and probably will be different to those used in the source language.'

The study of orality markers in dramatic translation is fundamental not only because of their inherent and specific value, but also because of their importance in the external communication system and the challenges they pose to translators. Yet, little research has been carried out to date on prefabricated orality in theatre translation, which contrasts with the attention that the topic has received in audiovisual translation (AVT), where numerous studies have been conducted on orality markers (Chaume 2004a; Baños 2009, 2013b, 2014; Arias-Badia 2017, 2020; Bruti 2019), discourse markers (Chaume 2004b; Mattsson 2006, 2009; Romero-Fresco 2009a, 2009b, 2012; Forchini 2010), foul language (Mattsson 2006; Ávila Cabrera 2015, 2023; Zamora and Pavesi 2021), interjections (Matamala 2008, 2009), vocatives (Forchini 2013), intensifiers (Baños 2013a; Marzà, 2016) and demonstratives (Pavesi 2014).

In the field of theatre, Kruger (2004a) looks at linguistic traits such as contractions, discourse markers, first and second person pronouns and time and place adverbs, and, in a similar publication, she examines the nature of discourse markers (Kruger 2004b). Brumme (2008, 2012a) focuses on discourse markers, foul language and phraseology in various language combinations and Ramos Pinto (2008) centres her research on the translation of linguistic varieties into Portuguese. Brumme and Bernal (2010) study both phatic markers and linguistic varieties; Cebrián (2011) discusses features such as repetition, vocatives and deixis; Stavinschi (2012) and Cebrián (2015) investigate the role of deixis; López Lapeña (2015) addresses issues such as fluency, linking devices, interjections and onomatopoeia; and Andaluz-Pinedo (2022) explores different syntactic and lexical-semantic features such as vocatives, repetitions, discourse markers, intensifiers and deixis. Most of these studies focus on a single play or on linguistic combinations other than English into Spanish, making the analysis of the translation of orality markers in a corpus that includes more than one play in this specific language pair a worthwhile academic pursuit.

2.2. TRACE-theatre studies (1939–1985)

Research carried out within the TRACE project – led by the University of the Basque Country and the University of León in Spain, between 1997 and 2015 – sheds light on the English to Spanish translations that were carried out between 1939 and 1985 in the areas of audiovisual culture and printed culture (Rabadán 2000b; Merino-Álvarez 2007b). The former encompasses theatre (Merino-Álvarez 2000, 2007a, 2016a, 2016b, 2016c; Pérez L. de Heredia 2001, 2003; Bandín 2007; Goñi 2017), cinema (Gutiérrez Lanza 1999, 2000; Fernández López 2000, 2007; Miguel González 2000; Santamaría 2000, 2007; Serrano 2003; Camus 2009) and television (Miquel 2011), while the latter includes narrative (Merino-Álvarez and Rabadán 2002; Pérez Álvarez 2003; Pajares 2007; Rioja Barrocal 2008; Camus 2009; Gómez Castro 2009) and poetry (Lobejón Santos 2013). The present research draws on results obtained in the TRACE-theatre studies and is envisioned as a continuation of these earlier works.

In the TRACE-theatre studies – and in TRACE in general – the main documentary source used to reconstruct the history of translated theatre during the Franco period is the Spanish Archivo General de la Administración (AGA) [General Administration Archive], as it provides valuable information 'beyond standard editions of dramatic works or the sources available in generalist libraries in order to examine carefully the relevance of translation and to identify foreign authors, works and genres which form part of Spanish theatre in the twentieth century' (Merino-Álvarez 2016c: 176). Authorization by the censors was compulsory for the performance and publication of theatre translations, and a rather convoluted process with records was therefore required. According to Merino-Álvarez (2017b: 440), 'since all productions had to seek official permission from the Francoist bureaucratic censorship offices, the traces left in the form of millions of documents are an exceptional documentary resource to mine.'

The committees responsible for censoring plays were different for performance and publication, meaning that there were in effect two different systems. Although the name changed over the years, during a large part of the Francoist period the *Dirección General de Cinematografía y Teatro* [General Directorate for Cinema and Theatre] was in charge of censoring theatrical productions, while the *Dirección General de Propaganda* [General Directorate for Propaganda] and the *Dirección General de Información* [General Directorate for Information] dealt with the censorship of books (Rabadán 2000b).[7] The documentation generated by the censorship boards dealing with productions and publications is held by the AGA under the umbrella archive of *(03) Cultura* [Culture], which includes a collection of censorship records of theatrical productions – *(03)046 Inventario de expedientes de censura de teatro* [Inventory of theatre censorship records] – and a different one for the censorship records of books – *(03)050 Inventario de los expedientes de censura literaria* [Inventory of literary censorship records].

In order to understand the Francoist regime, it is useful to remember the legislative developments, documented by Merino-Álvarez (1999; 2000) and Bandín (2007), that affected the censorship of performance- and reader-oriented translations. The *Ley de 22 de abril de 1938, de Prensa* [Law of 22 April 1938, on the Press] established the mandatory prior censorship of all cultural products including theatrical productions and books. With regard to productions, it is also worth noting the passing of censorship norms for the theatre (*Orden de 6 de febrero de 1964 por la que se aprueba el Reglamento*

7 See Merino-Álvarez (2000) and Pérez L. de Heredia (2004) for a detailed list of the different bodies in charge of censoring theatrical productions.

de Régimen Interior de la Junta de Censura de Obras Teatrales y las normas de censura [Order of 6 February 1964 approving the Internal Regulations of the Censorship Board of Theatre Plays and the censorship rules]), which drew on norms approved for the cinema the previous year (*Orden de 9 de febrero de 1963 por la que se aprueban las «Normas de censura cinematográfica»* [Order of 9 February 1963 approving the 'Film Censorship Rules']). In 1963, the *Junta de Censura* [Censorship Board], which specialized in the censorship of theatrical productions, was set up through the *Orden de 16 de febrero de 1963 por la que se constituye una Junta de Censura de Obras Teatrales* [Order of 16 February 1963 establishing a Censorship Board of Theatre Plays]. In the case of books, the *Ley 14/1966, de 18 de marzo, de Prensa e Imprenta* [Law 14/1966, of 18 March 1996, on the Press and Printing Industry] replaced previous legislation from 1938, allowing the editors to choose 'between submitting the text to "voluntary consultation" or carrying out the "direct deposit" of copies, risking the seizure of the book, its report and the well-known administrative sanction' (Bandín 2007: 58–59, my translation).

After Franco's death in 1975, the end of official censorship was marked by the *Real Decreto-ley 24/1977, de 1 de abril, sobre libertad de expresión* [Decree-Law 24/1977, of 1 April 1977, on freedom of expression], the *Real Decreto 262/1978, de 27 de enero, sobre libertad de representación de espectáculos teatrales* [Royal Decree 262/1978, of 27 January 1978, on the freedom of theatre performances], and the *Constitución Española* [Spanish Constitution]. However, the old, familiar bureaucratic procedures remained in force until 1985 (Merino-Álvarez 2000).

As Bandín (2007: 53, my translation) observes, 'censorship goes hand in hand with repression and propaganda and has as its primary aim the annihilation of the enemy by all possible means.' Merino-Álvarez's (2000) and Bandín's (2007) overview of the standard procedure for theatrical and literary censorship provides a clear picture of how this type of control operated. In the case of theatrical productions, the process began with the submission of a request for the performance of a play, signed by the petitioner, which included the details of the production as well as a copy of the corresponding text. Next, the appointed censors issued their individual reports on the text, in which they indicated their objections and proposed changes. Negotiations between the censors and the various agents involved in a theatrical production were possible both before and after the resolution of a case.

Finally, the petitioner was informed of the prohibition or authorization of the work. Authorization usually entailed conditions such as deletions and changes to a text, a viewing of the dress rehearsal to oversee the mise-en-scène before the première, indications as to whether the play could be broadcast on the radio and the required minimum age of spectators and whether the performance was to be restricted to *Teatros de cámara y ensayo* [chamber theatres] (Merino-Álvarez 2000). Being staged in one of these theatres was a common way for a play in English to be introduced into the country. Although the number of performances in chamber theatres was limited, it helped promote a favourable image of Spain abroad and gave theatre companies the opportunity to introduce avant-garde plays. On occasion, some plays obtained subsequent authorization for performance in commercial theatres (Merino-Álvarez 2005, 2017b). For books printed in Spain, as well as for those imported from abroad, the request for authorization came from the publisher and the censors issued their corresponding reports (Bandín 2007). The numerous translations published in Latin America had to undergo the same process when imported to Spain, although there is evidence that some fiction books were circulated illegally during the dictatorship (Abellán 1980; Gómez Castro 2009; Cornellà-Detrell 2015), and it is possible that this also happened with plays.

The documents generated during the censorship process were organized into censorship records and filed at the AGA. Records relating to the various productions include the mandatory request for a performance, which contains information especially useful for identifying the play, the translation and the theatrical production. They sometimes also include other documents of great help in understanding the censorship process such as reports made by the censors, in which they foreground the topics that were deemed dangerous, letters exchanged between the different agents, in which tensions and negotiations can be perceived, and the final decision as to whether a performance was prohibited or authorized, either conditionally or unconditionally. In some cases, the texts are also preserved and these are of great interest as a textual complement to the contextual study of a particular case. Censorship records relating to the publication of theatre translations tend to be less detailed and contain a compulsory section, with information on the source and target authors, the play and the publishers, as well as censorship reports, the decision, and, occasionally, also the actual text.

The TRACE-theatre studies focus on two main areas of research, namely, TRACEti (TRACE teatro inglés [TRACE English theatre]) and TRACEtci (TRACE teatro clásico inglés [TRACE classic English theatre]). The TRACEti catalogue covers the period 1939–1985 and focuses on English-speaking authors whose plays are registered in the AGA, while the TRACEtci catalogue concentrates on the translations of plays by Shakespeare and his contemporaries, performed and published between 1939 and 1985 (Bandín 2007). After the pre-TRACE study of Merino-Álvarez (1994b) laying the methodological groundwork for the cataloguing and subsequent selection of texts, catalogues are compiled in both areas (TRACEti and TRACEtci) to offer a glimpse of the data gathered on the censorship process. Corpora are then defined according to parameters such as the recurrent presence of certain titles and the identification of complex cases from the viewpoint of censorship, normally because of the topics dealt with in these works. Table 1 summarizes the areas of study in TRACE-theatre as well as the composition of the catalogues and corpora.

Table 1: TRACE-theatre catalogues and corpora, based on Merino-Álvarez (2009)

Names	Catalogues	Plays selected for the corpora
Pre-TRACE (1950–1990)	156 entries	*Educating Rita* by Willy Russell *Exiles* by James Joyce *Mulatto* by Langston Hughes *A View from the Bridge* by Arthur Miller *Passion* by Edward Bond *Roots* by Arnold Wesker *A Man for All Seasons* by Robert Bolt *Busybody* by Jack Popplewell
TRACEti (1939–1985)	875 entries	*Who's Afraid of Virginia Woolf?* by Edward Albee *Desire Under the Elms* by Eugene O'Neill *Sweet Bird of Youth* by Tennessee Williams *Five Finger Exercise* by Peter Shaffer *The Complaisant Lover* by Graham Greene *Equus* by Peter Shaffer *Waiting for Godot* by Samuel Beckett *The Zoo Story* by Edward Albee *The Royal Hunt of the Sun* by Peter Shaffer *Cat on a Hot Tin Roof* by Tennessee Williams *The Boys in the Band* by Mart Crowley *A Streetcar Named Desire* by Tennessee Williams

Names	Catalogues	Plays selected for the corpora
TRACEtci (1939–1985)	678 entries	*Hamlet* by William Shakespeare *The Taming of the Shrew* by William Shakespeare *Tis Pity She's a Whore* by John Ford *The Changeling* by Thomas Middleton and William Rowley *Othello* by William Shakespeare *Volpone* by Ben Jonson

The information included in the TRACEti catalogue, on which TEATRAD draws, has been obtained from sampling the AGA file boxes containing the censorship records, as well as from manual searches of card indexes according to author, title and nationality (Merino-Álvarez 2010, 2017b). In the TRACEti catalogue, each entry is organized around a censorship record and title and includes several fields, structured in three levels of information (Merino-Álvarez 2000; Pérez L. de Heredia 2004). The first level contains listed information that relates to source and target authors and plays, as well as to the Spanish première of the works (e.g. the year and the director of the production). The second level contains information on plays also circulated through printed editions or as films, such as the name of the publisher or director of the cinema adaptation, though the focus is on performance-oriented translations of plays. Finally, the third level contains extratextual information such as the censorship record number, the outcome (prohibition or authorization and any conditions), potential relation to other records and any other interesting details collected from additional documentary sources.

The TRACEti catalogue contains registers relating to authors such as Edward Albee, Samuel Beckett, Agatha Christie, Graham Greene, Patrick Hamilton, Arthur Miller, Eugene O'Neill, Harold Pinter, John Boynton Priestley, Terence Rattigan, Peter Shaffer, George Bernard Shaw and Tennessee Williams (Merino-Álvarez 2010; Pérez L. de Heredia 2004). Merino-Álvarez (2017b) notes that in the 1940s it is mainly British playwrights who appear in the records, whereas from the 1950s Americans predominate, with some Irish writers found scattered throughout the whole period. Some of the works which recur between 1939 and 1963, discussed by Pérez L. de Heredia (2004), include *The Trial of Mary Dugan* (Bayard Veiller, 1929), *Baby Mine* (Margaret Mayo, 1911), *Desire Under the Elms*

(Eugene O'Neill, 1924), *Angel Street* (Patrick Hamilton, 1938), *Our Town* (Thornton Wilder, 1938), *The Glass Menagerie* (Tennessee Williams, 1944) and *A Streetcar Named Desire* (Tennessee Williams, 1947). Target authors such as José Luis Alonso, Antonio de Cabo, Luis Escobar, José Gordon, José López Rubio and León Mirlas are also commonly found in the records (Pérez L. de Heredia 2004; Merino-Álvarez 2010).

Other than the TRACEti studies, research on English theatre translated during the censorship period generally focuses on specific authors or titles rather than offering an overview of translated theatre. For instance, work has been carried out on the translations in Spain of plays by Edward Albee (Espejo 1997, 1998), Samuel Beckett (Fernández-Quesada 2007, 2020; Fernández-Quesada *et al.* 2019; Fernández Sánchez 2020; Rodríguez Gago 2020a, 2020b), Arthur Miller (Mateo 2000; Espejo 2001, 2002, 2003, 2004, 2010a, 2010b, 2011, 2012), Harold Pinter (Martínez Luciano 2006), Sean O'Casey (O'Leary 2012, 2018), John Osborne (Isabel Estrada 2001), William Shakespeare (Campillo 2005), George Bernard Shaw (Isabel Estrada 2001; Goñi 2017), Oscar Wilde (Mateo 2010a, 2010b), Tennessee Williams (Espejo 2019; Vilaró 2017) and William Butler Yeats (Hurtley 2013). Other studies relate to the works of authors from a specific country, such as American writers in Spain (Espejo 2017) or Irish writers in Galicia (Serra Porteiro 2015). London (1997) explores the theatrical productions in Spain of plays by a variety of English-speaking authors, such as Samuel Beckett, Noël Coward, Graham Greene, Somerset Maugham, Arthur Miller, Eugene O'Neill, John Boynton Priestley, Peter Ustinov, Thornton Wilder and Tennessee Williams.

All in all, the information contained in TRACEti has been a solid starting point for the compilation of the TEATRAD catalogue, since it offers a very complete account of the playwrights, plays and translations introduced in Spain during the dictatorship. Furthermore, information on the target authors who signed the translations of plays has allowed comparisons to be made with the target authors responsible for the corresponding translations in the TEATRAD catalogue.

2.2.1. (Self-)censorship under the Francoist regime

According to Merino-Álvarez (2003), official censorship and self-censorship feature regularly in the TRACE-theatre catalogues and corpora, particularly when topics are deemed sensitive. Official censorship can be described as a set of restrictions imposed by censors after they have read a translation. This section is concerned with their linguistic manipulation of texts, although, as previously mentioned, the official censorship of performances also involved extratextual elements such as the viewing and control of dress rehearsals, the decision as to whether a text was suitable for broadcast on the radio or not, the minimum age of spectators and whether the performances would only be staged in chamber theatres.

Merino-Álvarez (2000: 143, my translation) defined self-censorship as 'a process that takes place prior to an actual request where the professionals involved intervene by removing or changing what they think the censors will remove, or trying to disguise and mask what might be censored so that it goes unnoticed.' Self-censorship, however, can also occur during or after the censorship process itself (*ibid.*) and offers a clear example of how target authors generate TTs under certain restrictions imposed by the system. This translational behaviour is conceptualized by Aaltonen (2000: 29) when she uses the 'tenants' metaphor: 'In translation, cultural, social, theatrical and linguistic systems work through the translators and in this way determine the terms of occupancy of the texts to be translated.' Some of the recurrent translation techniques which show possible traces of self-censorship, not only in theatre, but also in cinema, prose and poetry, have been categorized as the addition, omission or substitution of textual material (Gutiérrez Lanza 1999; Pérez L. de Heredia 2004; Merino-Álvarez 2007a; Gómez Castro 2009; Lobejón Santos 2013).

Official censorship and self-censorship paid special attention to topics that Abellán (1980) has grouped into four categories: sexual morality, politics, religion and foul language. These thematic filters recur regularly across research carried out into the translation of theatre (Merino-Álvarez 2000, 2003, 2005; Pérez L. de Heredia 2004; Bandín 2007), cinema (Gutiérrez Lanza 1999), prose (Merino-Álvarez and Rabadán 2002; Gómez Castro 2009) and poetry (Lobejón Santos 2013).

The topics are specifically mentioned in the censorship regulations for cinema (*Orden de 9 de febrero de 1963 por la que se aprueban las «Normas de censura cinematográfica»* [Order of 9 February 1963 approving the 'Film Censorship Rules']), which were applied to the theatre by the *Orden de 6 de febrero de 1964 por la que se aprueba el Reglamento de Régimen Interior de la Junta de Censura de Obras Teatrales y las normas de censura* [Order of 6 February 1964 approving the Internal Regulations of the Censorship Board of Theatre Plays and the censorship rules]. Among other issues, point 8 banned 'the justification of divorce, adultery, illicit sexual relations, prostitution and, in general, anything that violates the institution of marriage and the family'; point 13 forbade 'colloquial expressions and scenes or shots of an intimate nature that violate the most basic norms of good taste'; and clause 17 censored 'anything that in any way violates: first the Catholic Church, its dogma, morals and worship; second the fundamental principles of the State, national dignity and security; third the Head of State'.

Within the framework of TRACE-theatre, different case studies have been carried out in which these topics – whether part of the plot or present only in sporadic references – have encountered censorial obstacles in their translation. Some of these studies are outlined below.

a) Sexual morality is the topic with the largest number of examples of (self-)censorship found in performance-oriented translations in the TRACE-theatre studies. In this respect, Merino-Álvarez (2003: 648, my translation) observes that there was:

> an attempt to avoid certain topics affecting society such as homosexuality and extramarital relations, adultery in particular, and anything connected with sexual behaviour that departs from the edifying Catholic marriage advocated by the civil and ecclesiastical authorities.

In relation to homosexuality, Merino-Álvarez (2003, 2007a) documents the difficulties encountered by the performance-oriented translations of *Five Finger Exercise* (Peter Shaffer, 1958, transl. 1959), *The Zoo Story* (Edward Albee, 1959, transl. 1963) and *The Boys in the Band* (Mart Crowley, 1968, transl. 1970 and 1975). Pérez L. de Heredia (2004) outlines the cuts imposed by official censorship and the traces of self-censorship detected in *A Streetcar Named Desire* (transl. 1951 and 1956) and *Cat on a Hot Tin Roof* (transl. 1958 and 1959). Despite these obstacles, some plays like *Five Finger Exercise* and *The Boys in the Band* represented milestones in the introduction of the topic of homosexuality to the Spanish theatrical scene of the time (Merino-Álvarez 2007a; Merino-Álvarez and Andaluz-Pinedo 2017), thus attesting to the pivotal role of translation in bringing new subject matter to other cultures.

Official censorship and, especially, self-censorship are also observed in the case of extramarital relations in the translations of works such as *A Streetcar Named Desire* (transl. 1951 and 1956), *Desire Under the Elms* (transl. 1953 and 1961), *Cat on a Hot Tin Roof* (transl. 1959), *Sweet Bird of Youth* (transl. 1962) (Pérez L. de Heredia 2004) and *The Complaisant Lover* (Graham Greene, 1959, transl. 1968) (Merino-Álvarez 2000). Sporadic examples of (self-)censorship in the area of sexual morality can also be found in *Equus* (Peter Shaffer, 1973, transl. 1974) (Merino-Álvarez and Andaluz-Pinedo 2017) and in *Waiting for Godot* (Samuel Beckett, 1952, transl. 1955 and 1970) (Merino-Álvarez and Andaluz-Pinedo 2020). Bandín (2007) claims that in classical works, plays by Shakespeare for example, problematic references do not tend to be common, although some examples relating to sexual morality and foul language can still be found.

Pérez L. de Heredia (2004) contrasts the performance-oriented translations with the Argentinian reader-oriented translations of *A Streetcar Named Desire* (transl. 1961 and 1966), an example that reveals what appears to be a less strict censorial control of reader-oriented translations. She also observes that the way in which topics were addressed in performance-oriented translations changed in the late 1970s and 1980s and gives *Cat on a Hot Tin Roof* (transl. 1979 and 1984) and *A Streetcar Named Desire* (transl. 1988) as examples where references previously deemed inappropriate are generally restored and, in certain cases, even intensified.

b) With regard to politics, Abellán (1980) notes that any opposition to the governing regime was unacceptable. For instance, in the performance-oriented translation of *The Royal Hunt of the Sun* (Peter Shaffer, 1969, transl. 1969), self-censorship can be detected in fragments where Spain is criticized; yet, the censors still banned it because of the 'improper use of "the good name of Spain"' (Merino-Álvarez and Andaluz-Pinedo 2017: 252, my translation).

c) References to religion also constituted a delicate area. The previously mentioned translation of *The Royal Hunt of the Sun* (transl. 1969) includes traces where comments critical of religion were self-censored (Merino-Álvarez and Andaluz-Pinedo 2017). Pérez L. de Heredia (2004) detects the (self-)censorship of sporadic references to religious themes in *Desire Under the Elms* (transl. 1953 and 1961), and Merino-Álvarez and Andaluz-Pinedo (2020) make similar observations in *Waiting for Godot* (transl. 1955 and 1970).

d) The classification of offensive and taboo language put forward by Ávila Cabrera (2014, 2015) is useful for the discussion of the fourth sensitive topic: foul language. Offensive language includes subcategories such as cursing, derogatory tone, insult, oath, exclamatory swearword/phrase and subtle insult, whereas taboo language involves subcategories relating to animal naming, death/killing, drugs/excessive alcohol consumption, ethnic/racial/gender slur, filth, profanity/blasphemy, psychological/physical condition, sexual reference/body part, urination/scatology and violence. As Abellán (1980: 88–89, my translation) remarks, censors objected the 'use of language considered indecorous, provocative and improper concerning the good manners that ought to rule the behaviour of people who consider themselves decent'. Foul language is a feature of orality used to give the impression of naturalness, to evoke a certain atmosphere and as a characterization device (Baños 2014; Arias-Badia 2020), and its toning down will irremediably affect these aspects. A play that makes abundant use of this type of language is *Who's Afraid of Virginia Woolf?* (Merino-Álvarez 2016a).

According to Pérez L. de Heredia (2004), both official censorship and self-censorship were harsher in the case of performance-oriented translations than in reader-oriented ones. In this sense, as Gutiérrez Lanza (1999) points out, the control of public performances and screenings was particularly strict during the Francoist regime because of their potentially direct impact on the audience. The collective and mimetic character of performances (Merino-Álvarez 1994b) seems to have been a decisive factor in the tighter controls imposed on the theatrical system. Furthermore, a significant number of published theatre translations were carried out in Argentina, where various Spanish publishing houses – Losada and Sudamericana for example – had moved after the Spanish Civil War (Merino-Álvarez 1999; Pérez L. de Heredia 2004). It has been argued that the fact that these translations were produced in Argentina had an impact on the fewer instances of self-censorship carried out in plays (Pérez L. de Heredia 2004) and fiction (Gómez Castro 2009).

For Merino-Álvarez (2003), obtaining permission to stage a production was easier in cases where the representation of sensitive themes took place in contexts that did not involve Spain, as it was thought that the audience would find it more difficult to identify with them, or where they were discussed in a very implicit manner. In this regard, topics that would not have been acceptable in Spanish plays were sometimes allowed in foreign ones. This was also the case in the cinema, as is highlighted in Gutiérrez Lanza's (1999: 412, my translation) analysis of a corpus of films from the 1960s, in which some topics 'would not have reached the screen were it not for the fact that they were foreign which curiously turned them into examples of what was morally incorrect'.

The year in which a translation was submitted to the censors is another factor which affected the degree of manipulation exerted. In this respect, Muñoz Cáliz (2005) observes that the censorship period can be divided into the following five subperiods: autarchy (1939–1945), adaptation (1945–1958), development (1959–1968), decadence (1969–1975) and transition (1975–1978). Regarding the development period, Merino-Álvarez (2000) underlines the impact that the openness policy had on the censorship process for some performance-oriented translations.

Other factors that censors bore in mind involved box office success – especially on the New York, London or Paris stage and in the cinema – as well as any awards received by the author or play (Merino-Álvarez 2000, 2003). While censors tried to avoid certain topics from being presented before Spanish audiences, stakeholders such as producers, directors and target authors took the initiative to facilitate the staging of these plays. Apart from censoring some of the references themselves, they would also present the international awards and box office success of a particular play as an argument for its approval in Spain (Merino-Álvarez 2000, 2003, 2016c). Merino-Álvarez (2003) argues that the position of power held by the different agents and the mediation of prestigious figures from the theatrical world, acting as requesters or target authors, were crucial. In a later work, Merino-Álvarez (2017b) names Luis Escobar, director of one of Spain's national theatres, as one of the main figures behind the introduction of British plays into Spain. The success of film adaptations also played out as an argument for the authorization of plays. Merino-Álvarez (2001) discusses how, due to their fame on the silver screen, productions by Tennessee Williams and Arthur Miller were commonly staged at the beginning of the 1960s.

From a governmental viewpoint, allowing the performance of foreign plays that had been successful in other countries was a strategy used to project a pseudo-democratic image of Spain abroad, though the commercial interest of the producers cannot be underestimated, as highlighted by Merino-Álvarez (2016c: 177): 'theatre programming was guided by the hope of similar box office takings together with the desire to put the Spanish scene on an international level.' In this regard, Muñoz Cáliz (2006) observes a more tolerant treatment of prestigious foreign authors than of Spanish ones.

Self-censorship when translating sexual morality, politics, religion and foul language was a regular occurrence during Franco's regime, reflecting the restrictions made on freedom at that time. The question remains as to how these topics were dealt with in subsequent translations of the same plays. The current study explores whether translations censored during Franco's time are still used in the twenty-first century and whether (self-)censored references have been restored or not.

2.2.2. *After Franco*

As already noted, the TRACE-theatre studies focus on translations that circulated between 1939 and 1985, for which records are kept at the AGA. The catalogues show that some plays were translated and staged numerous times over the years, thus becoming an integral part of the Spanish theatrical culture. Plays have been retranslated, adapted and their original translations plagiarized (Pérez L. de Heredia 2004; Bandín 2007; Merino-Álvarez 2007a).

Merino-Álvarez (2016c) remarks that translated theatre was such an integral part of Spanish culture that some of the plays introduced during the dictatorship continued on into the democratic period. Given the enduring nature of printed texts, it is possible that translations published during Franco's time continue to circulate in reeditions or are used to generate new translations, whether performance- or reader-oriented. Cornellà-Detrell (2015: 49, my translation) claims that measures have not been taken to prevent the medium- or long-term impact of Francoist censorship, adding that 'when addressing the issue of censorship we should not limit ourselves to pointing out the cuts to, or prohibition of, a certain work; it is also necessary to research what happened to the text in the medium and long term.' As Gómez Castro (2008: 184) emphasizes, 'the action of the official censorship will endure as long as the bookshops continue to sell those works that had been subjected to it.' With regard to AVT, Díaz-Cintas (2019: 17) observes that the censored dubbed version of the film *The Barefoot Contessa* (Joseph L. Mankiewicz, 1954) is still widely available in the twenty-first century and argues that:

> If these nefarious changes could be somewhat justified on the basis of the historic-political context in which they took place, their perpetuation and commercial exploitation in the twenty-first century is less defensible. Censorship in Spain was officially nullified in 1978, soon after the country embraced democracy. And yet, as the film was marketed by MGM in 2004 with the same dubbed dialogue exchanges as the ones used for its theatrical release in troubled 1956, it could be argued that censorship continues to cast a shadow over the industry in the digital age and that film distributors have (un)wittingly become the censors of the present by repackaging the old, mutilated dubbed translations.

Studies on translations that are still in circulation after the censorship period suggest the need for further investigation into this issue. Gómez Castro (2008) demonstrates the longevity of censored translations with fragments from the novels *The Godfather* (Mario Puzo, 1969, transl. 1970) and *The Exorcist* (Peter Blatty, 1971, transl. 1972), which are still on sale at the beginning of the twenty-first century. In her comparison of the way in which sensitive topics were addressed in a translation of Woody Guthrie's (1943) autobiography, *Bound for Glory*, published in 1977 and a retranslation from 2009, Gutiérrez Lanza (2015) observes that the references to sexual morality, religion and politics were retained in both translations, while some instances of foul language were omitted only in the earlier version but restored in the later one. Despite limited research on the topic, the situation seems to be the same for theatrical works introduced during the dictatorship, which continue to be used in productions and publications to this day. In her analysis of a 1988 translation of *A Streetcar Named Desire*, Pérez L. de Heredia (2004) notes that elements that were previously censored had now been restored. All in all, little has been published on the English-language plays introduced during the censorship period and still performed or published in Spain, although work has been carried out on such playwrights as Samuel Beckett (Fernández-Quesada 2007; Fernández-Quesada *et al.* 2019), Arthur Miller (Mateo 2000; Espejo 2010b, 2011, 2012), George Bernard Shaw (Goñi 2017), Oscar Wilde (Mateo 2010b) and Tennessee Williams (Espejo 2019).

The present volume seeks to contribute towards filling this gap with the compilation and analysis of a catalogue and a corpus of theatrical plays which were first translated during the censorship period and have continued in circulation up until 2019. The following chapter describes the methodological framework adopted for the purposes of this research.

CHAPTER 3

Methodological considerations

This chapter discusses the themes fundamental to DTS and the TRACE protocol as well as the notions and tools from corpus linguistics on which the investigation is based. It then goes on to outline the different procedures for the creation and analysis of the TEATRAD catalogue and corpus.

3.1. Descriptive Translation Studies and the TRACE protocol

In 1972, Holmes (1988: 67) put forward the term Translation Studies (TS) as the name of the discipline concerned with 'the complex of problems clustered round the phenomenon of translating and translations'. He divided this research field into two interrelated branches: the pure branch and the applied branch, with the former subdivided into the theoretical and descriptive branches. The descriptive branch explores empirical phenomena related to translation as a product, function or process and provides data for the theoretical branch in which general or partial principles and models are developed. The results from these two branches inform the pure branch and are also of benefit to the applied branch, which deals with practical aspects such as training, tools, policy and criticism relevant to translation. The theoretical-methodological framework of this research draws on the descriptive branch of TS, generally known as DTS, as well as the TRACE protocol, which has its roots in DTS and proposes a sequence of research stages that help to organize the different phases of the investigation, facilitating the cross-fertilization of the results with other studies thanks to the application of a common methodology.

This research project therefore adopts a descriptive, empirical and retrospective approach. In contrast to the traditional prescriptive perspective, 'the descriptive method takes the translated text as it is and tries to determine the various factors that may account for its particular nature' (Hermans 1985: 12–13). In this respect, DTS examine 'empirical, observable facts, in other words, the reality that exists as opposed to speculation' (Rabadán and Merino-Álvarez 2004: 18, my translation), and these phenomena are analysed after the act of translation has been completed.

Toury (1997, 2004) argues that it is possible to study different empirical phenomena retrospectively, namely, assumed translations, that is, texts that function as translations in the target culture; the relationships that can be established between an assumed translation and its assumed ST or between components of both; the translation strategies that underlie those relationships and the functions that the assumed translations fulfil in the target culture. Toury (1997) then differentiates between entities that are observable (assumed translations) and those that are reconstructed (relations, strategies and functions), and suggests that, to study the latter, researchers have to start from the former.

The concept of assumed translation is worth a more detailed look, since it helps define the object of study in this work, namely, assumed translations of the plays introduced in Spain under the Francoist regime and still in circulation in the twenty-first century. Toury (2012: 31) explains this concept as follows:

> any target-culture text for which there are reasons to tentatively posit the existence of another text, in another culture/language, from which it has presumably derived by transfer operations and to which it is now tied by a set of relationships based on shared features, some of which may be regarded – within the culture in question – as necessary and/or sufficient.

Rabadán (2022: online) notes that Toury (1995) 'puts forward the notion of *assumed translation* to account for the relativity and variability inherent to any TT-ST dependency relationship(s)'. In the present research, the concept TT is used as a synonym, which Rabadán (1991: 297, my translation) defines as 'the result of a transfer process; that is, the "reconstruction" of a logically and chronologically previous text, belonging to a source polysystem, under the communicative conditions of the target polysystem at a certain time in history and directed at target readers'.

One of the critical concepts that articulates this approach to translation is that of equivalence, defined by Rabadán (2022: online) as:

> the relationship that binds any target text (TT) to the source text (ST) it derives from, and that accounts for both texts being 'the same' in different languages. Depending on the theoretical outlook and the text's specificity involved (e. g. literary, technical, multimodal), this dependency relationship may adopt different modes to ensure the successful TT's delivery to its intended recipients.

Equivalence is therefore a dynamic, functional and relational notion and, in order to identify the type of equivalence established in a translation, a retrospective analysis is required.

When it comes to the previously mentioned types of empirical phenomena (assumed translations, relations, strategies and functions), Toury (2012: 18) underlines the importance of their interrelations as follows:

> the position and functions that translations (as entities) and translating (as an activity) are designed to have in a prospective target culture, the form a translation would have (and hence the relationships that would tie it to its original), and the strategies resorted to during its production constitute an ordered set rather than a mere congeries of disconnected facts. Having accepted this as an axiom, it is *interdependencies* that will be the focus of our attention, the main intention being to lay bare the regularities marking the relationships assumed to obtain between function, product and process.

Toury's (2012: 18) proposal foregrounds the target-orientedness of any translation, which he regards as 'facts of the culture that would host them'. Seen from this perspective, TTs are produced by translators under a set of given circumstances, and:

> Translators never 'just translate'. They translate in the context of certain conceptions and expectations about translation, however much they may take them for granted or come to regard them as natural. Within this context translators make choices and take up positions because they have certain goals to reach, personal or collective interests to pursue, material and symbolic stakes to defend. (Hermans 1999: 60)

This conception of translations as belonging to the target cultural system derives from the polysystem theory developed by Even-Zohar (1990: 11), who defines *polysystem* as 'a multiple system, a system of various systems which intersect with each other and partly overlap, using concurrently different options, yet functioning as one structured whole, whose members are interdependent', underlining its dynamic and heterogeneous character and emphasizing that it is governed by norms pertaining to a given socio-historical context. As explained in section 2.1, Aaltonen (2000) is one of the scholars who applies the polysystem theory to the study of theatre translations and points out that they function in either the theatrical or the literary systems but are also connected to broader cultural and economic systems. In the case of the literary system, Lefevere (1992: 15) puts forward the term patronage, which he defines as 'the powers (persons, institutions) that can further or hinder the reading, writing and rewriting of literature'. As Díaz-Cintas (2004) suggests, this concept helps clarify the intervention and control of extratextual factors over translations, which can also be applied to the study of audiovisual and theatrical practices.

Two other pivotal notions in DTS are those of regularity and norm. Regularities, understood as 'recurrent patterns' in the behaviour of the translators (Toury 1997: 73), are the final stage in the DTS analytical sequencing: compiling data, analysing it and formulating regularities (Rabadán 2000a). As for norms, they 'occupy the middle-ground between more absolute rules present in a given culture or system and the idiosyncrasies which also take place during every translational activity' (Toury, 2012: 51). Within this conceptualization, the scholar distinguishes three types of norms: initial, preliminary and operational. The initial norm determines whether a translation prioritizes the source or the target pole, that is, whether it is adequate or acceptable. For Toury (2012: 79–80), adequacy means that 'the translation act will be dominated by attempts to have the ensuing text reflect the source text,' while acceptability suggests that 'target norms will be triggered and set into motion' and shifts from the ST 'would be an inevitable price for taking that course of action'. Aware of the impossibility of systematically adopting only one of these two approaches, Toury (1995: 57) points out that 'even the most adequacy-oriented translation involves shifts from the source text', placing the two concepts as part of a gradation. In this context, the role of the researcher is to establish the place that the translation occupies between these two opposing poles of adequacy and acceptability (Rabadán and Merino-Álvarez 2004).

The preliminary norms are related to the 'translation policy', that is, the cultural planning that leads to the choice of a certain text at a certain time, and to the issue of whether translations are transferred directly from the original language or indirectly via a pivot language. Finally, operational norms direct the decisions made during the translation act itself and are in turn divided into matricial and textual-linguistic norms. The former govern the distribution and segmentation of the textual material and are related mainly to the macrotextual level, whereas the latter 'govern the selection of linguistic material for the formulation of the target text, or the replacement of the original material' (Toury 2012: 83) and, hence, draw on translation solutions observed at the microtextual level. Norms can only be reconstructed retrospectively and formulated after the information contained in a data set has been analysed and significant regularities identified.

In accordance with the TRACE protocol, the first phase of the research consists in the compilation and analysis of a catalogue, a concept borrowed from DTS that refers to a set of entries where data about different types of assumed translations are registered (Rabadán and Merino-Álvarez 2004). The analysis of the catalogue offers an overview of the segment of the translated culture under study and allows the identification of regularities that, in turn, help extract criteria for the selection of a significant corpus. As Merino-Álvarez (2003: 641, my translation) argues, 'unless we have a global view of the translated products in a particular period and culture, the selection of specific facts constituting the subject of descriptive-comparative analyses becomes difficult.'

After the cataloguing, the second stage requires the building and analysing of a corpus, defined by Rabadán and Merino-Álvarez (2004: 24) as 'organised groups of texts, arranged according to a set of selection criteria'. These criteria, which are elicit from the analysis of a catalogue, are fundamental for the compilation of corpus 1, which is made up of whole texts, as well as corpus 2, which contains textual fragments from corpus 1 (Gutiérrez Lanza 2005). Sets of texts are made up of at least a ST and a TT and can include retranslations, understood as 'the second or subsequent translation(s) of the ST into the same target language' (Chaume 2018: 13). Although the inclusion of retranslations adds complexity to the analysis, it becomes highly relevant as a way of facilitating the study of how translations have evolved over time. As highlighted by Heylen (1993: 12), 'important conclusions about the change of norms can be drawn from the comparison of one source text with several translated texts.'

Since translations are considered to belong to a given target culture, Toury (2004) emphasizes the need for an initial contextualization prior to the analysis of the translations. Merino-Álvarez (1994b) warns that texts cannot be regarded in isolation since they are never produced nor perceived in that way, and endorses the exploration of contextual factors in any research into the nature of translation. Similarly, Díaz-Cintas (2004: 31) argues that 'linguistic and cultural approaches should not be viewed as antagonistic paradigms but, rather, complementary. By focusing on our object of study from several angles we can only gain a better knowledge of translation and translating.' To contextualize translations, Toury (2004) refers to Lambert and Van Gorp's (1985) contribution to the subject in which a framework for a descriptive analysis that integrates contextual and textual issues is offered. Paratexts are vital to the contextualization and are understood as 'presentational materials accompanying translated texts and the text-specific meta-discourses formed directly around them' (Tahir-Gürçağlar 2002: 44). In her work on theatre translation, Bandín (2007) offers numerous examples of paratexts used in productions and publications, such as programmes, introductions, posters, censorship records and the like.

Textual comparisons are also crucial in any translation enquiry, as they help to elucidate the relationship between the STs and the TTs and to establish which ST is at the origin of a given TT, an issue that is not always clear in the case of the theatre (Merino-Álvarez 1993b). In addition to evaluating pairs of texts in different languages, a comparison between various TTs of the same ST can also be very rewarding (Rabadán 2001).

Textual comparisons are normally drawn between segments of the TT and the ST, rather than between whole texts, since, as Toury (2012: 115) acknowledges, 'the mapping of an assumed translation onto its assumed source is impracticable unless both texts are broken down into smaller, and lower-level entities.' When deciding on the comparative units to be shortlisted, they should be 'relevant to the operations which would then be performed on them; in our case, this means an attempt to gradually reconstruct both translation decisions and the constraints under which they were made' (*ibid.*: 116).

In the current study, the use of a character's utterance as the minimal structural unit of comparison in the dramatic field is essential for the analysis of a text at the macrotextual level. In the words of Merino-Álvarez (1992b: 285):

> the utterance consists of both levels of theatrical language, dialogue and what is not dialogue: the frame. The name of the character and all stage directions and comments that are not to be verbally presented on the stage but rather performed are part of the frame and the words to be spoken by the actors are part of the dialogue. Each utterance is clearly indicated on the page by the name of the character which tells us when the turn for the said character to speak (and move) has come.

An operational concept for the microtextual analysis is that of transleme, defined by Rabadán (1991: 300, my translation) as a: 'bitextual unit, of any type or level, composed of the same content and two formal manifestations, different but connected, and whose existence depends on the global relation of equivalence underlying each ST-TT textual binomial'.

Through macrotextual and microtextual comparisons, the present work aims to detect regularities linked to possible matricial and linguistic-textual norms, respectively.

3.2. Corpus linguistics

The benefit of bringing together corpus linguistics and TS has been underlined in a number of works, giving rise to what is known as Corpus-based Translation Studies. According to Calzada Pérez and Laviosa (2021: 8), 'Corpus-based Translation Studies (CTS) denotes an area of research that adopts and develops the methodologies of Corpus Linguistics (CL) to analyse translation practices for theoretical, descriptive and applied purposes.'

The notion of corpus used in this research follows the definition suggested by Kenny (2009: 59), which aligns with the definition put forward by DTS and the TRACE protocol:

> A corpus (plural: corpora) is a collection of texts that are the object of literary or linguistic study. In contemporary corpus linguistics, such collections are held in electronic form, allowing the inclusion of vast quantities of texts [...] and fast and flexible access to them using corpus-processing software.

The criteria for the selection of the texts or text samples that are included in a corpus should be coherent with the objective for which that corpus has been compiled (*ibid.*). In this regard, McEnery *et al.* (2006: 5) argue that it is important that the definition of corpus is not restrictive and includes different sets of texts whose selection is based on justified criteria:

> while it may be appealing to define precisely what a corpus is, the criteria should not be applied with such zeal that terminology is used as a tool to exclude carefully composed collections of language data from corpus-based research. The term corpus, while useful, should always be viewed as a somewhat vague and inclusive term.

Another key trait is that the texts that compose the corpus are in digital format, so that they can be easily processed. As McEnery *et al.* (*ibid.*: 6) emphasize: 'Machine-readability is a *de facto* attribute of modern corpora. Electronic corpora have advantages unavailable to their paper-based equivalents.' The use of tools not only increases the speed and reliability of corpus exploration, but it also allows the texts to be enriched with the addition of annotations that expand the analytical options (McEnery *et al.* 2006; McEnery and Hardie 2012).

When it comes to types of corpora, Xiao and Yue (2009) offer a typology of those most widely used in TS, classified according to different parameters:

a) From the viewpoint of the number of languages, corpora can be monolingual, if they contain texts in one language; bilingual, in two languages; or multilingual, in more than two languages.
b) In accordance with their form, bi-/multilingual corpora can be comparable if they are composed of subcorpora created using the same sampling criteria or parallel if they contain aligned source texts and TTs. Parallel corpora can be unidirectional, with source texts in one language and TTs in another; bidirectional, with source and TTs in both languages; or multidirectional, with source texts in one language and TTs in several.
c) Depending on their fields or textual genres, corpora can either be general or specialized. The former include the highest possible number of fields and genres, in a proportional manner, since they strive to be representative of a language or a linguistic variety, while the latter focus on texts from a specific field or textual genre.

As discussed in section 3.4, the TEATRAD corpus built for the present research is bilingual, parallel, unidirectional and specialized, comprising of theatre texts originally written in English and aligned with their Spanish translations. As such, TEATRAD is one of the few parallel corpora of theatre plays that are aligned with their translations.[1] From a technical perspective, the current corpus has benefited from the development of the TAligner tool (Zubillaga *et al.* 2015; Sanz-Villar and Andaluz-Pinedo 2021). The use of software is essential to build and analyse corpora, as it enables the addition of annotations and, in the case of parallel corpora, the alignment of original texts and their translations. Furthermore, tools of this nature make it possible to use techniques such as concordances and statistics to examine large quantities of text at great speed and with a high level of accuracy, and they also facilitate the replicability of analyses (McEnery and Hardie 2012).

Tools can also impose limitations as their functionality 'largely dictates what corpus linguistics research methods are available to a researcher' (Anthony 2013: 141). The same concern is raised by Laviosa (2002: 6), who states that 'any corpus linguistic analysis is dependent on both the creation of its object of study – that is the corpus itself – and the development of software tools to observe, analyse and process it.' The software used to build parallel corpora needs to allow the alignment of texts and its processing. Currently, there are not many tools available that facilitate the analysis of parallel corpora, and there are even fewer that will allow the users to build them (Sanjurjo-González 2018). For instance, CQPweb and AntPConc include options for the analysis of parallel corpora, but not for text alignment, which means that this task has to be performed externally and the results then imported into the software applications. Sketch Engine, ACM and TAligner are some of the tools that provide options to both build and analyse parallel corpora.

As plays have a specific structure, it is crucial that the tools used for their manipulation should be able to support these characteristics. According to Merino-Álvarez (1994b), theatre texts are organized into global units such as

1 Most theatre corpora are monolingual and made up of original plays: *Enhanced Shakespearean Corpus* (<http://wp.lancs.ac.uk/shakespearelang/project-resources/data>), *Shakespeare Corpus* (<https://lexically.net/wordsmith/support/shakespeare.html>) and *Drama Corpora* (<https://dracor.org>). The platform of the project EMOTHE (<https://emothe.uv.es/biblioteca-digital>) allows the visualization of European plays from the sixteenth and seventeenth centuries and their translations.

acts or scenes, which contain utterances, speakers' names, stage directions and dialogue exchanges. For tools to accommodate this structural specificity, three functions are fundamental in addition to the options that are common to texts written in prose, namely, structural mark-up, alignment at the utterance level and analysis options that filter the results based on the aforementioned mark-up. TAligner has been adapted to incorporate these functions and has thus been chosen as the most suitable type of software for this research.

A parallel corpus of theatre plays can be built and analysed by using the following elements: (a) metadata, (b) structural mark-up, (c) linguistic annotation, (d) alignment at the utterance level and (e) concordances.

a) Metadata add information to the texts that can be of potential use to researchers, such as the name of the author, title of the work or language. In TAligner it is possible to include metadata while building corpora and later use them to filter queries about the corpora in question.
b) Structural mark-up enables the differentiation of units in theatre texts such as acts or scenes, utterances, speakers, stage directions and dialogue exchanges, thus facilitating the processing of these units in the phases of alignment and analysis. TAligner is based on the standard proposed by the Text Encoding Initiative (TEI Consortium 2021), which makes it possible to add these mark-up tags automatically.
c) Linguistic annotations add extra information about the textual segments, such as grammatical or semantic information (McEnery *et al.* 2006). Customized annotations can also be inserted into a corpus to encode other details considered relevant for a study.
d) Aligning means establishing correspondences between the units of the original texts and their translations, so that they appear together when the corpus is queried. While alignment is carried out at the level of the paragraph, sentence or word for texts written in prose, in the case of theatre texts it is more useful to enact it at utterance level (Bandín 2007; Merino-Álvarez 2007a). The lack of tools that allow the alignment of utterances meant that previous studies on theatre translations had to be carried out by means of tables in a text processor (Merino-Álvarez 2007a; Bandín 2007). TAligner improves the methodology by allowing this type of alignment, which is adjusted manually in the tool.
e) A concordance search function, or concordancer, has been incorporated into TAligner, as it:

> allows us to search a corpus and retrieve from it a specific sequence of characters of any length – perhaps a word, part of a word or a phrase. This is then displayed, typically in one-example-per-line format, as an output where the context before and after each example can be clearly seen. (McEnery and Hardie 2012: 35)

This query interface makes it possible to search by exact sequences of characters or regular expressions and to apply different filters, including the structural mark-up of stage directions and dialogues.

3.3. The TEATRAD catalogue

As already mentioned, this research aims to examine the survival into the twenty-first century of some of the translated plays introduced into Spain during the Francoist regime, whether as performances or publications. A list of plays was compiled first of all, drawing on records found in the AGA database and the TRACEti catalogue, which contained the relevant authors and plays originally written in English. Each entry corresponds to a production or publication still in circulation in the twenty-first century, more specifically between 2000 and 2019.

TRACEti was used as a reference to define the fields of the catalogue with the information considered to be most relevant to identify each translation: source author, source title, target title, target author, label and observations. The initial list of authors and plays provided the data for the first two fields, while the target title varied in different productions and publications. The notion of *target author* includes a wide range of professionals who take part in theatre translations. The field *label* indicates whether the transfer was presented as a translation, adaptation, version or under a different name. Finally, the field *observations* was introduced to record whether the names of the target authors registered for the TTs used in twenty-first century productions and publications coincided with those from the twentieth century, indicating whether the TTs had perdured in time. Another set of fields was included with information about the circulation of the translations, which could either be as theatre productions, including recorded performances and audio described or subtitled versions, or as publications, including electronic

Source author	Source title	Target title	Target author	Observations	Label	Means of circulation	Year	Producer/ Publisher	Director/ Series	Place of première/ publication	Source
Arthur Miller	*Death of a Salesman*	*La muerte de un viajante*	José López Rubio	Target author from the 20th century	Version	Theatre production, recorded performance	2000	Producer: Centro Dramático Nacional, Focus	Director: Juan Carlos Pérez de la Fuente	Place: Teatre Principal (Barcelona)	CDAEM
Arthur Miller	*The Crucible*	*El crisol*	Ramón Espejo Romero		Translation	Publication, electronic book	2011	Publisher: Cátedra	Series: Letras universales	Place: Madrid	CCBIP, ISBN, REBIUN

Figure 1: Examples of entries in the TEATRAD catalogue.

books. The year, the names of the producer and the director, as well as the place of the première were added in the case of theatre productions, while for written publications, the year, the publisher, the name of the book series and the place of publication were noted. The last field contained the source where the information was found. All these details were stored in a Microsoft Excel spreadsheet to facilitate its subsequent quantitative analysis. Figure 1 shows examples of the way entries used in the TEATRAD catalogue were formatted.

The TRACEti catalogue was pivotal for the compilation of the TEATRAD catalogue as it provided a list of original playwrights with their translated counterparts introduced in Spain between 1939 and 1985, to which a few more plays retrieved from the AGA database were then added. In total, the initial list comprised 154 authors and 323 plays. To complete the field *Observations*, the TRACEti catalogue and the AGA were also used to compare the names of the target authors from the twentieth century with those identified in the twenty-first century.

The main documentary source used to gather additional data on the initial list of plays that had made it into productions in the new century was the premières database of the Centro de Documentación de las Artes Escénicas y de la Música (CDAEM), the Spanish documentation centre for performing arts and music, which is under the Spanish Ministry of Culture. This can be considered the most reliable and complete source for the study of theatrical productions performed in Spain, since the information on offer has been compiled and checked by expert documentalists and covers the dissemination of theatre culture at a national level. The webpage of the project Teatro Accesible (<www.teatroaccesible.com>) was also consulted to trace plays for which accessible versions were created for people with sensory disabilities. Other relevant details were found in the press and on the websites of several theatres.

A valuable source of information for published translations was the Catálogo Colectivo de Bibliotecas Públicas (CCBIP, <http://catalogos.mecd.es/CCBIP/cgi-ccbip/abnetopac>), which hosts more than eight million entries from over three thousand public and specialist libraries in Spain. The ISBN database (Base de datos de libros editados en España, <www.culturaydeporte.gob.es/en/cultura/libro/bases-de-datos-del-isbn/base-de-datos-de-libros.html>) was equally important as it contained information about all the books published in Spain since 1972, although some entries of works published before that date were also found. Finally, the REBIUN collective catalogue (Catálogo Colectivo de la Red de Bibliotecas Universitarias, <https://rebiun.baratz.es/rebiun>) was consulted to cross-check some of the data and to detect potential new registers. This network brings together seventy-six libraries of Spanish universities as well as the National Library of Spain and holds over sixteen million entries.

The ensuing TEATRAD catalogue, containing 307 entries of theatre productions and publications, showed the authors, plays and TTs which survived into the twenty-first century. Regarding the catalogue analysis, the data in the fields of source authors and plays was also quantified to identify frequent cases. The authors and plays that make up the corpus were then selected on the basis of their presence and recurrence both as stage productions and as published texts, an indicator not only of their survival but also of their significance in the target culture.

3.4. The TEATRAD corpus

The TEATRAD corpus was built in different stages which included: selecting and obtaining copies of the texts, digitizing and cleaning them, adding structural mark-up and metadata and aligning the TTs with their corresponding STs at the utterance level. As previously discussed, the TAligner tool was used in this process.

The authors chosen for the corpus were Tennessee Williams, Arthur Miller, Samuel Beckett and Harold Pinter. For the textual analysis, one play was to be chosen per author, one that stood out regarding stage productions and written publications. The CCBIP and REBIUN catalogues, as well as the ISBN database, helped to locate different editions of the original texts in English and their translated versions. Most were reader-oriented TTs, although some were also performance-oriented. Censored performance-oriented TTs were found at the AGA, and more recent unpublished performance-oriented TTs were generously provided by the target authors. The main criterion for the inclusion of the specific translations of the plays was their availability. The final list was made up of four plays – *The Glass Menagerie*, *The Crucible*, *Happy Days* and *The Lover* – for which the following material was obtained: (a) all the published reader- and performance-oriented TTs and (b) the unpublished performance-oriented TTs available at the AGA or provided by the target authors themselves.

Table 2 shows the identifier of all the texts that make up the TEATRAD corpus. In the case of the STs, this includes the surname of the playwright followed by the date when it was first published. In the case of the TTs, the identifier contains the target author's surname, the year in which the play was first performed or published and whether it is performance (P) or reader (R) oriented. Furthermore, to refer to each set of texts, made up of the original STs and their corresponding TTs, a noun from the title has been used: MENAGERIE (*The Glass Menagerie*), CRUCIBLE (*The Crucible*), DAYS (*Happy Days*) and LOVER (*The Lover*).

Table 2: Sets of texts in the TEATRAD corpus

Sets of texts	STs	Performance-oriented TTs	Reader-oriented TTs	References to texts
MENAGERIE	WILLIAMS_1945 WILLIAMS_1948[2]	GORDON AND DE QUINTO_1950P VÁZQUEZ VIGO_1978P GALÁN_2014P	MIRLAS_1951R DIÉGUEZ_2007R ESPEJO_ 2019R	Censorship record 274–50; Williams (1951, 1975, 2007, 2011, 2014, 2019)
CRUCIBLE	MILLER_1953	HURTADO_1956P GONZÁLEZ VERGEL AND ESCRIBANO_2007P	MUCHNIK AND MUCHNIK_1955R LÓPEZ MUÑOZ_1997R ESPEJO_2011R	Censorship record 310–56; Miller (1955, 1997, 2003, 2007, 2011)
DAYS	BECKETT_1961	MARTÍNEZ TRIVES_1963P MARTÍNEZ LUCIANO_2011P	RODRÍGUEZ GAGO_1989R	Beckett (1961, 1963, 2011, 2020)
LOVER	PINTER_1963	BOHR_1966P ESCOBAR_1966P GÓMEZ AND CANO_2013P ALDEGUER_2017P	BARBERÁ_1965R SPREGELBURD_2005R	Censorship record 91–66, 343–66; Pinter (1965, 1996, 2005a, 2013, 2017)

2 WILLIAMS_1945 and WILLIAMS_1948 are two editions of the ST where distinct differences can be found.

As most texts were only available in paper format, it was necessary to digitize them before entering them in the corpus. An optical character recognition device was employed to extract the text in plain text format (.txt), which was then revised for errors. When uploaded to TAligner, the cleaning function allowed the correction of issues such as double spaces and the standardization of the signs used to indicate character names and stage directions. Some issues were detected that affected the signs used by TAligner for structural tagging. For instance, the colon that is often located right after the speaker's name is used by the tool to recognize and mark up this structural unit, but sometimes the colon appears after the first stage direction, making it necessary to resolve this before the texts could be marked up. In these cases, a text editor (Notepad++) was used for correction. Other errors were addressed by using the Spelling & Grammar checker in the Microsoft Word text processor.

Tagging the structural units of theatre texts (i.e. acts, scenes, utterances, speakers, stage directions and dialogue exchanges) was necessary for alignment at the utterance level and to filter searches in specific parts of the texts. In TAligner, the structural mark-up process is automatic, which means that users only have to load the texts in .txt format and select *Etiquetar texto* [markup text]. The result is a file in .xml format where tags differentiate acts, scenes, utterances, speakers, stage directions and dialogues, as shown in Figure 2.


```
<div type="escena"><head>CUADRO 1</head>
 <stage>Dormitorio en la casa del reverendo Samuel Parris, en Salem, Massachussets. Primavera de 1692. En escena está el reverendo
 <sp n="1"><speaker>TITUBA:</speaker><stage type="mixed">Temerosa.</stage> ¿Se pondrá bien mi niña?</sp>
 <sp n="2"><speaker>PARRIS:</speaker><stage type="mixed">Nervioso, de mal talante.</stage> ¡Vete!... ¡Fuera de aquí!</sp>
 <sp n="3"><speaker>TITUBA:</speaker><stage type="mixed">Retrocede.</stage> Mi Betty no va a morirse... ¿verdad?</sp>
 <sp n="4"><speaker>PARRIS:</speaker><stage type="mixed">Irguiéndose, le grita. TITUBA se va dócilmente. Entre sollozos, toma la m
 <sp n="5"><speaker>ABIGAIL:</speaker><stage type="mixed">Entra ABIGAIL, sobrina del reverendo. Es una chica de belleza impresiona
 <sp n="6"><speaker>PARRIS:</speaker> ¿Qué dice el médico?</sp>
 <sp n="7"><speaker>SUSANNA:</speaker><stage type="mixed">Intenta ver a BETTY.</stage> Que no encuentra en sus libros ningún remed
 <sp n="8"><speaker>PARRIS:</speaker><stage type="mixed">Excitado.</stage> ¡Pues que siga buscando! ¡Díselo de mi parte!</sp>
 <sp n="9"><speaker>SUSANNA:</speaker> Él me manda decirle que lo de Betty podría deberse a causas antinaturales.</sp>
 <sp n="10"><speaker>PARRIS:</speaker><stage type="mixed">Temeroso, con los ojos desencajados.</stage> ¡No, no! Aquí no hay causas
 <sp n="11"><speaker>SUSANNA:</speaker><stage type="mixed">Se vuelve para irse.</stage> Sí, señor.</sp>
 <sp n="12"><speaker>ABIGAIL:</speaker><stage type="mixed">Confidencial, a SUSANNA.</stage> No hables de esto con nadie en el pueb
 <sp n="13"><speaker>PARRIS:</speaker><stage type="mixed">Con firmeza.</stage> ¡Ni de nada sobrenatural! ¿Entiendes?</sp>
```


Figure 2: Fragment of an XML file with structural annotation.

In TAligner, metadata was also introduced to help identify the texts in the corpus and facilitate filter searches according to the information included. The following fields were indicated: source authors, target titles, target authors, years, languages, identifier of each text and, if available, the publisher and the censorship record.

The STs were then aligned with all their corresponding TTs at the utterance level, as recommended by scholars such as Merino-Álvarez (1994b) and Bandín (2007). In the specific case of *Happy Days*, due to the scarcity of utterances and their significant length, it was necessary to align the texts in smaller units, for which the stage directions inside the utterances were used as references. An added value of TAligner is that it allows to align simultaneously all the TTs of a given ST, thus facilitating comparisons not only between ST-TT pairs of texts but also among TTs, as displayed in Figure 3.

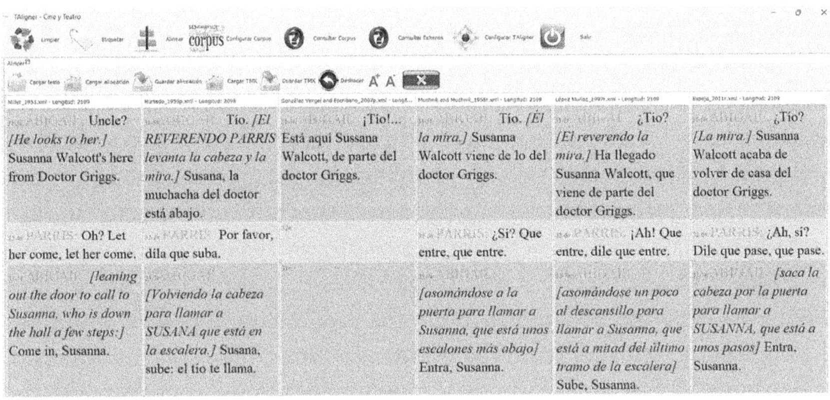

Figure 3: Aligning utterances in TAligner.

The last step consisted of linking the STs with their corresponding TTs within the tool. The ensuing parallel corpus contained a total of 463,012 words, of which 100,148 were in English and 362,864 were in Spanish.

The scrutiny of the corpus was conducted from two complementary angles. The first one seeks to offer a general characterization of the TTs in terms of the translation strategies implemented by the target authors. The second approach offers a diachronic snapshot of how sensitive topics have been dealt with across time.

The aim of the first analysis was to uncover whether the TTs were more adequate or more acceptable by crosschecking data obtained at the preliminary, macrotextual and microtextual levels. To this end, the methodology proposed by Lambert and Van Gorp (1985), and adapted by Merino-Álvarez (1994b) to the study of translated theatre, proved instrumental. During the preliminary contextualization, extratextual information about each TT was gathered from paratexts in order to better understand the TTs and interpret the results of subsequent textual analyses. The details collected included the name and profile of the target authors, their priorities and restrictions when translating, the geographical origin of the TT, the period when it was created, its performance or reader orientation, the name of the producer or publisher and, in the case of TTs from the dictatorship period, any references to the agents that had taken part in the censorship process and to any potential instances of (self-)censorship of the TTs. Different paratexts were examined including billboards, prologues, footnotes, press releases, programmes, dossiers and book covers.

As previously mentioned, all the texts included in the TEATRAD corpus were divided into utterances at the macrotextual level, which were then paired as ST and TTs to be able to identify deletions and additions. TAligner facilitated this task by showing the alignments, though it was still necessary to count manually the utterances added or deleted in each part of the play. A corpus containing 36,967 words (corpus 2) was then compiled and analysed at a microtextual level. It was made up of three fragments of about 500 words each, for each of the five STs (one from the beginning, another from the middle and the third one from the end, in line with McEnery *et al.*'s [2006] recommendations) together with the corresponding segments from the twenty TTs. In this selection, priority was given to the parts where differences between the STs and TTs were detected at the macrotextual level, as well as to the sections where indications of (self-)censorship could be detected. The transleme was used as the unit of comparison for the analysis of the linguistic data, while a set of translation techniques was borrowed from Santoyo (1980) and Merino-Álvarez (1994b). Special emphasis was placed on those techniques that had the potential of indicating the highest degree of divergence from the ST (addition, change in the order of utterances, omission and substitution). Finally, translational regularities were identified from a quantitative as well as a qualitative point of view.

The second approach to the corpus expands on a microtextual level by centring on an exploration of the diachronic evolution of the translation of certain sensitive topics that had been the object of (self-)censorship in the past: sexual morality, politics, religion and foul language. These topics were identified in the texts by searching for anchor words, described by Gómez Castro (2009: 375) as 'terms which are the physical representation of the problematic topics for the authorities of Franco's regime'.

Table 3, which is based on the complete list put forward by Gómez Castro (*ibid.*: 141–146), displays the anchor words found in the STs of the TEATRAD corpus, classified by topic and in which the asterisks represent any letter.

Table 3: English anchor words used in the analysis of the (self-)censored topics

Sexual morality			
*adulter** *affair** *bed** *bitch** *bod** *bosom** *divorce** *fornicat**	*gasp** *harlot** *illegitimate* *illicit* *kiss** *lay** *lecher** *leg**	*lover** *lust** *manly* *mistress** *negligee** *org** *passion** *pleasure**	*prostitut** *sex** *slut** *thigh** *touch** *underneath* *want** *whore**
Politics			
*Communis** *Franco* *government**	*ideolog** *King**	*law** *politic**	*Spain* *torture**
Religion			
faith *Almighty* *altar** *belie** *Catholic** *Christ**	*church** *demon** *Devil* *evil** *God* *Gospel*	*heaven* *hell* *holy* *irreverent* *minister** *pious*	*religio** *saint** *sect** *sin** *spirit**
Foul language			
*arse** *bastard** *bitch**	*bloody* *Christ*	*damn* *God*	*Goddamn* *Hell*

Using TAligner, the first passing focused on English anchor words contained in the STs, which brought up all the TTs aligned with the given ST anchor word, as displayed in Figure 4.

Figure 4: Search for (self-)censored topics in TAligner.

The concordances were then exported as Microsoft Excel spreadsheets to facilitate the analysis of the data, for which the following translation techniques were used: addition, omission (of a fragment or word), substitution and transfer. To better differentiate the translation outcomes, it was considered appropriate to split omission into omission of a fragment and omission of a word, while the category transfer was added to account for the solutions where no significant divergences from the ST were observed. As Gómez Castro (2009) remarks, the use of these techniques has certain textual-pragmatic consequences, such as reducing, maintaining or intensifying the supposedly dangerous content.

In both parts of the analysis of the TEATRAD corpus, the goal was to detect regularities not only within the textual sets but also in the corpus overall and to relate these results to those obtained in previous similar studies, as is discussed in the following chapters.

CHAPTER 4

From the TEATRAD catalogue to the corpus

This chapter focuses on the TEATRAD catalogue, which is made up of 307 entries for plays originally written in English and introduced to the Spanish theatre between 1939 and 1985 which are still being performed or published in printed form.

4.1. Survival of plays and their authors from Franco's censorship period

A careful analysis of the data in the TEATRAD catalogue shows that 31.1 per cent of the authors and 34.7 per cent of the plays introduced during the censorship period are still being performed on stage and/or are in circulation in published form today. Most of the playwrights and plays live on only in productions (22.7 per cent of authors and 21.4 per cent of plays), with a smaller number surviving both in productions and publications (7.8 per cent of authors and 10.2 per cent of plays) and only 0.6 per cent of authors and 3.1 per cent of plays being used in publications. Certain authors and plays are therefore in circulation in both the theatrical and literary systems, demonstrating their importance in Spanish culture.

Approximately a quarter of the playwrights (22.1 per cent) and plays (26 per cent) were identified solely through twentieth-century publications, many from the censorship period – 72.6 per cent of which had appeared between 1939 and 1978. The survival of these publications raises concerns about the lingering traces of textual manipulation from the Francoist censorship, an aspect examined in further detail in Chapters 5 and 6.

Figures 5 and 6 display the percentage of authors and plays initially introduced during the censorship period that have survived into the twenty-first century: (A) both productions and publications (black and dark grey stripes), (B) productions (black) or (C) publications (dark grey). They also show the percentage of (D) those only available as twentieth-century publications (light grey), and (E) those not registered in the present century (white).

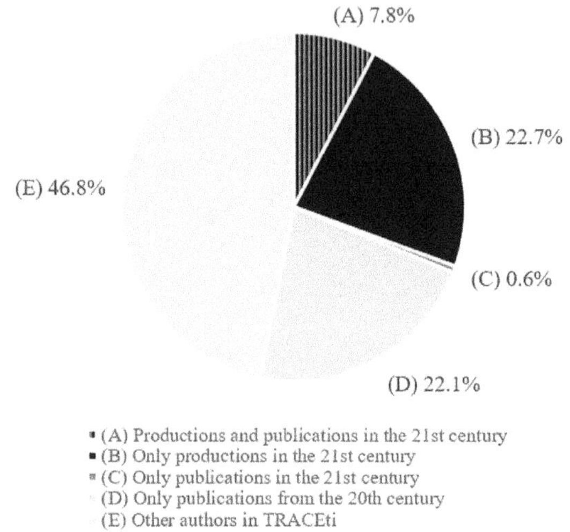

Figure 5: Presence of authors in publications/productions in the twenty-first century.

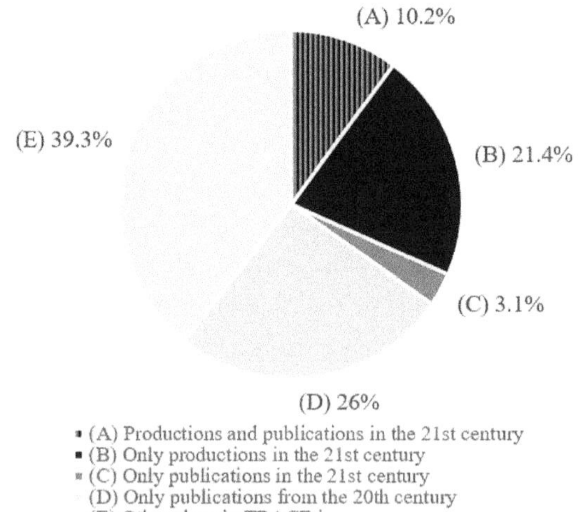

Figure 6: Presence of plays in publications/productions in the twenty-first century.

Figure 7 shows the number of plays in TEATRAD that have been staged and published during the first two decades of the twenty-first century.

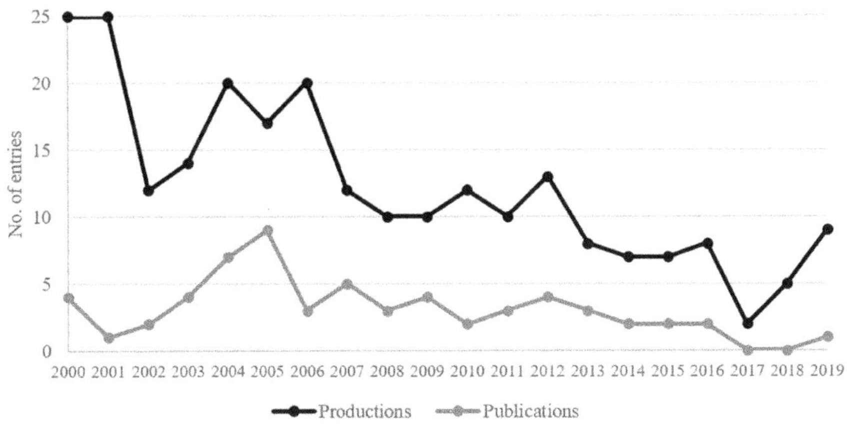

Figure 7: Distribution in years when the productions and publications took place.

The analysis of the TEATRAD catalogue shows that, between the years 2000 and 2019, the most frequently staged authors, with more than fifteen entries each, were Samuel Beckett, Tennessee Williams, Harold Pinter and Arthur Miller, followed by Edward Albee, Neil Simon, Agatha Christie, John Boynton Priestley, Peter Shaffer, Noël Coward, Eugene O'Neill and John Pielmeier, all of whom have more than five entries. As can be expected, the four most frequently staged authors are also the ones with the largest number of publications, with more than five entries apiece.

The plays with most performances, with more than five each, are: Beckett's *Waiting for Godot*, *Happy Days* and *Endgame*; Albee's *The Zoo Story*; Williams's *The Glass Menagerie*; Pinter's *The Lover*; Simon's *The Odd Couple*; Miller's *The Crucible* and Pielmeier's *Agnes of God*. The most popular printed titles, with at least three entries each, partially coincide with the most frequently acted ones, namely, Miller's *Death of a Salesman*, *The Crucible*, *All My Sons*, *A View from the Bridge* and *After the Fall*; Beckett's *Waiting for Godot*; Williams's *The Glass Menagerie*, *A Streetcar Named Desire* and *The Night of the Iguana* and Pinter's *A Slight Ache*. Other frequently performed titles, like Beckett's *Happy Days* and *Endgame* and Pinter's *The Lover*, also appeared in published form, albeit in a lower number, one or two entries each.

Table 4 summarizes the authors that made it to the stage on more than five occasions, together with a breakdown of some of the titles that were performed and published.

Table 4: Most recurrent authors and plays on stage (TEATRAD catalogue)

Pro.	Pu.	Authors	Pro.	Pu.	Plays
45	7	Samuel Beckett	17	4	*Waiting for Godot/Esperando a Godot*
			10	1	*Happy Days/Días felices*
			9	2	*Endgame/Final de partida*
			5	1	*Krapp's Last Tape/La última cinta de Krapp*
			3	1	*Come and Go/Ir y venir*
28	18	Tennessee Williams	7	3	*The Glass Menagerie/El zoo de cristal*
			5	2	*Cat on a Hot Tin Roof/La gata sobre el tejado de zinc caliente*
			3	2	*The Rose Tattoo/La rosa tatuada*
			3	3	*A Streetcar Named Desire/Un tranvía llamado Deseo*
			2	2	*Suddenly Last Summer/De repente, el último verano*
			2	0	*Talk to Me Like the Rain and Let Me Listen/Háblame como la lluvia*
			2	0	*The Lady of Larkspur Lotion/La marquesa de Larkspur Lotion*
19	6	Harold Pinter	7	1	*The Lover/El amante*
			5	1	*The Dumb Waiter/El montaplatos*
			2	1	*The Caretaker/El portero*
			2	0	*The Homecoming/Regreso al hogar*
17	15	Arthur Miller	6	4	*The Crucible/Las brujas de Salem*
			4	0	*The Price/El precio*
			3	6	*Death of a Salesman/La muerte de un viajante*
			2	4	*All My Sons/Todos eran mis hijos*
			2	3	*A View from the Bridge/Panorama desde el Puente*
14	2	Edward Albee	9	0	*The Zoo Story/Historia del zoo*
			4	1	*Who's Afraid of Virginia Woolf?/¿Quién teme a Virginia Woolf?*
12	0	Neil Simon	8	0	*The Odd Couple/La extraña pareja*
			3	0	*Barefoot in the Park/Descalzos por el parque*

Pro.	Pu.	Authors	Pro.	Pu.	Plays
9	3	Agatha Christie	3 3 2	2 0 0	*The Mousetrap/La ratonera* *And Then There Were None/Diez negritos* *The Unexpected Guest/La visita inesperada*
8	3	John Boynton Priestley	4 2 2	1 2 1	*Time and the Conways/El tiempo y los Conways* *An Inspector Calls/Llama un inspector* *Dangerous Corner/Esquina peligrosa*
8	1	Peter Shaffer	4 2 2	0 1 0	*Black Comedy/El apagón* *Equus/Equus* *Amadeus/Amadeus*
7	0	Noël Coward	4	0	*Blithe Spirit/Un espíritu burlón*
6	1	Eugene O'Neill	2	1	*Long Day's Journey Into Night/Largo viaje hacia la noche*
6	0	John Pielmeier	6	0	*Agnes of God/Agnes de Dios*

Figures 8 and 9 offer a more visual representation of the above data.

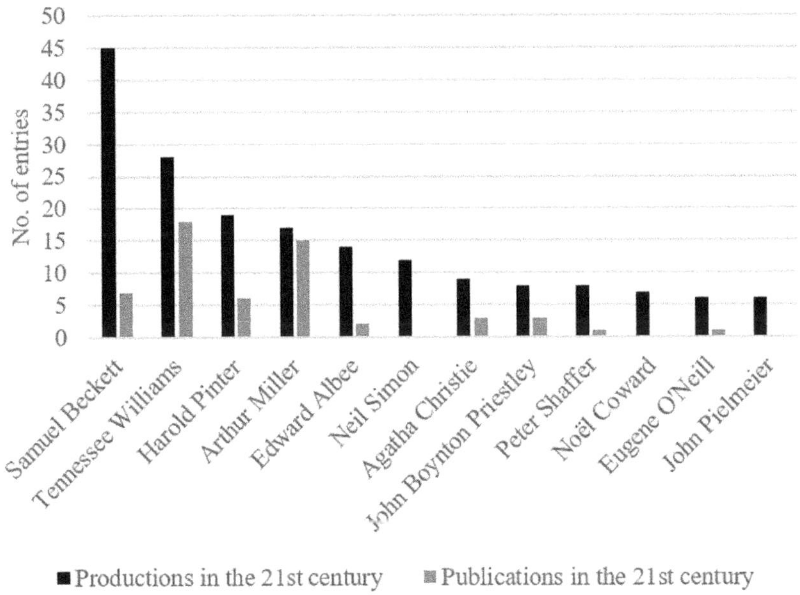

Figure 8: Most commonly staged authors.

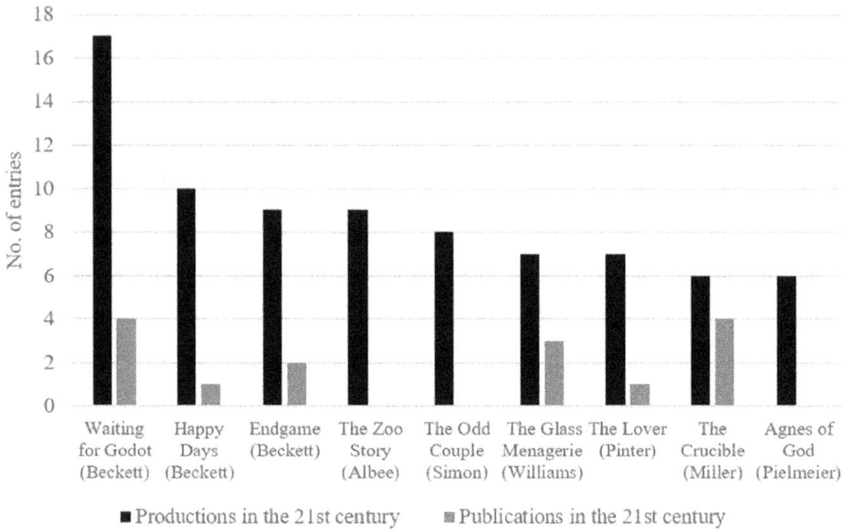

Figure 9: Most commonly staged plays.

As shown, Beckett, Williams, Pinter and Miller take the lion's share of the entries in the TEATRAD catalogue when it comes to both productions and publications. The plays selected for further analysis, based on the recurrent presence of the authors as well as the titles, as both staged and printed works, are Williams's *The Glass Menagerie*, Miller's *The Crucible*, Beckett's *Happy Days*[1] and Pinter's *The Lover*.

The Glass Menagerie, translated as *El zoo de cristal*, was one of Tennessee Williams's most frequently performed and published plays in the two centuries. Over forty staged productions of this play in Spanish, Basque and Catalan can be traced in the censorship record, 274–50, and the CDAEM database. The fact that by 1959, Tennessee Williams was an acclaimed author who had earned three New York Drama Critics' Circle Awards, two Pulitzer Prizes, three Donaldson Awards and a Tony Award might have contributed

1 Although *Waiting for Godot* appears more often than *Happy Days* in the TEATRAD catalogue, initial textual comparisons indicate that the available TTs seem to come from the French ST.

to his continual presence on stage. As Merino-Álvarez (2000) notes, having won awards was a line of argument used to convince the censors at the time. Regarding the publications of this play, four translations in Spanish and one in Catalan can be found in the CCBIP and REBIUN. The work was also broadcast on television in 1963 (Espejo, 2019), and two films based on the play, from 1973 and 1987, were also distributed in Spain (Harvey and Jordan 2006; Newman 2015). As is the case with other contemporary American plays, part of the success enjoyed by Tennessee Williams's plays on stage was largely on the back of the film adaptations of those works (Pérez L. de Heredia 2004).

Arthur Miller's *The Crucible*, translated as *Las brujas de Salem* or *El crisol*, was circulated through successive theatre productions. The censorship record, 310–56, and the CDAEM database register fourteen performances in Spanish and two in Catalan, some of which came with subtitles for the deaf and hard of hearing and audio description for the blind. The play saw five editions in print, according to the CCBIP. A film adaptation was directed by Nicholas Hytner in 1996 (Hytner 1996), once again showing the close relationship that exists between theatre and cinema. An adaptation in Spanish was broadcast by Radio Televisión Española (RTVE, 2022) in 1973 as part of their long-running anthology series *Estudio 1*. Apart from winning numerous international prizes, such as the New York Drama Critics' Circle Award and the Pulitzer Prize (Bigsby 2010), Miller also received the prestigious Spanish *Premio Príncipe de Asturias de las Letras* in 2002.

Samuel Beckett's *Happy Days*, *Días felices* or *Los días felices*, was frequently staged since its première in 1963. According to the censorship record, 47–63, and the CDAEM, twenty productions took place in Spanish and six in Catalan. The play was also circulated in print form, with two publications in Spanish and another two in Catalan, all of which were catalogued in the CCBIP and REBIUN. The awards received by Beckett throughout his professional career include the Nobel Prize in Literature in 1969.

According to the censorship records, 91–66 and 343–66, as well as the CDAEM database, *El amante*, the literal Spanish title for Pinter's *The Lover*, was widely performed, with sixteen productions in Spanish and four in Catalan. Written publications were less numerous, however, with two in Spanish, from Argentina, another two in Catalan and one in Basque; these were all registered in the CCBIP and the REBIUN. Among the awards obtained by Pinter, are the Nobel Prize in Literature in 2005 and the French *Légion d'Honneur* in 2007.

Merino-Álvarez (2021) argues that the status of an author or play as a classic derives from their continued presence within a given culture, often through adaptations. In this sense, the authors and plays selected for further analysis can be considered contemporary classics, both in terms of artistic quality as well as economic benefit (Espejo 2018). In short, their artistic and financial status may well have opened the doors to their continued presence in the new millennium.

Table 5 contains further information about the most frequent production companies, directors and venues (at least four entries) behind the plays in the TEATRAD catalogue.

Table 5: Production companies, directors and première venues

Production companies	Directors	Venues of premières
Centro Dramático Nacional (x10) Teatro Español (x7) Nearco Producciones (x6) Txalo Producciones (x6) Iniciativas Teatrales (x5) Juanjo Seoane Producciones (x5) Real Escuela Superior de Arte Dramático (x5) La Pajarita de Papel (x4) Nueva Comedia (x4)	José Carlos Plaza (x4) Ricard Reguant (x4) Rodolfo Cortizo (x4)	Teatro Palacio Valdés (Avilés) (x6) Teatro Valle-Inclán (Madrid) (x5) Teatro de La Abadía (Madrid) (x5) Teatro Español (Madrid) (x4) Palacio de Festivales de Cantabria (Santander) (x4)

The Centro Dramático Nacional and the Teatro Español, sometimes in coproduction with others, stand out as the main production companies. The former is dependent on the National Institute for Performing Arts and Music and the latter on the Madrid City Council, both based in the Spanish capital.

A close examination shows that some of the plays were made accessible to patrons through audio descriptions, subtitles for the deaf and hard of hearing or sign language, signalling a qualitative step in the dissemination of the plays to wider audiences. The numbers are low – only two per cent of the productions in TEATRAD – and correspond to initiatives of the project Teatro Accesible, led by the Centro Dramático Nacional. Some of the accessible versions are Miller's *The Crucible* and *A View from the Bridge*, Beckett's *Waiting for Godot* and Williams's *The Rose Tattoo*.

The catalogue also registers the video recordings of certain productions (26.8 per cent), including some accessible ones, which are available on the platform Teatroteca (<http://teatroteca.teatro.es>). As with the accessible shows, some of these recordings focus on the works of the most prominent playwrights, namely, Williams, Beckett, Pinter, Miller and Albee.

Table 6 includes the most frequent publishers and places of publication, with a minimum of four entries.

Table 6: Publishers and places of publication

Publishers	Places of publication
Losada (x20)	Barcelona (x20)
Tusquets (x10)	Buenos Aires (x20)
Cátedra (x7)	Madrid (x16)
Losada and Sagrafic (x5)	Buenos Aires and Barcelona (x5)

The publishing house with the most entries (twenty) is the Argentinian Losada, which, as Merino-Álvarez (1994b) observes, offered prototypical reader-oriented translations. Tusquets is the second most popular publisher, with ten entries, followed by Cátedra (7), characterized by the inclusion of critical studies about the plays. In addition to printed editions, electronic editions are also found (16.4 per cent), including plays by Arthur Miller and Tennessee Williams, usually in Cátedra and Alba.

4.2. Survival of target texts from the twentieth century

In the case of staged productions, only 6.5 per cent of the entries found in the twenty-first century use TTs from the preceding century, while

43.5 per cent seem to be TTs created in the new millennium. In the case of the remaining 50 per cent, it has not been possible to ascertain their origin since the name of the target author was not found in the consulted sources, a common occurrence highlighted by Pérez L. de Heredia's (2004) when working with performance-oriented TTs.

With regard to publications, the same TTs that were commercialized in the twentieth century are also being distributed in the twenty-first in 37.7 per cent of cases, while 62.3 per cent seem to be new retranslations. The name of the target author is systematically included in all the works so that it is possible to trace the survival of TTs in the literary system more accurately than in the theatrical system. Figure 10 shows the percentage of productions and publications according to the year in which the TTs appeared.

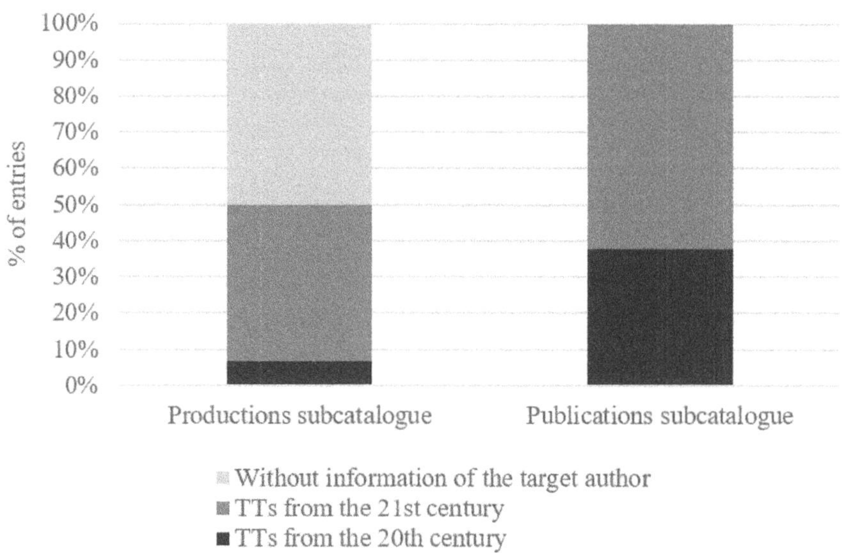

Figure 10: Use of TTs from the twentieth or the twenty-first centuries.

Table 7 contains a list of the most prolific target authors from the twenty-first century and shows that some of them, such as Eduardo Mendoza and Juan Vicente Martínez Luciano, were involved in productions and publications while the rest only participated in one of the creative processes.

Table 7: Target authors of TTs from the twenty-first century

Productions	Publications	Recurrent target authors
4	3	Eduardo Mendoza
3	1	Juan Vicente Martínez Luciano
4	0	Ricard Reguant
0	8	Cristina Piña
0	4	Ramón Espejo
0	4	Rafael Spregelburd

It was a common practice to translate works by the same playwright and, for instance, Ramón Espejo worked on different plays by Miller (*A View from the Bridge*, *The Crucible* and *Death of a Salesman*) and Williams (*The Glass Menagerie* and *A Streetcar Named Desire*); Juan Vicente Martínez Luciano translated Pinter's *A Slight Ache* and *One for the Road*; and Rafael Spregelburd also translated plays by Pinter, published in four books (*The Lover*, *Night School*, *Revue Sketches*, *The Birthday Party*, *The Room*, *A Slight Ache*, *The Black and White*, *The Examination*, *The Dumb Waiter*, *The Hothouse*, *A Night Out*, *Old Times*, *Betrayal*).

In half of the staged productions, the target author and director were the same person, and collaboration between target authors was more common in the case of productions (21.7 per cent) than publications (12.5 per cent). This teamwork approach in the theatrical sphere has also been observed by Merino-Álvarez (1994b) in Spain and by Perteghella (2004) and Brodie (2017) in Italy, Germany and the United Kingdom.

Different terms are used to refer to the TTs in the theatrical and literary systems, with a higher variability in the former, where the most frequent labels are *version*, *adaptation* and *translation*. When it comes to publications, all the TTs are referred to as *translation* except for two editions of performance-oriented TTs, for which *version* and *translation and version* are used. Brodie (2017: 3) regards the use of such nomenclature in the theatrical system as 'an attempt to highlight the creativity of the translation process'. Arguably, it could also point to different types of transfer but, since the use of these labels is far from being unified (Merino-Álvarez 1994b; Braga Riera 2006; Brodie 2017), further research should be conducted on the topic to elucidate whether different terms reflect different translational approaches.

The reutilization in the twenty-first century of TTs that had seen the light in the previous century is also a common occurrence, with most of these texts coming from the censorship period (in 87.5 per cent of the productions and 65.2 per cent of the publications) and having been translated by target authors such as Ana María Moix, León Mirlas, Manuel Barberá and José López Rubio, who got involved in productions and publications, and Miguel de Hernani and Aurora Bernárdez, who only worked on printed translations in the catalogue. Many signed more than one title by the same playwright, as in the case of Mirlas, who translated three plays by Tennessee Williams, one of which has been included in the corpus. Most of the TTs generated during the censorship period were reader-oriented texts in print, although some performance-oriented TTs were also published. Our data show that the literary system regularly provides translations for the theatrical system. Table 8 contains a list of the most prolific target authors with their works, the year of publication and the name of the publisher in the case of books, and the year and producer in that of staged plays, both in the twentieth and twenty-first centuries.

Table 8: Twentieth-century TTs (1939–1978) that survive in the twenty-first

Target authors	TTs	Twentieth century (1939–1978)	Twenty-first century
Manuel Barberá	*Incidente en Vichy* (*Incident at Vichy*)	1965 Losada 1967 Losada	2002 Losada
	Después de la caída (*After the Fall*)	1965 Losada 1967 Losada	2002 Losada 2004 Losada
	El precio (*The Price*)	1970 Tiempo Nuevo	2003 Bacanal Teatro
	La noche de la iguana (*The Night of the Iguana*)	1964 Losada 1966 Losada	2007 Losada
	Lo que no se dice (*Something Unspoken*)	1966 Losada	2006 Losada
	Súbitamente el último verano (*Suddenly Last Summer*)	1966 Losada	2006 Losada

Target authors	TTs	Twentieth century (1939–1978)	Twenty-first century
Aurora Bernárdez	*El tiempo y los Conway* (*Time and the Conways*)	1952 Losada 1959 Aguilar	2005 Losada
	Ha llegado un inspector (*An Inspector Calls*)	1952 Losada	2005 Losada
	La esquina peligrosa (*Dangerous Corner*)	1952 Losada	2005 Losada
	Yo estuve aquí una vez (*I Have Been Here Before*)	1952 Losada	2005 Losada
Miguel de Hernani	*Todos eran mis hijos* (*All My Sons*)	1953 Losada	2002 Losada 2004 Losada
	La muerte de un viajante (*Death of a Salesman*)	1953 Losada	2005 Losada
José López Rubio	*La muerte de un viajante* (*Death of a Salesman*)	1952 Lope de Vega 1952 Escelicer 1985 MK	2000 CDN and Focus
	Crimen perfecto (*Dial 'M' For Murder*)	1954 Lope de Vega 1955 Escelicer	2000 Compañía Manuel Canseco
León Mirlas	*El zoo de cristal* (*The Glass Menagerie*)	1951 Losada 1956 Losada 1978 Losada	2005 Centro de Nuevos Creadores 2007 Losada
	Verano y humo (*Summer and Smoke*)	1956 Losada 1964 Losada	2004 Losada
Ana María Moix	*Esperando a Godot* (*Waiting for Godot*)	1970 Ateneo de Bilbao 1970 Barral 1985 Tusquets 1989 Plaza & Janés	2005 Réplika Teatro 2013 CDN 2015 La Nuca Teatro 2003 Sol 90 2015 Tusquets 2017 Tusquets 2018 Austral
	Fin de partida (*Endgame*)	1970 Barral 1986 Tusquets 1989 Plaza & Janés 1999 Unidad Editorial	2010 Teatro de La Abadía 2015 Tusquets 2017 Tusquets

Table 9 shows that many TTs carried out in the twentieth century after the censorship and available in the twenty-first are publications, and most are reeditions by the same publisher, although some were also used in staged productions. Each target author appears in only one register, except for José Luis López Muñoz, who is found in two. Works by José Luis López Muñoz (1997) and Antonia Rodríguez Gago (1989) have been selected for further analysis in Chapters 5 and 6.

Table 9: Twentieth-century TTs (1979–1999) that survive in the twenty-first

Target authors	TTs	Twentieth century (1979–1999)	Twenty-first century
Mariano Antolín Rato	*La noche de la iguana* (*The Night of the Iguana*)	1998 Alba	2006 Random House Mondadori
Ana Antón-Pacheco	*Largo viaje hacia la noche* (*Long Day's Journey Into Night*)	1986 Cátedra 1995 Altaya	2014 Cátedra
Alberto Mira	*¿Quién teme a Virginia Woolf?* (*Who's Afraid of Virginia Woolf?*)	1997 Cátedra	2018 Arte&Desmayo 2015 Cátedra
León Mirlas	*Un tranvía llamado Deseo* (*A Streetcar Named Desire*)	1989 Losada	2008 Losada
José Luis López Muñoz	*Las brujas de Salem* (*The Crucible*)	1997 Tusquets	2017 CDN 2015 Tusquets
	La visita de un inspector (*An Inspector Calls*)	1996 Vicens Vives	2013 Vicens Vives
Antonia Rodríguez Gago	*Los días felices* (*Happy Days*)	1989 Cátedra	2020 Cátedra
Manuel Sáenz de Heredia	*Sueños de un seductor* (*Play It Again Sam*)	1983 Tusquets	2015 Tusquets

Collaboration between target authors is also observed in the works created in the twentieth century, albeit in a smaller scale than in the new millennium: 18.8 per cent of productions and 4.3 per cent of publications.

As for the terminology used to refer to the outputs, different options are noted in the case of the productions, while all publications appeared as *translations*. The diversity of labels operating in the theatrical system and the preference for *translation* in the literary one is a characteristic that cuts across time.

This first analysis has uncovered the authors, plays and TTs that were introduced in Spain during the censorship period and are still being used in productions and publications in the twenty-first century. The next chapters contain the analysis of a selection of works, the TEATRAD corpus, from two perspectives: an overview at the macro and micro levels of the main translation strategies adopted and an incursion at the micro level to ascertain the diachronic evolution of some (self-)censored topics.

CHAPTER 5

Characterization of target texts

This chapter focuses on uncovering whether the twenty TTs that make up the corpus tend to the pole of adequacy or acceptability. After gathering contextual data from these TTs, over 15,000 utterances (corpus 1) were paired, and textual fragments were compared at a microtextual level (corpus 2), where 650 translation techniques – additions, changes in the ordering of utterances, omissions and substitutions – were observed. The results of the analysis are explored in relation to each of the sets of texts in order to identify their characteristics as well as the trends in the corpus as a whole. A brief preliminary contextualization of each TT is included, starting with performance-oriented TTs and followed by reader-oriented TTs. Graphs are used to present the results of the study at a macrotextual level. Finally, the translation techniques are detailed at a microtextual level and global conclusions are drawn.

5.1. The Glass Menagerie

The MENAGERIE text set is composed of six TTs, three of which are performance-oriented (GORDON AND DE QUINTO_1950P, VÁZQUEZ VIGO_1978P and GALÁN_2014P) with a further three being reader-oriented (MIRLAS_1951R, DIÉGUEZ_2007R and ESPEJO_2019R). Figure 11 places the works in a historical context depending on whether they belong to the period of censorship (delimited by the discontinuous vertical line) or were produced afterwards.

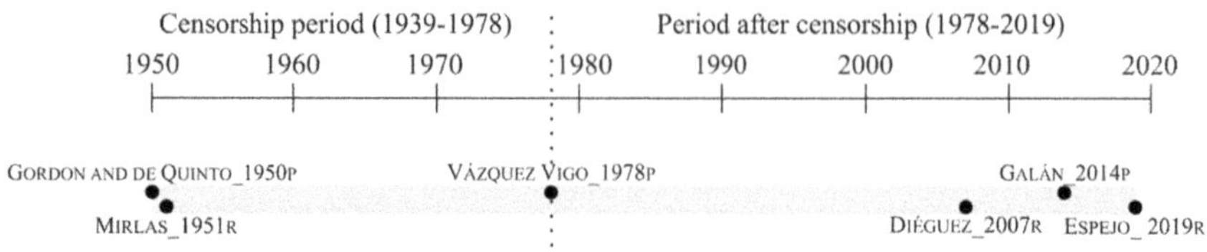

Figure 11: Menagerie text set.

Gordon and de Quinto_1950p

The first request for a performance of a TT of *The Glass Menagerie* to be listed in the AGA was presented in 1950 by José Gordon and José María de Quinto, directors of the theatrical company La Carátula and translators of the TT. The high number of requests filed in the censorship record (twenty-two before 1973) confirms the wide circulation of this TT on the stage. The first printed work of the play in Spain saw the light in 1960. The publisher was Escelicer and it came out as part of the Teatro series, which specialized in performance-oriented texts (Merino-Álvarez 1994b). A re-publication dating to 1964 also exists in the CCBIP and the ISBN database. It includes a preliminary note, signed by Gordon, offering information on the introduction of the play to the Spanish stage, which seems to indicate a target-oriented approach.

After being given an original English version of the play by Santiago Magariños (Gordon 1960), the target authors decided to stage it and submitted a request for its performance on 26 June 1950, which was then filed in the AGA as part of record 274–50. A censor's report was subsequently filed praising the beauty of the play but noting that it should only be performed before a minority audience because the psychology of the characters was deemed more interesting than the action. On 1 July 1950, the censors authorized it for audiences over sixteen years of age, without any deletions. The first première of the translated play took place at the Salón de Actos del P. M. M. in Madrid in 1950, as noted by Sainz de Robles (1950). For over two decades, requests for performances were filed annually by a number of companies. The first première to take place in a commercial theatre was in 1957 at the Teatro Eslava in Madrid (Espejo 2019). Interestingly, to encourage patrons to see this particular production of Williams's play, it was stressed that it did not resemble other plays by the same author – for example,

A Streetcar Named Desire or *Cat on a Hot Tin Roof* – insofar as it did not contain anything scandalous (Espejo 2019). Most of these productions were performed in Madrid and Barcelona, although other smaller cities were also listed in the censorship record 274–50.

VÁZQUEZ VIGO_1978P

In 1978, the year that marked the legislative end of the Francoist censorship, the impresario Andrés de Kramer requested the use of a TT of the play *The Glass Menagerie*, signed by Carmen Vázquez Vigo, for a production directed by José Luis Alonso at the Teatro Marquina in Madrid. Vázquez Vigo, who appears as both a target author and an actor in this production, had taken part in previous productions of the play which used the GORDON AND DE QUINTO_1950P TT. The programme openly indicates that VÁZQUEZ VIGO_1978P was an adaptation of this earlier TT.

The request for a performance of VÁZQUEZ VIGO_1978P was filed in the same censorship record as GORDON AND DE QUINTO_1950P (record 274–50). The documentation includes a letter in which Kramer makes a case for a change of classification: 'taking into account [the fact] that this comedy deserves a new classification in the current circumstances, due to its content as well as its presentation and values, we ask that it be authorized for all audiences' (record 274–50, my translation). In their reports, the censors, Fernando Mier and Antonio Albizu, note that they do not have any objection to the play being authorized to all audiences, though they also insist that establishing a minimum age for viewing the play seems more appropriate to them. A new classification for all audiences was therefore granted on 3 March 1978. According to Espejo (2019), the production took a conventional approach and was a success, leading to the revival of various plays by Tennessee Williams up until the 1980s.

GALÁN_2014P

In 2014, a production by Secuencia 3 took place under the direction of Francisco Vidal and using a TT by Eduardo Galán. The play premièred at the Palacio de Festivales de Cantabria in Santander and was subsequently performed at the Teatro Fernán Gómez in Madrid. Eduardo Galán, a writer, producer and teacher, is a figure of considerable prestige in the world of Spanish theatre. He founded Secuencia 3 (<www.secuencia3.es/eduardo-galan>), held the position of *Subdirector General de Teatro* [Deputy Director General of Theatre] at the National Institute for Performing Arts and Music from 1996 to 2000 and is a founding member of the Academia de las Artes Escénicas de España (n.d.a). The involvement of theatrical professionals as target authors of performance-oriented TTs is a common occurrence, which has been identified in previous studies (Merino-Álvarez 1994b).

The website of Secuencia 3 includes paratexts on this production, such as the billboard, the dossier and a promotional video. The first lines of the billboard mention the starring of Silvia Marsó in *The Glass Menagerie* by Tennessee Williams, probably in an attempt to attract the spectator's attention through the use of three names well-known in theatrical culture. The status of the playwright and the play itself seem to have been key factors in its survival over the years, and the choice of a well-known actor as the protagonist is another marketing trick to attract a larger audience. Both the image and the name of the actor Silvia Marsó are in larger print than for other members of the cast, making her prominent role in the production abundantly clear. The target author is listed along with the name of the director and stage designer, something that does not always happen in the theatre, but in this case seems to indicate the high standing of this target author in the theatrical sphere. The dossier and promotional video offer a historical overview of the play in previous American and Spanish stages, as well as information on its adaptation for the cinema. The production aroused the interest of the press – thirty-seven articles have been found in the database of the CDAEM – and received positive reviews. Savirón (2014, my translation) welcomes it as: 'An adaptation that stands out for its correct staging, and for seemingly being made by and for Silvia Marsó, who uses this excellent opportunity perfectly and brings to life an exquisite Amanda'.

Galán (personal communication, April 2020), the target author who acted as producer, acknowledges having consulted the two previously published TTs in Spanish, MIRLAS_1951R and DIÉGUEZ_2007R, and having set himself clear priorities that favoured the target pole, namely, changing the focus from the character of Tom to that of Amanda, providing moments of humour, using dynamic dialogue exchanges and adjusting the timing of the performance so that it lasted ninety minutes.

MIRLAS_1951R

The oldest TT found in the CCBIP is by León Mirlas and dates to 1951. It was published by Losada – one of the main Argentinian publishers to provide reader-oriented TTs of plays at that time (Merino-Álvarez 1994b) – as part of their series Clásicos Universales and reedited in 1999 and 2006. Mirlas is a frequent target author of translations that circulated in Spain in the twentieth and the twenty-first centuries, and his translations include other plays by Tennessee Williams.

The first registered translations of the MENAGERIE set were a performance-oriented TT created in Spain (GORDON AND DE QUINTO_1950P) and a reader-oriented TT imported from Argentina (MIRLAS_1951R). These 'foreign' translations had to be registered with the censors as soon as they arrived in Spain, although some books also circulated illegally (Cornellà-Detrell 2015). In this case, two censorship records relating to MIRLAS_1951R (5862–53 and 251–58) have been found. The first request (record 5862–53) for the distribution of this TT, which appeared in the same volume as the plays *A Streetcar Named Desire* and *Summer and Smoke*, was presented to the literary censors in 1953. Reference is made in this record to the issues raised by the censors of the plays for performance, even though the TT presented to the theatrical censors was, in fact, a different one. The resolution states that the text of *The Glass Menagerie* is harmless and can therefore be authorized, although objections were raised to the other two plays, in particular *A Streetcar Named Desire*, for which a reader-oriented publication was authorized provided it was not performed, thus illustrating how norms were different for performance-oriented and reader-oriented TTs. The second censorship record (251–58) simply refers to the previous decision.

DIÉGUEZ_2007R

In 2007, a TT signed by Amado Diéguez was published by Alba in Barcelona as part of the series Artes Escénicas, together with a TT of *A Streetcar Named Desire*. The DIÉGUEZ_2007R TT continued to be republished over the ensuing years (a sixth edition from 2017 was identified in libraries and an electronic publication from 2013 in the ISBN database). Diéguez appears in the CCBIP and REBIUN as the translator of TTs of different textual genres.

The book containing the DIÉGUEZ_2007R TT also includes paratexts about the chronology of Williams's life and works, as well as introductions to each play and two texts written by Williams and associated with the plays. The introduction to *The Glass Menagerie* is the translation of a text originally written by Robert Bray – director of *The Tennessee Williams Annual Review* – covering aspects of the première, the author and the play and Williams's text *The Catastrophe of Success* comments on his popularity as a writer. Notes by the translator are also included to elaborate further on certain cultural references. On the whole, the nature of these paratexts points to a source-oriented approach.

ESPEJO_2019R

The most recent TT in the MENAGERIE text set, authored by Ramón Espejo, was published in 2019 in print and electronic format by Cátedra as part of the series Letras Universales, which specializes in literary classics. It is a critical edition that also includes a translation of the play *A Streetcar Named Desire*. The target author is a professor at the University of Seville and an expert in twentieth-century American theatre and its reception in Spain (Espejo 2010b, 2017). His work as a translator of plays by Miller (2010, 2011, 2012) is also of particular note. This edition is significant not only because it offers new translations, but also because of the vast amount of paratextual information and its high quality.

Indeed, the TTs include numerous notes by the translator, an introduction, a list of bibliographical references and a section about the edition itself. The translator's notes cover a variety of aspects, such as explanations of cultural references and traits specific to Williams's plays. The introductory chapter explores the playwright's life and work in the theatre and includes an in-depth study of the two plays, thus providing an abundance of data about the author and the works themselves. Regarding *The Glass Menagerie*, aspects such as the plot and the structure are examined, as well as the characters and dramatic technique, all of which foster a better understanding of the play both from a textual and contextual perspective. Some influential productions of the play in Spain are also examined. The documentation is completed with a series of recommended bibliographical references about the author and play. These paratexts point to the source-orientedness of the TT.

The section about the edition offers pertinent data on the translation. Espejo (2019) observes that the ST is the reader-oriented edition (WILLIAMS_1948), which is the one preferred by Williams and included in his complete works published by New Directions in 1971. Espejo (2019: 111, my translation) spells out his priorities when tackling the translation and emphasizes the importance of maintaining in Spanish the fluency of the English dialogue:

> Any translator has to make numerous decisions with which then to be consistent. In this case, I understood that the translation of Williams's plays required faithfulness to the original and meticulousness at the same time as fluency. I have tried to achieve these three things, maintaining not only what Williams tells us, but also the whole variety of nuances that he presents us with. This was not always easy. At the same time, it was important for me that the Spanish text sounded fluent in keeping with the spirit of Williams's dialogues.

Furthermore, Espejo (*ibid.*) describes specific translation decisions with regard to certain features of the ST, such as unfinished sentences and idioms, demonstrating a thorough understanding of how theatrical texts operate. Espejo (personal communication, January 2020) firmly believes that the translation must make it easy for the reader to imagine how the text would sound on stage. For him, theatre translations have to be performable, even if they are not initially intended for a specific production. For this reason, he always strives to make dialogue exchanges sound natural and believable and to ensure that, in broad terms, they will have a similar effect on the audience or readers as that of the ST.

His translational approach seems to have paid off, according to Ballesteros Dorado's (2021: 835, my translation) review: 'today, finally, readers can enjoy two of the greatest plays by Tennessee Williams in a reliable and rigorous Spanish version, with the guarantee of these having been prepared by an outstanding expert on American theatre.'

5.1.1. Macrotextual analysis

The pairing of utterances in MENAGERIE shows the complexity of this text set. First, the identification of the ST edition used for the TTs was crucial. The evidence derived from the comparison at the macrotextual level – as well as at the microtextual level, to be presented in the next section – points to the use of two different editions of the original play: the performance-oriented edition (WILLIAMS_1945) for MIRLAS_1951R and the reader-oriented edition (WILLIAMS_1948), or a combination of this edition and previous TTs, in the case of the rest of the TTs.

The three performance-oriented TTs tend towards acceptability at a macrotextual level. GORDON AND DE QUINTO_1950P is the performance-oriented TT where the fewest omissions of utterances from the ST are observed, although the number is still higher than in any of the reader-oriented TTs. When compared to the ST, almost all the differences found in VÁZQUEZ VIGO_1978P consist of omissions of utterances, notably in the second act. In the case of GALÁN_2014P, which shows the most differences, a substantial number of additions and omissions can be observed throughout the whole play, an approach that seems to relate to the specificity of the mise-en-scène. For instance, many of the additional utterances correspond to the character of Amanda, on which this production focuses, as discussed in the preliminary contextualization (Section 5.1).

The three reader-oriented TTs contain only a few occasional deletions, sometimes of repeated content that appears in consecutive utterances, thus bringing the TTs to the adequacy pole.

Drawing on the data obtained, the following visualization illustrates the levels of omission and addition of utterances observed in the TTs, as well as their distribution in the specific acts of the play (Figures 12 and 13). Each unit of the horizontal axis represents an utterance from the play. The ST utterances that have been omitted in the TTs are marked in darker grey, and the utterances added in the TTs are noted in black. Overall, these graphs show a higher number of omissions and additions in the performance-oriented than in the reader-oriented TTs.

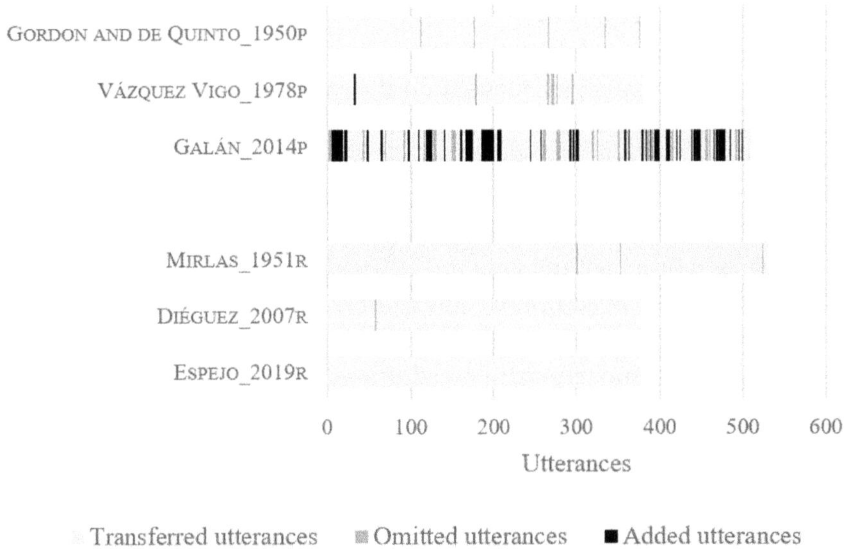

Figure 12: Omissions and additions of utterances in Menagerie, Act 1.

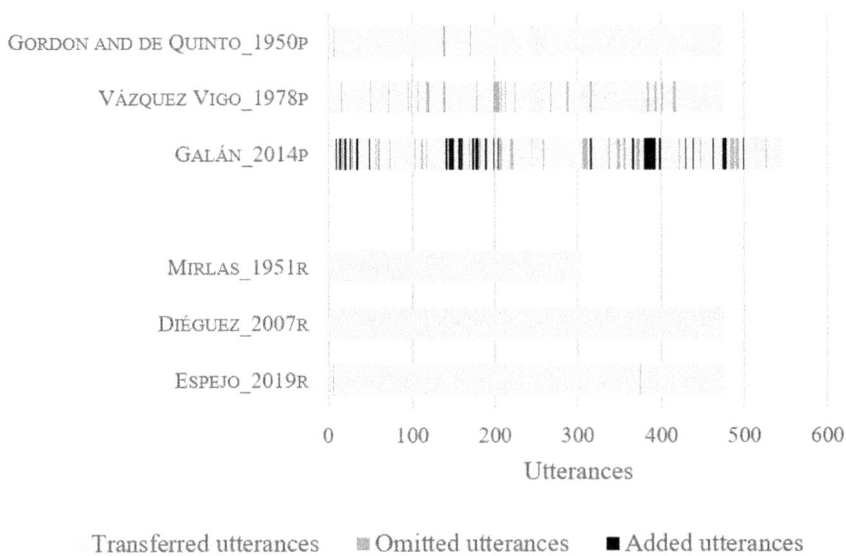

Figure 13: Omissions and additions of utterances in Menagerie, Act 2.

5.1.2. Microtextual analysis

The microtextual analysis, focused on the translation techniques implemented by the various translators, aligns with the results obtained in the macrotextual analysis: the three performance-oriented texts show a tendency towards acceptability, while the three reader-oriented versions lean towards adequacy. As illustrated in Figure 14, the first group of TTs is characterized by a high frequency of omission of textual material, as well as by the presence of additions, substitutions and, in some cases, changes in the order of some utterances. The reader-oriented TTs display fewer, minor omissions and, crucially, no additions, substitutions or changes in the order of utterances.

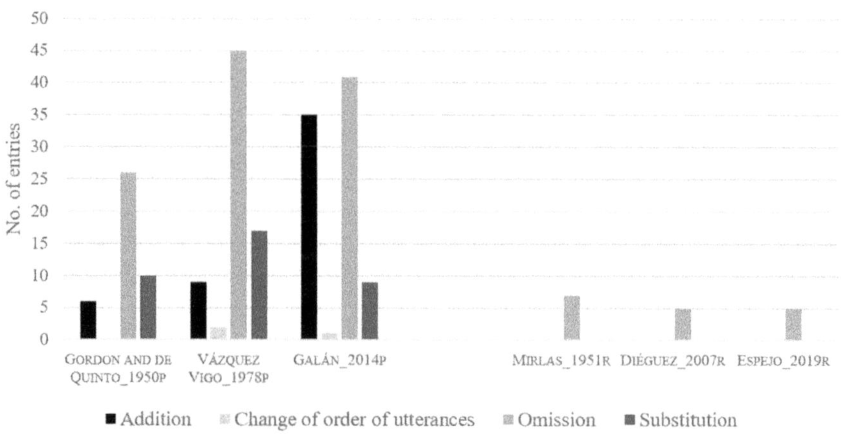

Figure 14: Translation techniques in Menagerie.

The following paragraphs take a closer look at the three translation techniques that stand out due to the degree of textual alteration they involve and their recurrence in the performance-oriented TTs, namely, omission, addition and substitution.

a) Omission

In the three stage-oriented translations, several words, phrases and sentences have been omitted, especially in the dialogues, and whole utterances are also absent. From a qualitative viewpoint, some of the deletions found in

GORDON AND DE QUINTO_1950P seem to be linked to self-censorship, unlike in the case of the two other versions, and GALÁN_2014P displays a higher number of omissions than the other two texts. Table 10 shows instances of these differences across the three TTs.

Table 10: Examples of omission in Menagerie

WILLIAMS_1948	TOM: [...] In Spain there was Guernica! But here there was only hot swing music and liquor, dance halls, bars, and movies, and sex that hung in the gloom like a chandelier and flooded the world with brief, deceptive rainbows ...
GORDON AND DE QUINTO_1950P	TOM: [...] Pero aquí solamente había música de jazz y licores, salones de baile y sensualidad, sensualidad correspondida en la penumbra opaca, como una lámpara que inundase el mundo de fugitivos arco iris engañosos. [TOM: [...] But here there were only jazz music and liquor, dance halls and sensuality, requited sensuality in the opaque gloom, like a lamp that flooded the world with fugitive, deceptive rainbows.]
VÁZQUEZ VIGO_1978P	TOM: [...] En España, Guernica era destruida. Pero aquí aún había jazz y whisky, salones de baile, sexo, cine ... [TOM: [...] In Spain, Guernica was destroyed. But here there were still jazz and whisky, dance halls, sex, movies ...]
GALÁN_2014P	Ø
DIÉGUEZ_2007R	TOM: [...] ¡En España estaba Guernica! Y aquí solo teníamos swing y alcohol, bailes, bares y películas, y el sexo, que pendía en la penumbra como una lámpara e inundaba el mundo de breves y engañosos arco iris ... [TOM: [...] In Spain there was Guernica! And here we only had swing and alcohol, dances, bars and movies, and sex, which hung in the gloom like a lamp and flooded the world with brief and deceptive rainbows ...]
ESPEJO_2019R	TOM: [...] ¡En España, Guernica! Pero aquí había solo música de swing, alcohol, salas de baile, bares, películas y el sexo sobre nuestras cabezas como una lámpara de araña que inundaba el mundo de luz, aunque era un arco iris efímero y engañoso ... [TOM: [...] In Spain, Guernica! But here there were only swing music, alcohol, dance halls, bars, movies and sex over our heads like a chandelier that flooded the world with light, although it was a brief and deceptive rainbow ...]

(Continued)

Table 10: Continued

Williams_1945	TOM: [...] In Spain there was Guernica! Here there was only hot swing music and liquor, dance halls, bars, and movies, and sex that hung in the gloom like a chandelier and flooded the world with brief, deceptive rainbows ...
Mirlas_1951r	TOM: [...] ¡En España estaba Guernica! Aquí, sólo había frenética música de jazz y licor y salones de baile y bares y películas, y el sexo suspendido en la sombra como un candelabro y que anegaba al mundo con breves y engañosos arco iris ... [TOM: [...] In Spain there was Guernica! Here there were only frenetic jazz music and liquor and dance halls and bars and movies, and sex that hung in the darkness like a candelabra and flooded the world with brief and deceptive rainbows ...]

In Gordon and de Quinto_1950p, the expression *In Spain there was Guernica!*, a direct reference to the bombing of civilians in the Basque town, instigated by Franco during the Spanish Civil War, has been deleted, presumably to avoid any confrontation with the censors. The expression is, however, retained in Vázquez Vigo_1978p, which shows a lengthier omission in the following part (*that hung in the gloom like a chandelier and flooded the world with brief, deceptive rainbows*). In Galán_2014p, several sentences within an utterance have been deleted, reflecting a broader trend of adjusting the textual material for the stage production. The TT combines the first utterance of the ST with an utterance from scene five, incorporating additions, rewrites and omissions, as illustrated in the example.

b) Addition

Galán_2014p is the performance-oriented text with the highest number of additions, followed, in decreasing order, by Vázquez Vigo_1978p and Gordon and de Quinto_1950p. In all of them, the additions are mostly observed in the dialogues and vary from the introduction of single words to fragments of text. Table 11 illustrates the introduction of sentences in Gordon and de Quinto_1950p and Vázquez Vigo_1978p. In the first TT, the idea from the previous question is repeated in *¿Has formulado algún deseo*? [Have you made a wish?], while the second adds new content, *Ya sabes que lo concede* [You know that she grants it].

Table 11: Examples of addition in Menagerie

Williams_1948	AMANDA: So it is! A little silver slipper of a moon. Have you made a wish on it yet?
Gordon and de Quinto_1950p	AMANDA: ¡Aquí está! Igual que una pequeña pantufla de plata. ¿Le has pedido ya algo? <u>¿Has formulado algún deseo?</u> [AMANDA: Here it is! Like a little silver slipper. Have you asked her for anything yet? <u>Have you made a wish?</u>]
Vázquez Vigo_1978p	AMANDA: ¡Ah, sí, ahí está! Como un zapatito de plata. ¿Le has pedido algo? <u>Ya sabes que lo concede.</u> [AMANDA: Ah, yes, there it is! Like a little silver slipper. Have you asked her for anything? <u>You know that she grants it.</u>]
Galán_2014p	AMANDA: ¿Ah, sí? ¿Has pedido ya un deseo? [AMANDA: Ah, yes? Have you made a wish yet?]
Diéguez_2007r	AMANDA: ¡Ah, sí! Una luna que parece una pequeña zapatilla de plata. ¿Ya has pedido un deseo? [AMANDA: Ah, yes! A moon that looks like a little silver slipper. Have you made a wish yet?]
Espejo_2019r	AMANDA: ¡Ah, sí! Es como una zapatillita plateada. ¿Has pedido ya un deseo? [AMANDA: Ah, yes! It's like a little silver slipper. Have you made a wish yet?]
Williams_1945	AMANDA: Oh! So it is! Such a little silver slipper of a moon. Have you made a wish on it?
Mirlas_1951r	AMANDA: ¡Ah! ¡Es cierto! Una luna que parece una pequeña chinela de plata. ¿Has pedido un deseo? [AMANDA: Oh! It's true! A moon that looks like a little silver slipper. Have you made a wish?]

Table 12 illustrates the recurrent additions associated with the character of Amanda in Galán_2014p. This focus on Amanda is evident not only in the use of paratextual material but also at both macro and microtextual levels, with the inclusion of additional text specifically for this character.

Table 12: An example of addition in Menagerie

WILLIAMS_1948	Ø
GORDON AND DE QUINTO_1950P	Ø
VÁZQUEZ VIGO_1978P	Ø
GALÁN_2014P	AMANDA: *(A LAURA)* ¿Sabes lo que me ha dicho hoy el doctor Hamilton? LAURA: ¿Has ido a verle? AMANDA: Dice que me encuentra como si tuviera treinta años ... Fuerte, juvenil, atractiva, qué sé yo ... No hacía más que halagarme ... Claro, que quien tuvo retuvo ... Y este hombre siempre me miró con buenos ojos ... Desde que se quedó viudo no ha hecho más que insinuarme proposiciones ... Pero yo no le hago caso, es un viejo chiflado ... De todas maneras, Laura, me ha gustado ... Siempre está bien que un hombre nos diga galanterías. LAURA: Debe de ser tan bonito oírlas ... AMANDA: También te las dirán a ti. LAURA: ¿A mí? No lo creo ... AMANDA: Eres una buena chica ... TOM: ¿Te ha propuesto matrimonio el Doctor Hamilton? AMANDA: ¡Qué va! Ha sido una galantería del doctor. No hay que hacerle caso. [AMANDA: *(To LAURA)* Do you know what doctor Hamilton said to me today? LAURA: Did you go to see him? AMANDA: He said I look as though I were thirty years old ... Strong, youthful, attractive, and so on ... He did nothing but flatter me ... Well, some things remain with you forever ... And this man always looked on me favourably ... Since he became a widower he has done nothing but make me propositions ... But I don't listen to him, he's a crazy old man ... Anyway, Laura, I liked it ... It's always nice when a man flatters us. LAURA: It must be so nice to hear it ... AMANDA: Men will also flatter you. LAURA: Me? I don't think so ... AMANDA: You're a good girl ... TOM: Has Doctor Hamilton proposed to you? AMANDA: No! The doctor was just being flattering. Don't mind him.]

Diéguez_2007r	Ø
Espejo_2019r	Ø
Williams_1945	Ø
Mirlas_1951r	Ø

c) Substitution

In Gordon and de Quinto_1950p some substitutions are seemingly due to self-censorship. In Vázquez Vigo_1978p, there are a few more substitutions, although there do not seem to be any clear cases of self-censorship. In both TTs most instances of substitution are found in the dialogues. In Galán_2014p certain utterances or parts of utterances also seem to stem from substituted material. Table 13 shows an example of substitution from Vázquez Vigo_1978p, where *Is my head so transparent?* is translated as *¡Tú qué vas a saber!* [What do you know!].

Table 13: Examples of substitution in Menagerie

Williams_1948	AMANDA: Is my head so transparent?
Gordon and de Quinto_1950p	AMANDA: ¿Es que soy tan transparente? [AMANDA: Am I so transparent?]
Vázquez Vigo_1978p	AMANDA: <u>¡Tú qué vas a saber!</u> [AMANDA: <u>What do you know!</u>]
Galán_2014p	AMANDA: ¿Tanto se me nota? [AMANDA: Am I that obvious?]
Diéguez_2007r	AMANDA: ¿Tanto se transparenta mi pensamiento? [AMANDA: Is my thinking so transparent?]
Espejo_2019r	AMANDA: ¿Tan transparente soy? [AMANDA: Am I so transparent?]
Williams_1945	AMANDA: Why, is my head transparent?
Mirlas_1951r	AMANDA: ¡Qué! ¿Acaso es transparente mi cabeza? [AMANDA: What! Is my head transparent?]

To conclude, in the MENAGERIE set, a gradation can be observed in how the TTs diverge from the ST. In GORDON AND DE QUINTO_1950P, the translation techniques generally affect less textual material than in the other two TTs, though still more than in the case of the reader-oriented versions. In this particular TT, unsurprisingly given the time of production during the dictatorship, self-censorship traces can be detected, thus reinforcing the acceptable nature of the end product, an aspect that is examined in further detail in Chapter 6.

VÁZQUEZ VIGO_1978P seems to have taken GORDON AND DE QUINTO_1950P as its starting point and used it to work on the reader-oriented edition of the original play (WILLIAMS_1948). The TT author not only restores parts that had been self-censored in GORDON AND DE QUINTO_1950P, but also introduces new additions and omissions, ultimately resulting in a greater textual divergence from the ST. Some of the translation techniques observed in both TTs coincide, whereas others only appear in one or the other. The extratextual data obtained by consulting the censorship record associated with these two TTs (record 274–50) shows that Vázquez Vigo was part of the cast of actors in the première of GORDON AND DE QUINTO_1950P. The fact that this new translation was carried out in 1978, the year that marked the abolition of censorship in Spain, justifies the updating of the censored excerpts from the 1950 version.

The study of the translation techniques activated in GALÁN_2014P reveals a particularly high incidence of additions and omissions at microtextual level, a conscious decision taken by the target author, who was also the producer, to give prominence to the character of Amanda, infuse humour to the dialogue and guarantee that the TT would be long enough for a ninety-minute performance.

Regarding the reader-oriented TTs, MIRLAS_1951R generally follows not only the meaning but also the syntax of the ST. This closeness to the structure of the English language has also been noted in other twentieth-century Argentinian theatrical (Mateo 2000) and narrative (Gómez Castro 2009) TTs. The two other translations (DIÉGUEZ_2007R and ESPEJO_2019R), published in typical reader-oriented editions and accompanied with source-oriented paratexts, lean towards adequacy at both macro and microtextual levels.

5.2. The Crucible

As illustrated in Figure 15, the CRUCIBLE set of texts comprises five TTs, two of which are performance-oriented (HURTADO_1956P and GONZÁLEZ VERGEL AND ESCRIBANO_2007P) and three reader-oriented (MUCHNIK AND MUCHNIK_1955R, LÓPEZ MUÑOZ_1997R and ESPEJO_2011R).

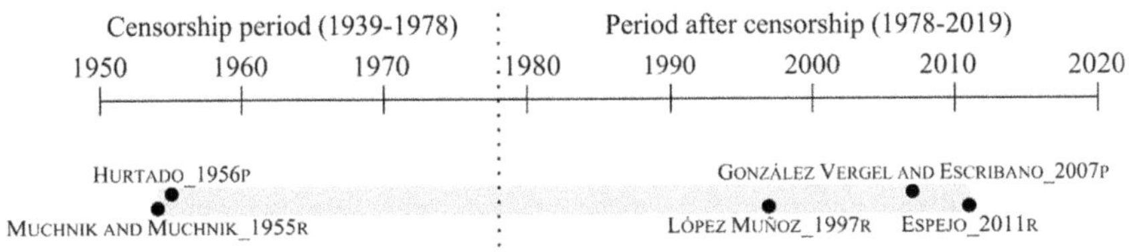

Figure 15: Crucible text set.

HURTADO_1956P

According to the CDAEM, the first staging of *The Crucible* in Spain took place in 1956, using a TT signed by Diego Hurtado, a frequent twentieth-century target author. In addition to being used in productions, this TT quickly established its presence in print, in 1957, when it was published in the second issue of the well-known theatrical journal *Primer Acto*. A few years later, in 1963, Escelicer printed it as part of their Teatro collection and included information on the première of the play at the Teatro Español in Madrid. Reprints of this book are registered in the CCBIP up until 1972.

The censorship record associated with this TT (record 310–56) includes documents that are key to understanding the emergence of the play on the Spanish stage during the 1950s. The company Lope de Vega, directed by José Tamayo,[1] filed a request for a performance on 7 November 1956.

1 Before introducing the play *The Crucible* in Spain, José Tamayo directed the première of *Death of a Salesman*, which increased his reputation (Espejo 2017) and set a positive precedent for the production of HURTADO_1956P (Gil Fombellida 2002).

The censorship process shows evidence of tension because of the controversial nature of the play on the political and religious fronts. For instance, in the record (310–56, my translation), it is noted that in France 'it was received with great applause by all communist and communist-loving people', and it also mentions a 'protest against this performance because its author is "an adherent of communism and is being investigated by the American authorities due to his doctrinal and political position"'. To counterargue these claims, more favourable arguments were put forward by the director:

> Mr. Barton, Cultural Attaché to the Embassy of the United States of America, [...] expressed the view that the cited author, considered one of the most significant figures in North America, recently declared before a Commission of the American Senate that he was not a communist, a statement that was reproduced in the press worldwide, that the play has no political message, that it has been performed almost everywhere the world over, and that audiences and press did not associate any political meaning either with the play or with the author. (Record 310–56, my translation)

In general, the reports deemed that the topics were not dangerous and the ecclesiastical censor Avelino Esteban Romero noted in his report that the community depicted was Protestant and, as such, the play was unrelated to Catholic matters. Despite the controversy that surrounded it, certain factors seem to have favoured its authorization, notably, the setting of the plot abroad, the standing of the playwright – Miller was already a well-known figure in the target context – as well as the box office success of the play in other countries around the world. In the end, the request was authorized without deletions, for audiences over sixteen years old, and the play premièred at the Teatro Español in Madrid on 20 December 1956 (Gil Fombellida 2002). The censorship record contains the material from three other applications submitted to the censorship board for performances to be staged throughout the 1960s, until 1967.

The première ran for more than 120 performances in Madrid and almost 100 in Barcelona, with the production and the TT being praised by the critics (Espejo 2004). As Espejo (2017) remarks, during the introduction of this play into Spain, several agents from the theatrical sphere – among them, Hurtado, the target author – sought to avoid its political connotations. In this sense, Espejo (2004: 135, my translation) observes that the TT 'shows a significant lack of respect for the original, which has been subjected to wild mutilation, and from which the target author, Diego Hurtado, tried to delete everything that lent itself to a political reading'.

González Vergel and Escribano_2007P

Fifty years had to pass until another major production of *The Crucible* was staged in Spain, in 2007, at the Teatro Español in Madrid, directed by Alberto González Vergel (Espejo 2010b). The performance-oriented TT used in this production was presented as a version, created by González Vergel and based on a previous translation by Julián Escribano, thus illustrating the fruitful collaboration between two target authors, a feature also observed by Brodie (2017) in the UK. González Vergel enjoyed a long career in the theatre. He was the director of the Teatro Español between 1970 and 1974, taught at the Real Escuela Superior de Arte Dramático [Royal School of Dramatic Art] and directed numerous productions, several of which were plays by American authors (Espejo 2010b). Escribano, who had previously collaborated on other plays directed by González Vergel, is a playwright and has also worked on the scripts and direction of film productions (Miller 2007).

The programme for the play and the published copy of the TT have certain elements in common. For instance, their covers are almost identical and they contain photographs of the performance and information on the members of the cast and the mise-en-scène, pointing to a target-oriented approach. In addition to the TT, this edition includes a general introduction signed by González Vergel and Escribano, information about the two witch hunts of the play (in Salem at the end of the seventeenth century and in the American cinema during the period of McCarthyism in the 1940s and 1950s), as well as details about the production, the translation used, the lighting, the rehearsals, the stage design, the costumes and the music.

González Vergel (2007) explicitly mentions that he directed the play on the suggestion of Mario Gas, at the time director of the Teatro Español. On the general strategy for the play, Escribano (2007: 265, my translation) observes that:

> [Alberto González Vergel] asked me for a close translation without flourishes. He combed the text, omitted repetitions, chose words that facilitated the delivery of the actors and shaped the work to suit his ideas for the staging of the play, creating a version that emphasized the expressionist theatrical concepts on which he had decided to base it.

González Vergel (2007: 260) describes Escribano's translation as 'literal and faithful to the text in English' and goes on to explain the changes introduced in the translation: 'I will point to some omissions, changes of structure and intensification of scenes and speech from the original text which, I think, do not alter its essence.' The profile of González Vergel as a prestigious theatrical director might have influenced his free rendering of the text, a trend also observed in the twentieth century by Merino-Álvarez (1994b). In his discussion about the play, González Vergel (2007: 260, my translation) notes that additions and omissions were incorporated to intensify the end of the appendix of the second act: 'it was lightened of some repetition and certain adjectives that unnecessarily lengthen the brilliantly frenetic dramatic action, whose lacklustre ending we substituted by the more intense and aggressive one written by Miller himself in previous paragraphs.' He highlights an attempt at intensification in the third act through the omission of the final utterances and the addition of a stage direction and an utterance for the character of Abigail:

> At the end of this act, we are shocked by Proctor's utterance *God has died!*, which Miller gives to the character minutes before the conclusion. It is now strengthened by the fall of the huge cross and the *Nooooo!!* uttered by Abigail, aware that her ex-lover has sentenced himself to death. (*ibid.*)

The following is another example of the changes incorporated by the target author and director, González Vergel (*ibid.*), which illustrates the relationship between the theatre and cinema: 'In the prison, the original text is somewhat lighter, and its end is exchanged for that written by Miller in the script for the film directed by Nicholas Hytner, notably when the cart takes the condemned to the gallows.' In relation to the textual alterations found in the text, Espejo (2010b) makes particular note of the omissions affecting a significant number of fragments.

Muchnik and Muchnik_1955R

The oldest TT of *The Crucible* registered in the CCBIP, signed by Jacobo and Mario Muchnik, dates back to 1955. It was published by the Argentinian Compañía General Fabril Editora and various reruns are found up until 1964. The play appears in a book entitled *Teatro*, together with four other translated works by Miller: *All My Sons, Death of a Salesman, A Memory of Two Mondays* and *A View from the Bridge*. The editor and writer, Mario Muchnik, signed the translation with his father Jacobo Muchnik, who was also an editor and had previously translated Miller's *A View from the Bridge* (Merino-Álvarez 1993c).

In addition to the five TTs, the book includes an introduction by Miller, translated by Juan Carlos Pellegrin. It is a further example of a reader-oriented TT from Argentina that was published only a short time after the ST and almost at the same time as the première of the performance-oriented TT created in Spain.

López Muñoz_1997r

Just over four decades after the play was first introduced in Spain, Tusquets published the TT by José Luis López Muñoz in 1997, of which reruns saw the light up until 2015. The translation was also used for an adaptation by Eduardo Mendoza that premièred in the Centro Dramático Nacional in 2017, and for which the project Teatro Accesible created intralingual subtitles for the deaf and hard of hearing and audio description for the blind and partially sighted (Centro de Documentación de las Artes Escénicas y de la Música 2017a). López Muñoz is a professional translator whose work has been recognized with prestigious Spanish awards such as the *Premio Nacional de Traducción* and the *Premio Nacional a la Obra de un Traductor*.

The CCBIP includes two editions of this translation, which Tusquets published in different series. The first one, from 1997, was published as part of the Marginales series, together with the Spanish translation of the cinema script, also carried out by López Muñoz (Miller 1997). In 2015, on the occasion of the centenary of Miller's birth, Tusquets launched an edition entitled *Teatro Reunido* as part of the series Andanzas, which brought together five major plays by Miller: *All My Sons, Death of a Salesman, The Crucible, A View from the Bridge* and *After the Fall* (Miller 2015).

Espejo_2011r

As in the case of Menagerie, the most recent TT available in the Crucible set is by Ramón Espejo, also published in Cátedra's series Letras Universales, preceded by a critical study. After its publication in 2011, an electronic edition from 2017 appeared in the ISBN database. As already discussed, Espejo specializes in research and translation work relating to twentieth-century

American theatre, particularly Miller's plays, and apart from *The Crucible* (Miller 2011), he has produced translations and critical studies of *Death of a Salesman* (Miller 2010) and *A View from the Bridge* (Miller 2012), and has made valuable contributions to the scholarly literature on this author in Spain (Espejo 2001, 2002, 2003, 2004, 2010b, 2017).

In contrast to the other TTs in CRUCIBLE, where the title appears as *Las brujas de Salem* [*The Witches from Salem*], influenced by the French title *Les Sorcières de Salem*, in ESPEJO_2011R the title is translated more literally as *El crisol* [*The Crucible*], which Espejo (2010b: 169, my translation) considers 'less sensationalist but a lot more evocative', though the first title is also included between brackets: *El crisol (Las brujas de Salem)*. The critical analysis preceding the TT provides information on the double context of the play, that is, the witch hunt in Salem in the seventeenth century and the anti-communist persecutions in the United States during the 1940s and 1950s, as well as on diverse aspects of the play (the première in the USA, the plot, the structure, the themes and the characters, the language and the dramatic techniques), and concludes with a list of bibliographical references for readers interested in broadening their appreciation of the work. The Cátedra edition, therefore, not only offers a new translation of the ST, but also provides a very rich and informative contextual framework. The presence of translator notes throughout the play offers an analytical view of different aspects of the play, also clarifying cultural and historical references from the source context to the reader. These paratextual devices contribute to making the translation an output clearly adequate to the ST.

Espejo (personal communication, January 2020) points out that similar to the work of an archaeologist the translation process required the identification of multiple layers of meaning as well as a thorough understanding of the subtext, rich in ironic statements, the intentionality of the plot and the duality of the characters. As Espejo (2019) himself claimed in relation to his translation of *The Glass Menagerie*, meticulousness, faithfulness to the original and linguistic fluency seem to be the articulating principles of his translation of *The Crucible*.

5.2.1. Macrotextual analysis

Textual comparison indicates that the TTs in the CRUCIBLE set take Miller's revision of the ST (MILLER_1953) as their starting point, which contains an appendix added to the second act. In this cluster of translations, even more noticeably than in MENAGERIE, the data of the macrotextual analysis reveal stark differences between the two groups of TTs, with the performance-oriented ones distinctly leaning to acceptability and reader-oriented ones to adequacy.

Figures 16, 17, 18 and 19 show the main differences between these two groups of TTs after the pairing of utterances and according to the different acts.

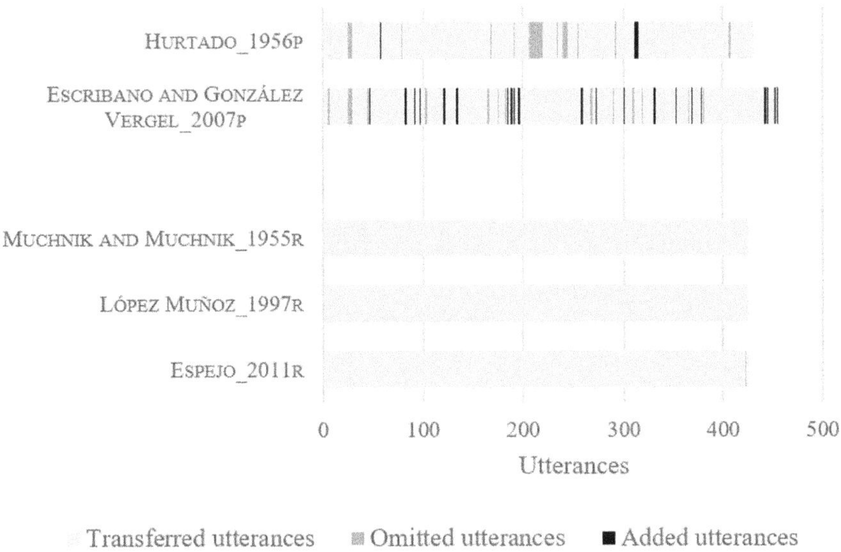

Figure 16: Omissions and additions of utterances in Crucible, Act 1.

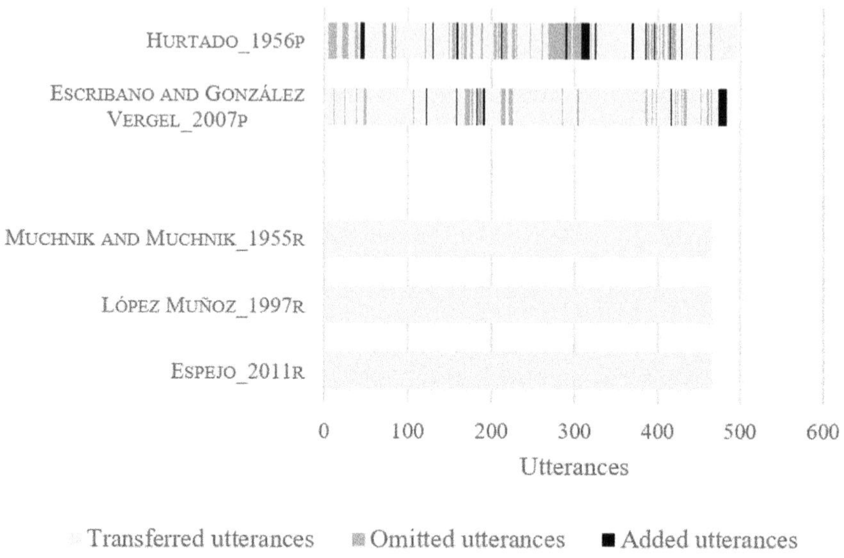

Figure 17: Omissions and additions of utterances in Crucible, Act 2.

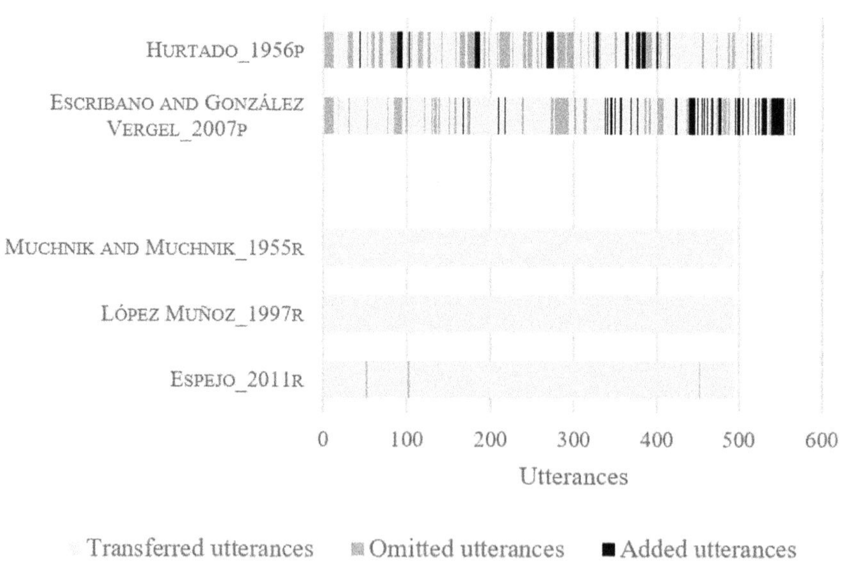

Figure 18: Omissions and additions of utterances in Crucible, Act 3.

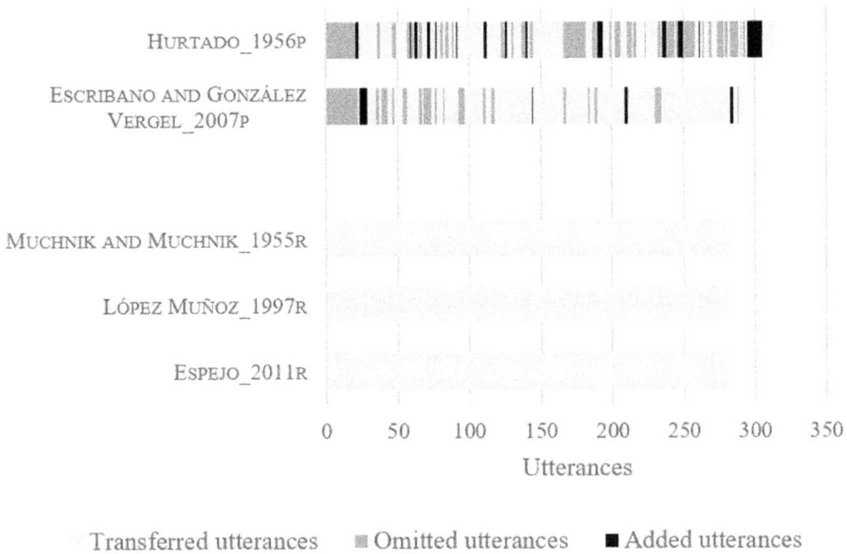

Figure 19: Omissions and additions of utterances in Crucible, Act 4.

HURTADO_1956P and GONZÁLEZ VERGEL AND ESCRIBANO_2007P are examples of texts containing a large number of omissions and additions of utterances. At the macrotextual level, the graphs corroborate Espejo's (2017: 442) observation that from Act Two onwards, Hurtado 'decides to re-write it to suit his tastes, following the storyline provided by Miller but wording it differently'. The number of changes observed in these TTs appears even more striking when compared with the reader-oriented ones, which tend to reproduce faithfully the utterances contained in the ST. As in the case of MENAGERIE, some of the instances of omission involve the deletion of content that is repeated in other utterances.

5.2.2. Microtextual analysis

The descriptive, comparative analysis of the CRUCIBLE set at the microtextual level confirms the trends identified at the macrotextual level. On the one hand, the two performance-oriented TTs show a recurrent use of translation techniques (additions, omissions, substitutions and, in some cases, changes in the order of utterances) that results in a high degree of divergence from the ST and brings the texts closer to the acceptability pole. On the other hand, the three reader-oriented TTs embrace the adequacy pole. Figure 20 displays the translation techniques activated in the various TTs.

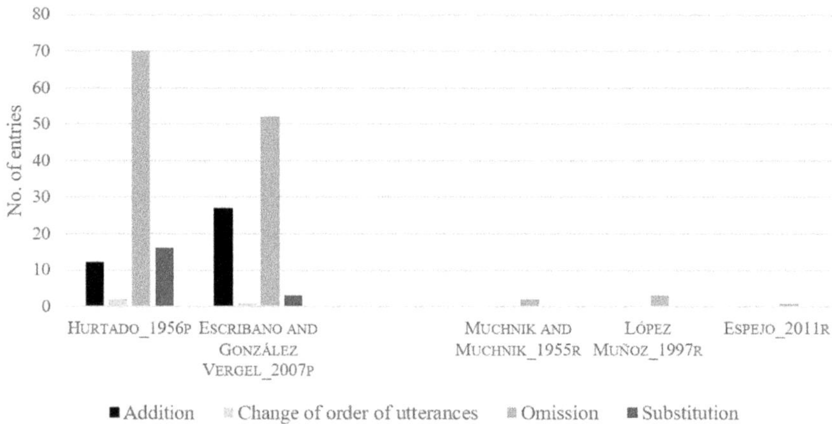

Figure 20: Translation techniques in Crucible.

a) Omission

Omission, the technique with the highest incidence in the two performance-oriented TTs, usually entails a significant alteration of the ST. In HURTADO_1956P, omissions mainly involve the disappearance of whole utterances or parts of dialogue, although there are also instances when stage directions are left out. Some of these seem to bear the traces of self-censorship. The analysis also shows that almost half of the omissions affect a specific orality marker, that is, vocatives, whether they appear independently or as part of a larger structure, a practice also observed in dubbing (Baños 2009; Cabanillas 2016). In GONZÁLEZ VERGEL AND ESCRIBANO_2007P, omissions are detected in dialogues and affect a wide range of structures, from single words to full sentences, with occasional deletions of stage directions and whole utterances. In this TT, omissions do not seem to be due to self-censorship but rather respond to the target authors' artistic preferences in relation to the mise-en-scène of the play. The first example contained in

Table 14 involves an omission of an utterance in HURTADO_1956P, possibly an instantiation of self-censorship of the criticism raised by Proctor against the minister.

Table 14: Examples of omission in Crucible

MILLER_1953	PROCTOR: You are a coward! Though you be ordained in God's own tears, you are a coward now!
HURTADO_1956P	Ø
GONZÁLEZ VERGEL AND ESCRIBANO_2007P	PROCTOR: *(Tras un silencio.)* ¡Es usted un cobarde! ¡Aunque le hubieran ordenado sacerdote con las lágrimas de Dios, es usted un cobarde! [PROCTOR: *(After a silence.)* You are a coward! Though you be ordained minister in God's tears, you are a coward!]
MUCHNIK AND MUCHNIK_1955R	PROCTOR: ¡Sois un cobarde! ¡Aunque hayáis sido ordenado con las propias lágrimas de Dios, ahora sois un cobarde! [PROCTOR: You are a coward! Though you be ordained in God's own tears, now you are a coward!]
LÓPEZ MUÑOZ_1997R	PROCTOR: ¡Es usted un cobarde! ¡Aunque le ordenaran ministro con las lágrimas mismas de Dios, ahora no es usted más que un cobarde! [PROCTOR: You are a coward! Though you be ordained minister in God's own tears, now you are nothing but a coward!]
ESPEJO_2011R	PROCTOR: ¡Es usted un cobarde! ¡Aunque haya sido ordenado con las mismas lágrimas de Dios, ahora no deja de ser usted un cobarde! [PROCTOR: You are a coward! Though you be ordained in God's own tears, now you are a coward!]

b) Addition

In HURTADO_1956P, addition is less frequent than in GONZÁLEZ VERGEL AND ESCRIBANO_2007P, although there are additions of whole utterances or parts of utterances, while in GONZÁLEZ VERGEL AND ESCRIBANO_2007P almost all the cases identified are stage directions, most of these brief indications of the attitudes and reactions of the characters. The fact that such a large number of stage directions are added to the text can be directly linked to the dual role of González Vergel as target author and director of the production. Table 15 contains the addition of the stage direction *Como si PROCTOR no entendiera* [As if Proctor did not understand] in González Vergel and Escribano_2007p.

Table 15: Examples of addition in Crucible

Miller_1953	PARRIS: Proctor, the village must have proof that –
Hurtado_1956p	PARRIS: Es el pueblo el que debe leerlo. [PARRIS: It is the village that must read it].]
González Vergel and Escribano_2007p	PARRIS: *(Como si PROCTOR no entendiera.)* Proctor, el pueblo debe tener la prueba de ... [PARRIS: *(As if PROCTOR did not understand.)* Proctor, the village must have proof that –]
Muchnik and Muchnik_1955r	PARRIS: Proctor, el pueblo debe tener pruebas de ... [PARRIS: Proctor, the village must have proof that –]
López Muñoz_1997r	PARRIS: El pueblo, Proctor, ha de tener prueba de que ... [PARRIS: The village, Proctor, must have proof that –]
Espejo_2011r	PARRIS: Proctor, el pueblo necesita pruebas de que usted ... [PARRIS: Proctor, the village needs proof that you –]

c) Substitution

The substitution instances found in Hurtado_1956p affect relatively long fragments in dialogue and stage directions or even whole utterances, whereas fewer cases have been detected in González Vergel and Escribano_2007p, with these involving shorter linguistic structures, such as words or clauses, in dialogue and stage directions. Table 16 illustrates some of these substitutions, notably the replacement of almost the whole ST fragment for another of Hurtado's own invention. In González Vergel and Escribano_2007p, the stage direction *He cannot bear to look at her* has intriguingly been transformed into *No soporta mirar a su marido* [She cannot bear to look at her husband], thus making her the agent of the action.

Table 16: Examples of substitution in Crucible

Miller_1953	ELIZABETH: John-I think I must go with them. *(He cannot bear to look at her.)* Mary, there is bread enough for the morning; you will bake, in the afternoon. Help Mr. Proctor as you were his daughter-you owe me that, and much more.

Hurtado_1956p	ISABEL: Juan, piensa en los niños. *(A MARY.)* Dios te perdone la ruina y la desolación que has traído a esta casa. [ISABEL: Juan, think of the children. *(To Mary.)* May God forgive you for the ruin and desolation you have brought to this home.]
González Vergel and Escribano_2007p	ELIZABETH: John, creo que debo ir con ellos ... *(Serena. No soporta mirar a su marido.)* Mary, tendrás que cocer pan. Ayuda al señor como si fueras su hija; me debes eso, y quizá algo más. [ELIZABETH: John, I think I must go with them – *(Calm. She cannot bear to look at her husband.)* Mary, you will have to bake bread. Help the master as if you were his daughter-you owe me that, and maybe something more.]
Muchnik and Muchnik_1955r	ELIZABETH: John ..., creo que debo ir con ellos. *(Él no puede soportar su mirada.)* Mary, hay pan suficiente para la mañana; pondrás el horno por la tarde. Ayuda al señor Proctor como si fueses su hija ... Me debes eso, y mucho más. [ELIZABETH: John-I think I must go with them. *(He cannot bear her look.)* Mary, there is bread enough for the morning; you will bake in the afternoon. Help Mr. Proctor as if you were his daughter-you owe me that, and much more.]
López Muñoz_1997r	ELIZABETH: John ..., creo que debo ir con ellos. *(Proctor no es capaz de mirarla.)* Mary, hay pan suficiente para mañana por la mañana; tendrás que volver a cocer por la tarde. Ayuda al señor Proctor como si fueses su hija ..., me debes eso, y mucho más. [ELIZABETH: John-I think I must go with them. *(Proctor cannot look at her.)* Mary, there is bread enough for tomorrow morning; you will have to bake again in the afternoon. Help Mr. Proctor as if you were his daughter-you owe me that, and much more.]
Espejo_2011r	ELIZABETH: John ... Creo que debo ir con ellos. *(No soporta mirarla.)* Mary, hay pan suficiente para por la mañana; por la tarde tendrás que cocer más. Ayuda al señor Proctor como si fueras su hija ... me lo debes, eso y mucho más. [ELIZABETH: John-I think I must go with them. *(He cannot bear to look at her.)* Mary, there is bread enough for the morning; you will have to bake more in the afternoon. Help Mr. Proctor as if you were his daughter-you owe me that, and much more.]

All in all, the microtextual analysis reveals a significant degree of manipulation in HURTADO_1956P, which is commensurate with the results obtained in the macrotextual study and the observations made during the preliminary contextualization. The alterations show that the TT is a product of the time in which it was created, since there are several traces of self-censorship, a common practice in the Spain of the 1950s. Some of the changes can also be put down to the performance-orientedness of the translation at a time when faithfulness to the ST was not among the primary objectives of the target authors (Merino-Álvarez 1994b, 1992a; Espejo 2004). Hurtado (1957, in Espejo 2004) himself acknowledges the extent of these textual alterations and justifies them as necessary adjustments to fit the socio-cultural target context.

The preliminary and macrotextual studies pointed to numerous departs from the ST in GONZÁLEZ VERGEL AND ESCRIBANO_2007R, which were also exposed at the microtextual level. In some of the paratexts consulted, the director González Vergel (2007) explains that he took Escribano's literal translation as a starting point and modified it in line with his own idea of the production, which led to extensive changes to the text. The ensuing TT seems to confirm Aaltonen's (1996: 204) observation that 'vertical deletion as well as the insertion of new lines or entire episodes are options in the theatrical polysystem, but only for those translators whom the polysystem has granted the power to effect them.'

In a similar way as in the MIRLAS_1951R translation of MENAGERIE, MUCHNIK AND MUCHNIK_1955R is a typical Argentinian reader-oriented edition of the time, characterized by its close proximity to the ST, to the extent that: 'what stands out most in this TT is […] the unnatural language resulting from an excessively literal rendering' (Mateo 2000: 156, my translation). The textual analysis uncovers that the other two reader-oriented texts, LÓPEZ MUÑOZ_1997R and ESPEJO_2011R, adopt a translational approach that gives priority to the adequacy pole.

5.3. Happy Days

The DAYS set includes three TTs: two performance-oriented (MARTÍNEZ TRIVES_1963P, MARTÍNEZ LUCIANO_2011P) and one reader-oriented TT (RODRÍGUEZ GAGO_1989R), as displayed in Figure 21.

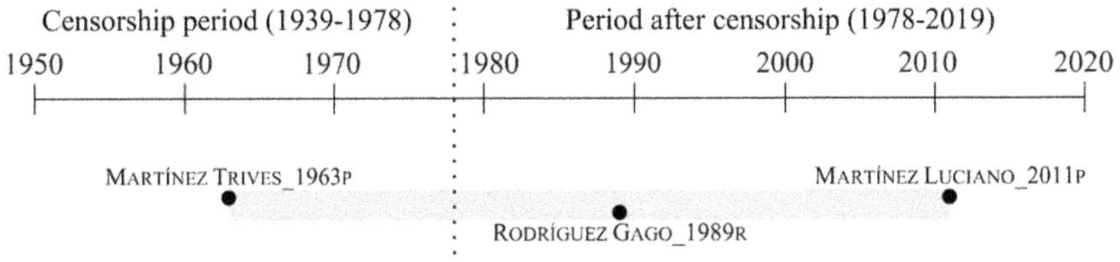

Figure 21: Days text set.

MARTÍNEZ TRIVES_1963P

The first TT of the play *Happy Days* to be performed and printed in Spain was by Trino Martínez Trives, in 1963. The TT author was pivotal in the introduction of Beckett's plays in Spain, and worked as a translator, director and producer. The censorship records relating to the works of Beckett show that, prior to translating this play, Martínez Trives had already translated *Waiting for Godot* in 1955 and *Endgame* in 1958 (Andaluz-Pinedo and Merino-Álvarez 2020). The TT has not been kept in the application submitted to the board of censors and the version used for this analysis is the one that appeared in issue 39 of *Primer Acto*, under the section 'Teatro de vanguardia' [avant-garde theatre]. The translation was accompanied by a prologue in which Martínez Trives (1963) states that Beckett sent him a personal copy of the play. By 1963, *Primer Acto* had already published TTs of other plays by Beckett, including *Waiting for Godot* (1957) and *Endgame* (1959).

Censorship record 47–63 starts with two applications for two different performances of the TT by Martínez Trives. The first one was submitted on

11 February 1963 by the theatrical group La Máscara, requesting approval for its performance in a chamber theatre in Gijón, the Ateneo Jovellanos. The play was eventually authorized, with no deletions, on 12 March 1963, albeit only for a single performance. The second application was presented the day after, on 12 February 1963, by the group Teatro Nacional Universitario for the performance of the play at the Teatro María Guerrero in Madrid. The reports issued by the censors regarding this latter request include allusions to Beckett as a well-known author in the Spanish theatrical world, where he had enjoyed a strong presence since the première of *Waiting for Godot* in 1955, and refer to the play as 'a form of avant-garde theatre, as is characteristic of Samuel Beckett' (censorship record 47–63). The production was authorized on 26 February 1963, without the need for any changes and for audiences over eighteen years of age, and the première took place on 20 March 1963 (Álvaro 1963). The censorship record for this play registers another three applications up to 1972.

Martínez Luciano_2011P

In 2011 the company Come y Calla premièred a production of *Happy Days* in the Teatros del Canal, Madrid, directed by Salva Bolta. The production was based on a TT by Juan Vicente Martínez Luciano, who, among many other professional achievements, taught at the University of Valencia, translated numerous works by anglophone authors, was a member of theatre organizations such as the Instituto Shakespeare and the Academia de las Artes Escénicas de España, and, in 2010, received the theatre translation award *Premio María Martínez Sierra a la Mejor Traducción Teatral* (Academia de las Artes Escénicas n.d.b).

The programme of the production shares information not only about the director, the actors and the producer, but also about the target author, which is indicative of the latter's importance in dramatic circles. It also contains reflections by the director about the general approach to the play and his admiration of the work:

> for those of us who enjoy the theatre, *Happy Days* is a treasure. [...] My intention as director is to make my hand invisible, to show the sense of the text imparted by the author, to confer breath and flexibility on the script, and to endow it with the powerful dynamics with which it is organized. (Centro de Documentación de las Artes Escénicas y de la Música 2017c, my translation)

In an article about the translation of Pinter's works, Martínez Luciano (2006: 106, my translation) speculates about the task of the drama translator, which can arguably be applied to his translation of *Happy Days*:

> the translator (or adaptor) who renders it into another language has to recognize the distinctive features of that text and of that author in order to transfer them, so that a text by Pinter sounds in Spanish – or in Catalan, or in any other language into which they are translating – like it sounds in its original language and so that it is recognizable in a way that, ideally, if someone listens to the text in that other language, they can recognize Pinter's voice in the translated text.

Rodríguez Gago_1989r

The frequent staging of the play *Happy Days* contrasts with the few publications available in Spain, especially if we compare them to the previous case studies analysed in these pages. Apart from the publication in *Primer Acto* of the performance-oriented TT Martínez Trives_1963p, only one other output has been found: a reader-oriented TT signed by Antonia Rodríguez Gago and first published in 1989 by Cátedra as part of their *Letras Universales* series. This TT has known numerous reruns up until 2020 and has been used in theatrical productions by Compañía Tabanque in 1993, Sala Círculo in 1996 and El Canto de la Cabra also in 1996 (Rodríguez Gago 2020b). As registered in the CDAEM premières database, the TT was also used in 2020 for a co-production by the Centro Dramático Nacional and Buxman Producciones, directed by Pablo Messiez. Rodríguez Gago (2010, 2020a, 2020b), an emeritus professor at the Universidad Autónoma of Madrid, has focused her research on anglophone theatre with a special emphasis on Beckett, on whom she has published a number of studies.

Like other TTs published in the Cátedra series *Letras Universales*, this book contains an introduction, which is organized around four themes: Beckett's life and works, the play *Happy Days*, its presence in Spain and previous editions. The title of the TT makes use of the definite article, that is, *Los días felices* [The Happy Days], unlike the previous TT by Martínez Trives_1963p, in which the article is missing in Spanish, that is, *Días felices* [Happy Days]. On this choice, and rather arguably, Rodríguez Gago (2020b: 24, my translation) points out that 'the article in Spanish is completely necessary – and not only from a grammatical viewpoint – since the play does not deal with certain happy days, but *all* Winnie's happy days.' The book is a bilingual edition that includes texts in English and in Spanish arranged on parallel pages. The TT also includes translator's notes on aspects relating to the way in which Beckett staged the play, as well as on translation decisions. Rodríguez Gago (*ibid.*: 23–24) states that she used the ST in English as a starting point to create her TT and only consulted Beckett's self-translation in French to resolve some of the difficulties she encountered:

> Some of the problems I found are discussed in the annotations, as well as the little 'treasons' I committed, due to the frequent impossibility of translating certain polysemic words or phrases, when sometimes – though very rarely – I had to resort to the French version.

In the introduction, she shows a profound understanding of the play and offers key details that shed light on the way in which she approached the translation. For example, she remarks that:

> Stage directions in Beckett's plays are an *integral* part and cannot be understood as mere suggestions for the director – the play under discussion in these pages is a good example. If we were to omit or change the stage directions of *Happy Days*, we would have a completely different play. When we read the text, we cannot dispense with the stage directions either, which tell us what Winnie does, since her gestures are as important as her words. (*ibid.*: 80–81)

In another publication, Rodríguez Gago (2020a: 17, my translation) stresses that for Beckett: 'form was as important as meaning, and he constantly revised his texts to achieve the musical structure of echoes and repetitions that characterizes them.' She suggests that the significance that Beckett assigns to form could well be one of the reasons behind his self-translation activity:

> There has been much speculation concerning the reasons that led Beckett to self-translate his works; however, due to the importance that this author gave to form, it was a way of making sure that, at least in two different languages, English and French, the reader would be able to enjoy the original texts as he had conceived them, preserving not only the meaning but also their formal structure. (Rodríguez Gago 2020b: 18, my translation)

In the specific case of *Happy Days*, Rodríguez Gago (*ibid.*: 83) describes Beckett's creative process in the following terms: 'he started by writing a monologue [...]. This preliminary monologue of twenty pages was followed by seven manuscripts, three holographs and four typed texts, which clearly show us the detailed Beckettian creative process.' She also explains that it was the complexity of the translation itself, and her intention to transmit the ST as faithfully as possible, which prompted her to opt for a bilingual edition, thus giving priority to a source-oriented approach:

> Like all poets, Beckett is difficult to translate; for this reason, I opted for a bilingual edition where the readers themselves can at all times compare the translated text with the original and check for themselves for mistakes and good decisions, at the same time as experiencing the beauty of Beckettian writing, its poetic intensity and its musicality, which make the task of translating almost impossible. (*ibid.*: 23)

5.3.1. Macrotextual analysis

A textual comparison shows that all the TTs take the same English ST (BECKETT_1961) as their starting point. Having used this text for the pairing of textual binomials, the results show an inclination towards acceptability in the case of the only performance-oriented TT from the censorship period and, as could be expected, the reader-oriented TT RODRÍGUEZ GAGO_1989R leans to the adequacy pole. What is different from the previous case studies of MENAGERIE and CRUCIBLE is the fact that one of the performance-oriented versions, MARTÍNEZ LUCIANO_2011P, displays a tendency towards adequacy rather than acceptability.

The utterances in the DAYS set had to be treated differently to the other plays because of their scarcity and considerable length, and the decision was taken to combine each stage direction and the following dialogue as a unit in this analysis. As the data obtained show in Figures 22 and 23, numerous elements were omitted in both acts of MARTÍNEZ TRIVES_1963P, revealing a trend for acceptability at the macrotextual level. The other two translations remained quantitatively faithful to the original text, with hardly any omissions, thus confirming their tendency towards adequacy.

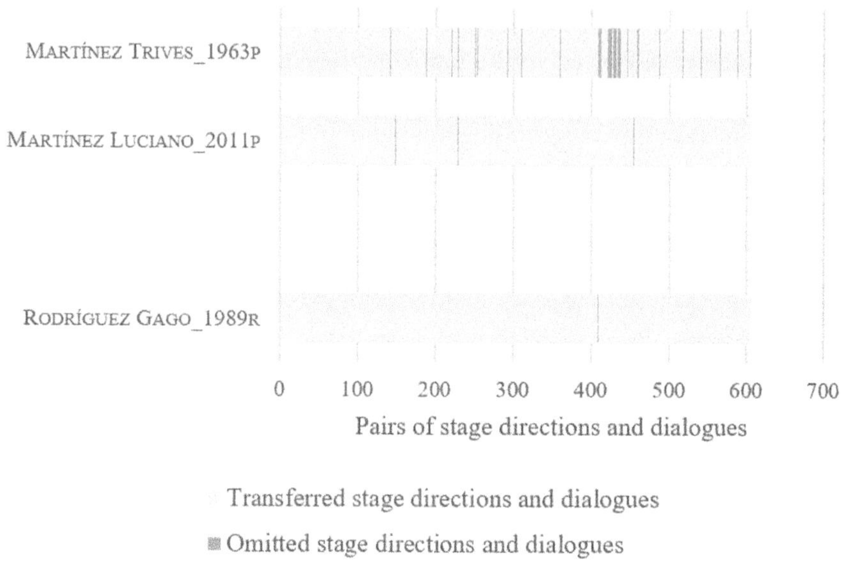

Figure 22: Omissions and additions of stage directions and dialogues in Days, Act 1.

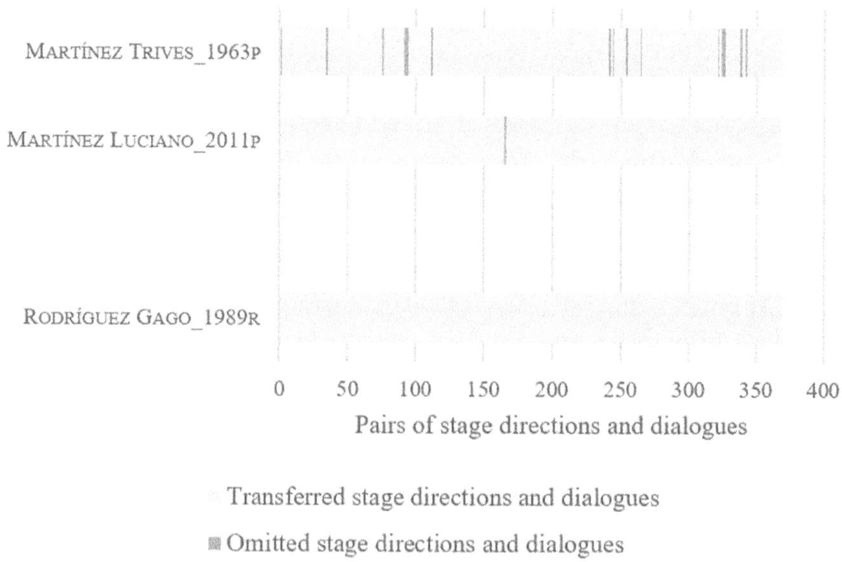

Figure 23: Omissions and additions of stage directions and dialogues in Days, Act 2.

5.3.2. Microtextual analysis

Figure 24 offers a detailed account of the frequency of the translation techniques detected in the various TTs of DAYS.

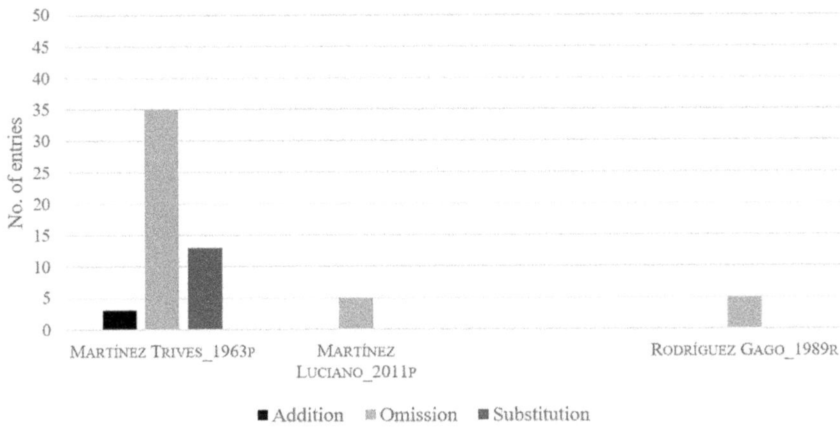

Figure 24: Translation techniques in Days.

As can be seen, and rather unsurprisingly, the most manipulated text is the one from the dictatorship period, MARTÍNEZ TRIVES_1963P. The next paragraphs discuss some of the most telling examples encountered in this translation.

a) Omission

The greatest number of omissions are detected in the stage directions, though these deletions are restricted to single terms or short phrases. Table 17 contains the example of an omission. In MARTÍNEZ TRIVES_1963P, pauses, which are classified as an orality marker by Baños (2014), and which appear frequently in the ST stage directions, are considerably reduced in number.

Table 17: An example of omission in Days

BECKETT_1961	WINNIE: […] Dim. *(Pause.)* Then gone. *(Pause.)* Last human kind – to stray this way.
MARTÍNEZ TRIVES_1963P	WINNIE: […] Confuso. [WINNIE: […] Blurred.]

(Continued)

Table 17: Continued

Martínez Luciano_2011p	WINNIE: […] Borrosos. *(Pausa.)* Hasta que desaparecen. *(Pausa.)* Los últimos seres humanos … que pasaron por aquí. [WINNIE: […] Dim. *(Pause.)* Until they disappear. *(Pause.)* Last human beings – to pass this way.]
Rodríguez Gago_1989r	WINNIE: […] Borrosos. *(Pausa.)* Luego nada. *(Pausa.)* Los últimos seres humanos perdidos por estos parajes. [WINNIE: […] Dim. *(Pause.)* Then nothing. *(Pause.)* The last human beings strayed in this place.]

b) Addition

Only a few instances of addition have been observed in the translation. In Table 18, the stage direction *Pausa* [Pause] has been included, presumably as an attempt to compensate for the numerous deletions of the term in other sections of the play.

Table 18: An example of addition in Days

Beckett_1961	WINNIE: […] One cannot sing … just like that, no. *(Pause.)* It bubbles up, for some unknown reason, the time is ill chosen, one chokes it back.
Martínez Trives_1963p	WINNIE: […] Una no puede cantar … cuando apetece, no. *(Pausa.)* Lanzas gorgoritos y por razones desconocidas una lo aguanta. *(Pausa.)* Está mal elegido el momento. [WINNIE: […] One cannot sing … when one feels like it, no. *(Pause.)* You warble away and for unknown reasons you hold it back. *(Pause.)* The time is ill chosen.]
Martínez Luciano_2011p	WINNIE: […] Una no puede cantar … así, de pronto, no. *(Pausa.)* Te viene a los labios, por alguna razón desconocida, eliges mal el momento, y se te atraganta. [WINNIE: […] One cannot sing … just like that, all of a sudden, no. *(Pause.)* It comes up to your lips, for some unknown reason, you choose the time badly and it gets choked.]
Rodríguez Gago_1989r	WINNIE: […] Uno no puede cantar … así como así, no. *(pausa.)* Sube a tus labios, por razones misteriosas, has elegido un mal momento, te lo tragas de nuevo. [WINNIE: […] One cannot sing … just like that, no. *(pause.)* It comes up to your lips, for mysterious reasons, you have chosen a bad time, you swallow it back.]

c) Substitution

One aspect that stands out in the MARTÍNEZ TRIVES_1963P TT is that in certain cases the meaning of the ST is not adequately communicated, as in the example contained in Table 19.

Table 19: An example of substitution in Days

BECKETT_1961	WINNIE: [...] *(examines tube, smile off)* – running out – *(looks for cap)* – ah well – *(finds cap)* – can't be helped –
MARTÍNEZ TRIVES_1963P	WINNIE: [...] *(Examina el tubo y deja de sonreír.)* ¡No puedo prescindir ... *(Encuentra el tapón.)* ... de este gasto! [WINNIE: [...] *(Examines the tube and stops smiling.)* I can't do without ... *(Finds the cap.)* ... this expense!]
MARTÍNEZ LUCIANO_2011P	WINNIE: [...] *(Examina el tubo. Su sonrisa se apaga.)* Se está acabando ... *(Busca el tapón.)* En fin ... *(Encuentra el tapón.)* ¿Qué le vamos a hacer ...? [WINNIE: [...] *(Examines the tube. Her smile fades.)* It's running out ... *(Looks for the cap.)* Ah well ... *(Finds the cap.)* What can we do ...?]
RODRÍGUEZ GAGO_1989R	WINNIE: [...] *(examina el tubo, deja de sonreír)* – acabándose – *(busca la tapa)* – en fin – *(encuentra la tapa)* – no tiene remedio – [WINNIE: *(examines the tube, stops smiling)* – running out – *(looks for the cap)* – ah well – *(finds the cap)* – it can't be helped –]

Despite containing a relatively low number of translation techniques, when compared to other texts that tend towards acceptability, MARTÍNEZ TRIVES_1963P is the TT that deviates the most from the ST in the DAYS set. The sporadic instances of self-censorship are to be expected in a text created during the Francoist censorship period, as was noted in the MENAGERIE and CRUCIBLE sets with regard to the GORDON AND DE QUINTO_1950P and HURTADO_1956P TTs, respectively.

The analysis shows that MARTÍNEZ LUCIANO_2011P text goes against the grain of what has been found in other performance-oriented works. Indeed, despite having been written to be performed, the text leans towards adequacy at both the macro and the microtextual levels, particularly in its adherence to the ST. Rodríguez Gago_1989r, on the other hand, is a typical reader-oriented TT that contains translator's notes, follows the ST closely, possibly because it was published as a bilingual edition, and, as such, tends towards adequacy.

5.4. The Lover

The Lover set of texts is comprised of four performance-oriented (Bohr_1966p, Escobar_1966p, Gómez and Cano_2013p and Aldeguer_2017p) and two reader-oriented (Barberá_1965 and Spregelburd_2005r) texts, as shown in Figure 25.

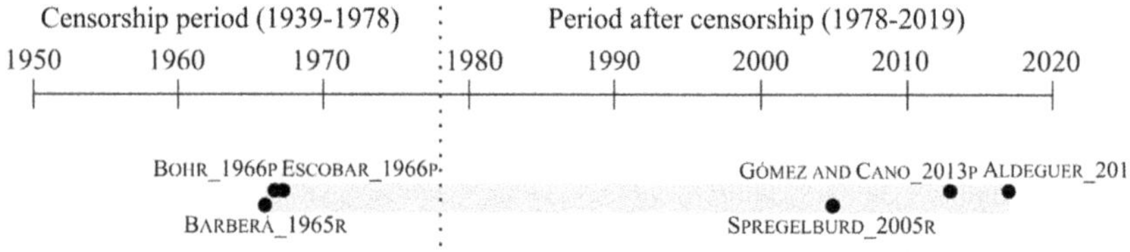

Figure 25: Lover text set.

Bohr_1966p

Censorship record 91–66 is dated back to 1966 and is connected to a TT signed by Daniel Bohr – director, playwright and founder of the theatrical company Nuevo Teatro Experimental (Gómez García 1998). This TT appears both as a version and adaptation by him in the censorship record and as a translation by Manuel Barberá, which was published in 1965 in Nueva Visión, as part of the programme for the Nuevo Teatro Experimental's 1966 production of the play (Centro de Documentación de las Artes Escénicas y de la Música 2017b). Consulting censorship record 91–66 provides further clarification regarding the identity of the target authors of this TT.

On 17 March 1966, Bohr requested a performance of *The Lover* by the group Teatro Nacional de Cámara y Ensayo at the Teatro Infanta Beatriz in Madrid. The first TT filed in record 91–66 matches that by Manuel Barberá (BARBERÁ_1965R). The reports made by the censors highlight concerns regarding the erotic tone of the stage directions and the violation of Censorship Rule 8, which addressed extramarital relations. The reports also note that the play could be authorized for a select intellectual audience, as 'the delicate nature of the topic is diluted in its own atmosphere of imaginative reality' (record 91–66, my translation). On 1 April, the performance was authorized under certain conditions: it was to be staged only in a chamber theatre, with prior supervision of the dress rehearsal. However, no omissions have been observed.

Bohr's achievement in transitioning the piece from a chamber to a commercial theatre, as documented in record 91–66, is especially noteworthy. On 4 April 1966, Nuevo Teatro Experimental, directed by Bohr, filed a request for a performance in the Teatro Infanta Beatriz, in Madrid, as well as in the Teatro Romea and the Teatro Windsor in Barcelona. In the document sent to the board of censors asking for permission to stage the play in commercial theatres, Bohr offers to modify the TT BARBERÁ_1965R, particularly in the parts deemed by the censors to be the most problematic, and proposes version BOHR_1966P. The target author admits the manipulation of the TT in the following terms:

> The play *The Lover* by Harold Pinter has been authorized for performance in chamber theatres in a direct translation from the original version. I now take the liberty of signing an adaptation of the same play, carried out specifically to obtain the authorization necessary for its commercial use in Madrid, Barcelona and the provinces [...].
>
> The version authorized for selected sessions was the text derived from the English original and the subsequent adaptations were not presented to the censors, as these modifications were made on stage, in rehearsals, to deal with difficulties relative to staging and to facilitate the understanding by the average audience. (Record 91–66, my translation)

The textual analysis of these *adaptations*, which are obvious instances of edits made to the previous TT, will be presented in sections 5.4.1, 5.4.2 and 6.4. By way of example, Figure 26 illustrates how the original question *How is your whore?* has been substituted by the euphemistic *¿Cómo están tus amigas?* [How are your girlfriends?].

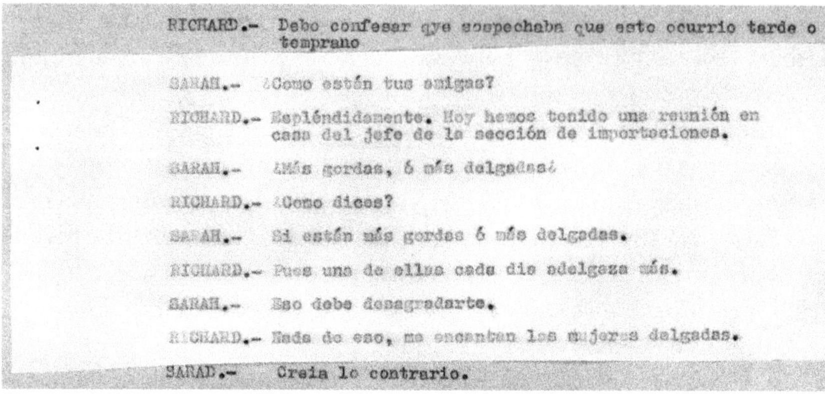

RICHARD.- Debo confesar qye sospechaba que esto ocurrio tarde o temprano

SARAH.- ¿Como están tus amigas?

RICHARD.- Espléndidamente. Hoy hemos tenido una reunión en casa del jefe de la sección de importaciones.

SARAH.- ¿Más gordas, ó más delgadas¿

RICHARD.- ¿Como dices?

SARAH.- Si están más gordas ó más delgadas.

RICHARD.- Pues una de ellas cada dia adelgaza más.

SARAH.- Eso debe desagradarte.

RICHARD.- Nada de eso, me encantan las mujeres delgadas.

SARAD.- Creia lo contrario.

Figure 26: Textual changes in BOHR_1966P.

By way of reply to Bohr's request, censorship record 91–66 includes a letter dated 15 April, in which José María García Escudero praises both the new text and the work of the theatrical group. The record also contains reports by the censors expressing a favourable opinion after the manipulation of the stage directions:

> the correction to the stage directions, which previously contained instances of strong sensuality, and the change of such passages into pantomime, considerably softens the formal flaws denounced in the previous report. Furthermore, the identification of the husband with the lover is now clearer. (Record 91–66, my translation)

In the end, authorization was granted without omissions, but with a series of conditions, namely, supervision of the dress rehearsal and inclusion, in the programme, of a note clarifying the identification of the husband with the lover. The first censorship guide was issued on 16 April 1966, allowing the performance of the play in commercial theatres. Understanding this process is crucial for grasping the reasons behind the significant textual alterations discussed in Chapter 6, which focuses on self-censorship.

ESCOBAR_1966P

Some months later in 1966, a TT of *The Lover* was presented to the censors signed by Luis Escobar, an important figure in the theatre during the Francoist period (Centro de Documentación Teatral 2017). The production premièred in the Teatro Eslava in Madrid in 1967 and was directed by the target author (Álvaro 1967). According to censorship record 343–66, like in the case of HURTADO_1956P and MARTÍNEZ TRIVES_1963P in the CRUCIBLE and DAYS sets, the same TT was used in subsequent productions in the following years and was published in *Primer Acto* (Pinter 1967), ensuring that access to this printed TT has remained available to the present day. Between 1940 and 1952, before becoming the director of the Teatro Eslava, Escobar was co-director, with Huberto Pérez de la Ossa, of the Teatro María Guerrero, an official theatre at that time (Espejo 2017). His role as a mediator in the introduction of British plays, some of which he also translated, is particularly noteworthy, as highlighted by Merino-Álvarez (2017b: 440–441):

> Although Escobar sided ideologically with the Franco government after the war, and was even deemed pro-German (Quirós 2010), as head of the María Guerrero Theatre he tried to continue the theatrical tradition first established by La Barraca group with whom he had cooperated, albeit without the group's ideological agenda. Escobar's Anglo-Spanish origin favoured his role as influential mediator and successful translator. As director of one of the national theatres, he was persuaded to import most British plays from London's West End, as a means to counteract German influence on Madrid's stages at critical moments for the allies in WWII (García 2007, 96; London 1997, 41), and he also spent some time in London with funding from the British Council in the mid 1940s.

The company of the Teatro Eslava filed the first request for a performance of ESCOBAR_1966P (record 343–66). Three reports by the censors mention the previous authorization of BOHR_1966P as a reason for authorizing ESCOBAR_1966P, although it was, in fact, a different TT. However, in one of the reports, the censor Sebastián Bautista de la Torre states that it would be necessary to watch the staging 'in order to clear up what happened exactly when the couple went under the table' and wonders whether the last utterance in ESCOBAR_1966P coincides with that of BOHR_1966P (record 343–66, my translation). On 19 December 1966 the authorization was issued without omissions for audiences over eighteen years old, with the prior supervision of the dress rehearsal and a note stipulating that an eye should be kept on the scene under the table. The influential position occupied by Escobar within the theatrical system might have facilitated the authorization, although the

TT arrived in Spain during a period of increased openness, with José María García Escudero as *Director General de Cinematografía y Teatro* [Director General of Cinema and Theatre] (Merino-Álvarez 2000). Six more requests to perform ESCOBAR_1966P are filed in record 343–66, and all were authorized. Until 1972, the year of the last recorded request, several companies staged *The Lover* at various venues, making this the most frequently performed TT on the Spanish stage during the censorship period.

GÓMEZ AND CANO_2013P

In 2013, the company Funfanfarria produced Pinter's play *The Lover*, which was directed by Susana Gómez at La casa de la portera in Madrid. The dossier for this production specifies that the translation was carried out by Susana Gómez and Jorge Cano, but the billboard states that the TT was by Susana Gómez, a professional who defines herself as a director, playwright and translator (Gómez 2022).

Gómez (Centro de Documentación de las Artes Escénicas y de la Música 2017d, my translation) highlights the importance of pauses in the text: 'Pinter immerses us in the enigma of words and silences; he presents the ambiguity of the implicit aspects on which a relationship is built and that we, as spectators, think we can decipher.' She also underlines that *The Lover* offers the typical dissection of characters and situations that characterize Harold Pinter's work and shows her admiration for the ST, describing it as 'theatre in one of the most lucid contemporary conceptual realizations' (*ibid.*). Gómez (2019, personal communication) acknowledges that one of her main objectives was to depart from the previous TTs that had been published in Argentina, by bringing the language closer to the present-day spectator in Spain. The dossier also includes positive reviews of the production, some of which point out the fact that the play was staged in La casa de la portera (<https://lacasadelaportera.wordpress.com/acerca-de>), an intimate space favouring the patrons' immersion.

ALDEGUER_2017P

In 2017, a production of *The Lover* took place at El Pavón Teatro Kamikaze in Madrid. It was directed by Nacho Aldeguer and Álex García and produced by El Loco Produce and Bella Batalla, founded by the two directors respectively. The TT was signed by Aldeguer, a theatre professional who was also the director and producer of this performance. The play was staged again in 2018.

On the theatre's website (<https://teatrokamikaze.com>, my translation), the production was described as 'a gastro-theatrical experience based on the text by Harold Pinter'. Aldeguer confirms that he remained very faithful to the original text, observing that 'Pinter is a surgeon of words' (Campos 2017, my translation).

BARBERÁ_1965R

The oldest TT of *The Lover* found in the CCBIP and REBIUN catalogues is by Manuel Barberá and was published in 1965 by the Argentinian publisher Nueva Visión as part of the Teatro Universal series (Pinter 1965), which specialized in reader-oriented translations (Merino-Álvarez 1994b). The publication also contains other plays by Pinter translated by the same target author, namely *The Caretaker* and *The Dumb Waiter*. The CCBIP shows that Barberá is the target author of several plays in the censorship period, and some of these (*The Night of the Iguana* by Tennessee Williams and *After the Fall* and *The Price* by Arthur Miller) were still in use in the twenty-first century, as the TEATRAD catalogue shows. Apart from the translated plays, the back cover of the book contains information about Pinter. Like MIRLAS_1951R and MUCHNIK AND MUCHNIK_1955R, in the MENAGERIE and CRUCIBLE sets respectively, BARBERÁ_1965R constitutes another example of the circulation of theatre TTs from Argentina in Spain during the dictatorship.

SPREGELBURD_2005R

After the reader-oriented BARBERÁ_1965R and the performance-oriented ESCOBAR_1966, no other published translations of *The Lover* are found for several decades. The only TT published in the twenty-first century appeared in 2005, signed by Rafael Spregelburd, as part of the Gran Teatro series brought out by the Argentinian publisher Losada. The book includes two other plays by Pinter and translated by Spregelburd – *Night School* and *Sketches* – and contains references to productions of the original plays, as well as translator's notes explaining words or expressions, indicating a source-oriented tendency. Spregelburd (2005: 14, my translation) adds a preface in which he describes his first contact with Pinter's theatre, as well as with the playwright himself, and points out some Pinterian traits, such as the 'indication of the point at which the world is a construction of language'. He also underlines the need for these retranslations to address the limited availability of Pinter's plays in Spanish: 'These plays that – in theory – all writers for the theatre have already read, these plays that have been studied so much, and whose influence has spread like wildfire to hundreds of contemporary playwrights, these plays are no longer easily found in Spanish' (*ibid.*: 12).

5.4.1. Macrotextual analysis

A textual comparison shows that the TTs in the LOVER set either take the ST published by Faber and Faber as their starting point or a TT based on this ST, as in the case of BOHR_1966P.[2] Similarly to the trend observed in DAYS, the performance-oriented TTs of the censorship period (BOHR_1966P and ESCOBAR_1966P) tend to acceptability, while the performance-oriented TTs of the post-censorship period (GÓMEZ AND CANO_2013P and ALDEGUER_2017P) and the reader-oriented TTs (BARBERÁ_1965R and SPREGELBURD_2005R) tend towards adequacy.

The pairing of utterances (Figure 27) shows that BOHR_1966P and ESCOBAR_1966P contain numerous omissions – especially BOHR_1966P – as well as a few additional utterances. By contrast, the macrotextual study of GÓMEZ AND CANO_2013P, ALDEGUER_2017P and SPREGELBURD_2005R

2 Another English version of the ST was published by Samuel French, and where it differed from the Faber and Faber edition, the TTs followed the latter version.

shows almost no such changes. Finally, in BARBERÁ_1965R some utterances have been omitted, although in some cases the content of the deleted utterances is incorporated into neighbouring ones. These omissions are fewer than in the TTs categorized as tending towards acceptability.

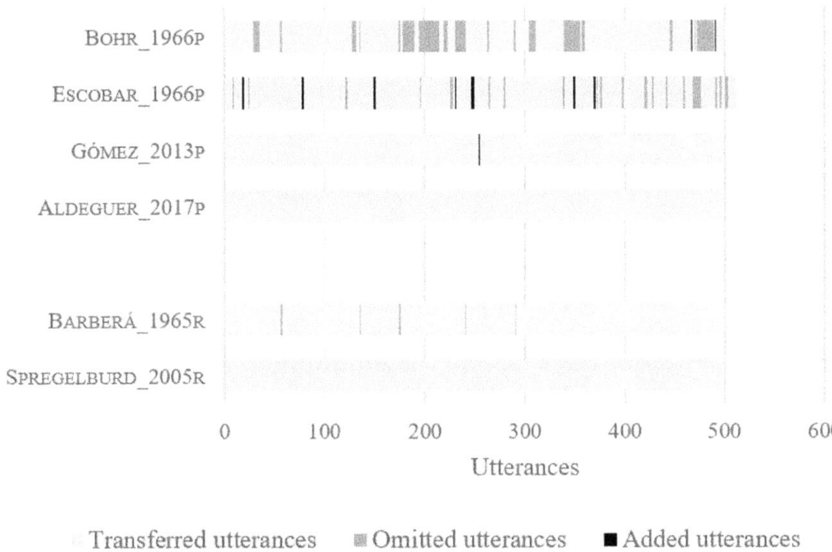

Figure 27: Omissions and additions of utterances in Lover.

5.4.2. Microtextual analysis

As in MENAGERIE, CRUCIBLE and DAYS, the results of the macrotextual study of the LOVER set are consistent with the microtextual one. Two groups of TTs can be distinguished. BOHR_1966P and, to a lesser extent, ESCOBAR_1966P display a high number of textual alterations – addition, omission and substitution – that render the TTs acceptable, while the rest of TTs can be considered adequate. Figure 28 illustrates the various translation techniques applied in each of the TTs belonging to the LOVER set.

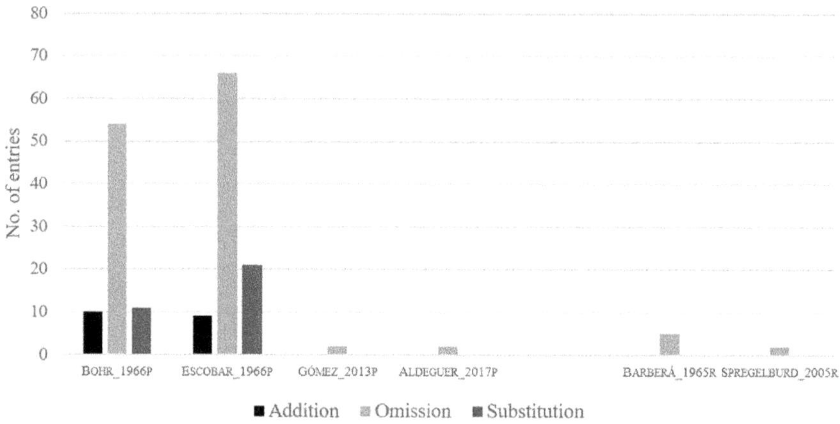

Figure 28: Translation techniques in Lover.

The numerous omissions, additions and substitutions in BOHR_1966P and ESCOBAR_1966P merit further examination.

a) Omissions

In BOHR_1966P two types of omission can be identified: the removal of words, phrases and sentences, primarily occurring in dialogue exchanges, and the deletion of longer text blocks. Textual evidence indicates that these omissions reflect the two stages followed in the creation of the TT. Many of the brief structures were omitted in the initial TT, BARBERÁ_1965R, while the more substantial deletions occur in BOHR_1966P and appear to result from self-censorship, as they address themes of sexual morality, particularly adultery, which were considered problematic by Spanish censors. In ESCOBAR_1966P, a significant number of omissions occur not only in the dialogues and stage directions, but entire utterances are also erased. Some of the deletions seem to have been caused also by self-censorship, albeit to a lesser extent than in BOHR_1966P. Table 20 illustrates how the term 'adulteress' has been omitted or translated in the various Spanish versions.

Table 20: Examples of omission in Lover

Pinter_1963	RICHARD: *(softly)*. Adulteress.
Bohr_1966p	Ø
Escobar_1966p	RICHARD: Adúltera. [RICHARD: Adulteress.]
Gómez and Cano_2013p	RICHARD: *(suavemente)* Adúltera. [RICHARD: *(softly)* Adulteress.]
Aldeguer_2017p	RICHARD: *(suavemente)*. Adúltera. [RICHARD: *(softly)* Adulteress.]
Barberá_1965r	RICHARD: *(quedamente)* ¡Adúltera! [RICHARD: *(quietly)* Adulteress!]
Spregelburd_2005r	RICHARD: *(en voz baja)* Adúltera. [RICHARD: *(in a low voice)* Adulteress.]

b) Additions

Additions play an essential role in Bohr_1966p. As documented in censorship record 91–66 itself, the hazardous topic of the lover is diluted by introducing stage directions that, among other things, make it clear that a game is being presented in which the husband and the lover are, in fact, the same person. In Escobar_1966p, there are fewer additions than in Bohr_1966p, with full sentences introduced in dialogues and stage directions and words added in dialogue exchanges. These additions do not appear to be linked to self-censorship, and, in some stage directions, they reflect an intention to clarify that certain actions are performed in the staging, as was also observed in González Vergel and Escribano_2007p (Crucible). Table 21 illustrates the additions encountered in Bohr_1966p, which can be understood as a strategy to soften the content of the play to satisfy the censors.

Table 21: Examples of addition in Lover

Pinter_1963	RICHARD: Why not?
Bohr_1966p	RICHARD: *(Volviendo al aire de farsa de la escena de los amantes)* ¿Y por qué no? [RICHARD: *(Going back to the sense of farce in the scene of the lovers)* And why not?]

(Continued)

Table 21: Continued

ESCOBAR_1966P	Ø
GÓMEZ AND CANO_2013P	RICHARD: ¿Por qué no? [RICHARD: Why not?]
ALDEGUER_2017P	RICHARD: ¿Por qué no? [RICHARD: Why not?]
BARBERÁ_1965R	RICHARD: ¿Por qué no? [RICHARD: Why not?]
SPREGELBURD_2005R	RICHARD: ¿Por qué no? [RICHARD: Why not?]

c) Substitutions

In BOHR_1966P, the examples observed involve the replacement of allusions to the lover or the prostitute with content that softens the tone of the play as in the example contained in Table 22. In ESCOBAR_1966, most substitutions appear to be an adjustment for the theatrical production, especially in the case of stage directions, although the change shown in Table 22 seems to be linked to self-censorship.

Table 22: Examples of substitution in Lover

PINTER_1963	SARAH: A whore?
BOHR_1966P	SARAH: ¿<u>Unas ... amigas</u>? [SARAH: <u>Some ... girlfriends</u>?]
ESCOBAR_1966P	SARAH: <u>Pero admites ... Tienes que admitir ... que tienes ...</u> [SARAH: <u>But you admit-You have to admit-that you have-</u>]
GÓMEZ AND CANO_2013P	SARAH: ¿Una puta? [SARAH: A whore?]
ALDEGUER_2017P	SARAH: ¿Una prostituta? [SARAH: A prostitute?]
BARBERÁ_1965R	SARAH: ¿Una ramera? [SARAH: A whore?]
SPREGELBURD_2005R	SARAH: ¿Una puta? [SARAH: A whore?]

The textual deviations detected in BOHR_1966P are identical to those found in BARBERÁ_1965R, except for some self-censored fragments. ESCOBAR_1966P displays changes that can be also linked to self-censorship, though fewer than in BOHR_1966P. GÓMEZ AND CANO_2013P and ALDEGUER_2017P are the other performance-oriented TTs from the twenty-first century which, like MARTÍNEZ LUCIANO_2011P in DAYS, tend towards adequacy. They follow the original very closely both in meaning and syntax, as do the reader-oriented TTs from Argentina, BARBERÁ_1965R and SPREGELBURD_2005R. The fact that the works from the censorship period show a high degree of manipulation justifies the need for subsequent retranslations, as also observed in the other text sets examined (MENAGERIE, CRUCIBLE and DAYS).

5.5. General trends

This study of the TTs in the TEATRAD corpus has revealed consistent patterns across the four text sets examined. TTs with similar extratextual traits – for example, their performance or reader orientation or the historical context in which they were produced – also exhibit shared linguistic characteristics.

The performance-oriented TTs produced during the censorship period tend to favour acceptability and are influenced by (self-)censoring to varying degrees. The approach taken to the performance-oriented TTs belonging to the subsequent period varies between acceptability and adequacy in consonance with the target authors' priorities and restrictions. The reader-oriented TTs in the corpus tend to be adequate, and, in general, those produced during the censorship period exhibit a greater proximity to the syntax of the ST than those of the later period, which aim for a more fluent expression in the target language.

Finally, the fragments from corpus 2 include recurrent references to sexual morality, politics, religion and foul language which were self-censored in the performance-oriented TTs of the censorship period. These topics are examined in greater depth in Chapter 6.

CHAPTER 6

The translation of sensitive topics

This chapter offers a diachronic analysis of the way in which certain topics, which were (self-)censored between 1939 and 1978, have been translated after the dictatorship. It looks specifically at sexual morality, politics, religion and foul language in 1,243 fragments of translations obtained by searching anchor words in the corpus. Focusing on topics deemed to be controversial by the censors, this chapter describes the most frequent translation techniques applied in the TTs and presents them in graph form, with examples showing the treatment of these topics over time. The analysis takes into account whether the texts are performance- or reader-oriented and whether they were produced during the Francoist regime or later.

6.1. The Glass Menagerie

The TTs for which a censorship record (274–50) exists are GORDON AND DE QUINTO_1950P, which was used for more than two decades, and VÁZQUEZ VIGO_1978P, a revision of the previous TT. Of the twenty-two requests filed for performance of GORDON AND DE QUINTO_1950P, one asked for the omission of the allusions to the female body. When it comes to books, records (5862–53 and 251–58) have been found for the Argentinian reader-oriented edition MIRLAS_1951R, published by Losada, which has endured in the theatrical and literary systems well into the twenty-first century, as well as for the performance-oriented edition of GORDON AND DE QUINTO_1950P, published by Escelicer (records 2982–60 and 1732–65). A textual analysis shows that GORDON AND DE QUINTO_1950P has been altered more than the censorship records would suggest, which can be attributed to self-censorship. In eleven cases, GORDON AND DE QUINTO_1950P softens the content of the ST (WILLIAMS_1948) in references to sexual morality (2 cases), politics (4) and foul language (5). The relatively low number of instances found in the MENAGERIE set may be attributed to the play's fewer themes deemed problematic by the censors compared to the CRUCIBLE and LOVER sets. However, an analysis of the concordances reveals distinct differences between the performance-oriented and reader-oriented TTs, reflecting the trends towards acceptability and adequacy discussed in the previous chapter.

6.1.1. Sexual morality

In GORDON AND DE QUINTO_1950P, suggestive content has been reduced in two cases with the word *bosom* being translated as *escote* [neckline] and *sex* as *sensualidad, sensualidad correspondida* [sensuality, requited sensuality], in an attempt to mitigate the force of the original words. It is plausible that these changes were made because the target authors assumed that the censors would find such references problematic and receiving authorization for the performance of the TT was a priority. In VÁZQUEZ VIGO_1978P, the substitution of *bosom* is retained, while transfer is used to translate the reference to *sex*. During the post-censorship period, the fragments in which both references appear were deleted in the performance-oriented TT GALÁN_2014P. Such an approach does not seem to have been motivated by censorship but rather by the decision to adapt the ST to a specific theatrical production.

In the reader-oriented TT from the censorship period, MIRLAS_1951R, transfer is used for both anchor words, most likely because the text was prepared abroad, in Argentina, and because the controls for books were generally less severe than for performances. This trend extends to other textual genres, as has also been noted in relation to Argentinian narrative TTs, despite the fact that they were sometimes manipulated by the publisher afterwards (Gómez Castro 2009). As Gómez Castro (*ibid.*: 407) observes: 'these translations had been done in a context different to the one Spanish translators working under Francoism were used to, and therefore their authors had not felt compelled to exert any kind of previous self-censorship.'

The reader-oriented TTs of the post-censorship period, DIÉGUEZ_2007R and ESPEJO_2019R, also resort to transfer to translate both references, showing their adequacy. The restrictions relating to controversial topics from the censorship period seem to have disappeared in the twenty-first century and the target authors of these reader-oriented translations could prioritize fidelity to the ST, as Espejo (2019) notes in the introduction to his TT.

Figure 29 shows the techniques used in each TT to translate the anchor words relating to sexual morality.

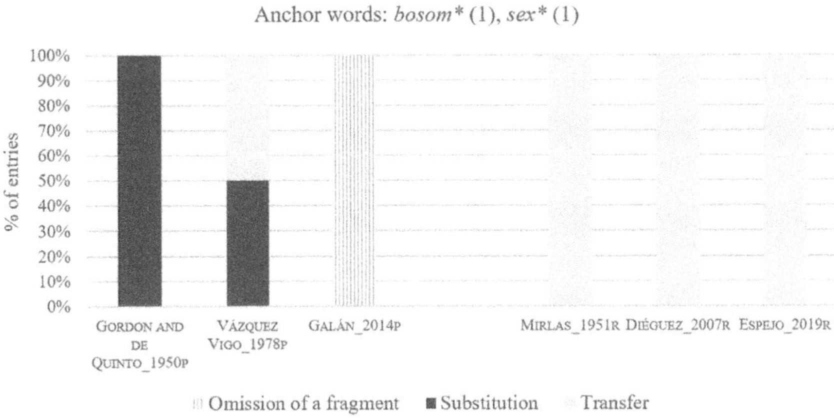

Figure 29: Translation techniques used to deal with sexual morality (Menagerie).

To showcase the differences among the TTs, Table 23 illustrates an utterance containing the anchor word *sex**. The word has been substituted in GORDON AND DE QUINTO_1950P, a fragment of text has been deleted in GALÁN_2014P; and in VÁZQUEZ VIGO_1978P, MIRLAS_1951R, DIÉGUEZ_2007R and ESPEJO_2019R, transfer has been used.

Table 23: An example of a reference to sexual morality in Menagerie

WILLIAMS_1948	TOM: [...] In Spain there was Guernica! But here there was only hot swing music and liquor, dance halls, bars, and movies, and <u>sex</u> that hung in the gloom like a chandelier and flooded the world with brief, deceptive rainbows ...
GORDON AND DE QUINTO_1950P	TOM: [...] Pero aquí solamente había música de jazz y licores, salones de baile y <u>sensualidad, sensualidad correspondida</u> en la penumbra opaca, como una lámpara que inundase el mundo de fugitivos arco iris engañosos. [TOM: [...] But here there was only jazz music and liquor, dance halls and <u>sensuality, requited sensuality</u> in the opaque gloom, like a lamp that flooded the world with fugitive, deceptive rainbows.]

(Continued)

Table 23: Continued

Vázquez Vigo_1978p	TOM: [...] En España, Guernica era destruida. Pero aquí aún había jazz y whisky, salones de baile, sexo, cine ... [TOM: [...] In Spain, Guernica was destroyed. But here there was still jazz and whisky, dance halls, sex, movies ...]
Galán_2014p	Ø
Diéguez_2007r	TOM: [...] ¡En España estaba Guernica! Y aquí solo teníamos swing y alcohol, bailes, bares y películas, y el sexo, que pendía en la penumbra como una lámpara e inundaba el mundo de breves y engañosos arco iris ... [TOM: [...] In Spain there was Guernica! And here we only had swing and alcohol, dances, bars and movies, and sex, which hung in the gloom like a lamp and flooded the world with brief and deceptive rainbows ...]
Espejo_2019r	TOM: [...] ¡En España, Guernica!. Pero aquí había solo música de swing, alcohol, salas de baile, bares, películas y el sexo sobre nuestras cabezas como una lámpara de araña que inundaba el mundo de luz, aunque era un arco iris efímero y engañoso ... [TOM: [...] In Spain, Guernica! But here there were only swing, alcohol, dance halls, bars, movies and sex over our heads like a chandelier that flooded the world with light, although it was a brief and deceptive rainbow ...]
Williams_1945	TOM: [...] In Spain there was Guernica! Here there was only hot swing music and liquor, dance halls, bars, and movies, and sex that hung in the gloom like a chandelier and flooded the world with brief, deceptive rainbows ...
Mirlas_1951r	TOM: [...] ¡En España estaba Guernica! Aquí, sólo había frenética música de jazz y licor y salones de baile y bares y películas, y el sexo suspendido en la sombra como un candelabro y que anegaba al mundo con breves y engañosos arco iris ... [TOM: [...] In Spain there was Guernica! Here there were only frenetic jazz music and liquor and dance halls and bars and movies, and sex that hung in the darkness like a candelabra and flooded the world with brief and deceptive rainbows ...]

6.1.2. Politics

In Gordon and de Quinto_1950p, the search for the anchor words *Spain* (three instances) and *Franco* (one instance) uncovered four references to politics, where sensitive content has been deliberately softened. The three mentions of Spain pertain to the Civil War and the bombing of Guernica, while the fourth refers to Franco in a newspaper headline. The translation employs two primary techniques – omission (75 per cent of the cases) and substitution (25 per cent) – which mitigate the content in a likely attempt to secure its authorization.

Vázquez Vigo_1978p, which was produced during a more liberal context, that is, the transition period between dictatorship and democracy, presented the impresario Andrés de Kramer with the opportunity to ask for a new rating of the play in light of the historical changes taking place, as indicated in record 274–50. The approval resulted in all references to politics being kept in the ensuing translation by means of transfer.

An examination of the way in which these anchor words have been handled in Galán_2014p, another performance-oriented TT produced after the censorship era, reveals that three fragments have been omitted, and a fragment referencing Mussolini and Hitler has been introduced following a mention of the Spanish Civil War, thereby intensifying a reference that had been softened in the first TT.

The reader-oriented Mirlas_1951r employs the transfer technique in all instances found in the performance-oriented edition of the ST (Williams_1945), which contains only half the controversial political references encountered in the reader-oriented ST (Williams_1948). These references may have been allowed during the censorship period because they targeted an individual readership rather than a collective theatre audience. Similarly, in Diéguez_2007r and Espejo_2019r, the same technique has been applied to translate all the references included in Williams_1948.

The way in which political references have been dealt with during and after the censorship period reveals trends similar to those discussed in the section on sexual morality. For instance, sporadic political references self-censored in Gordon and de Quinto_1950p were later restored in the late 1970s (Vázquez Vigo_1978p) and approached more freely in the twenty-first century (Galán_2014p). In reader-oriented TTs from both periods – Mirlas_1951r, Diéguez_2007r and Espejo_2019r – the consistent trend is the use of transfer, as displayed in Figure 30.

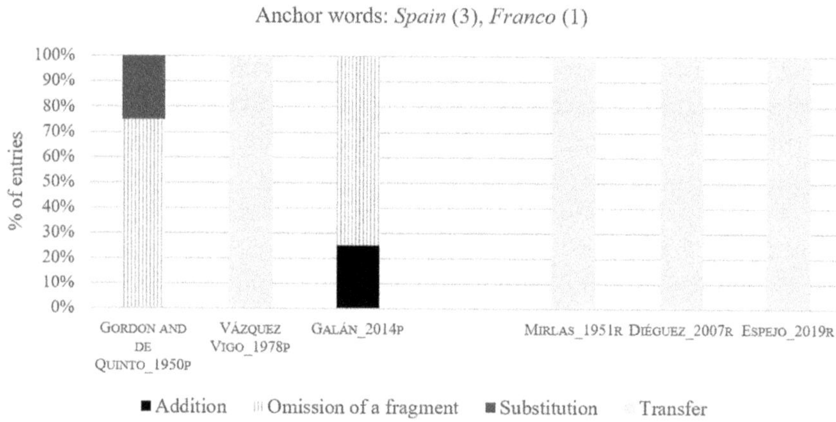

Figure 30: Translation techniques used to deal with political references (Menagerie).

To illustrate the different translational approaches applied at different historical periods, Table 24 shows how the sentences *In Spain there was revolution*, *Here there was only shouting and confusion* and *In Spain there was Guernica* have been addressed in the various TTs, with some of them opting for omission, others for literal transfer and yet others including additional references to totalitarian regimes to intensify the content that was deemed dangerous in the first TT. This latter approach presumably aims to provide a twenty-first-century audience with greater historical context about the political climate of the 1930s and 1940s, the period in which the play is set.

Table 24: An example of a reference to politics in Menagerie

Williams_1948	TOM: [...] In Spain there was revolution. Here there was only shouting and confusion. In Spain there was Guernica.
Gordon and de Quinto_1950p	TOM: [...] En Europa había mucho jaleo y mucha confusión. Ø [TOM: [...] In Europe there was a lot of mess and confusion.]

Vázquez Vigo_1978p	TOM: [...] En España había una guerra. Aquí, en América, gritos y confusión. En España bombardeaban Guernica [TOM: [...] In Spain there was a war. Here, in America, shouting and confusion. In Spain, Guernica was bombed.]
Galán_2014p	TOM: [...] Europa estaba convulsa. Era un polvorín a punto de estallar. El fascismo de Mussolini y el nacional socialismo de Adolf Hitler amenazaban con arrasar Europa. España estaba en guerra. [TOM: [...] Europe was in upheaval. It was a powder keg about to explode. Mussolini's fascism and Adolf Hitler's national socialism threatened to sweep through Europe. Spain was at war.]
Diéguez_2007r	TOM: [...] En España se libraba una revolución; aquí no había más que alboroto y desconcierto. En España estaba Guernica. [TOM: [...] In Spain a revolution was being fought; here there was only uproar and confusion. In Spain there was Guernica.]
Espejo_2019r	TOM: [...] En España había una revolución. Aquí solo griterío y confusión. En España lo de ... Guernica. [TOM: [...] In Spain there was a revolution. Here only shouting and confusion. In Spain ... Guernica.]
Williams_1945	TOM: [...] In Spain there was revolution. Here there was only shouting and confusion.
Mirlas_1951r	TOM: [...] En España, había revolución. Aquí, sólo había gritos y confusión. [TOM: [...] In Spain there was revolution. Here there was only shouting and confusion.]

6.1.3. Foul language

The search for anchor words in the ST yielded five occurrences of foul language, which, in Ávila Cabrera's (2015) classification of taboo language, are the insult *bastard* (two instances), the profane expressions *what in Christ's name* (one instance) and *who in hell* (one instance), and the derogatory *that Goddamn 'Rise and Shine'* (one instance). In the ST, all these cases of foul language are associated with the character of Tom and are used to convey strong emotions.

Rather unsurprisingly, all five instantiations have been mitigated in GORDON AND DE QUINTO_1950P, either through substitution (three instances) or omission (two instances), resulting in a loss of intensity of the character and the situations, despite their importance to the plot. In addition to their relevance to the affective dimension (Gómez Castro 2009; Arias-Badia 2020), foul language is also used as an orality marker (Baños and Chaume 2009), nuances that are irremediably lost with its omission in the TT.

Foul language differs from the previous topics of sexual morality and politics, as it reveals traces of possible self-censorship not only in GORDON AND DE QUINTO_1950P but also in VÁZQUEZ VIGO_1978P. In the latter TT, techniques such as substitution (three instances) and omission of a word (one instance) are employed, reducing the problematic content. However, transfer is also used in one instance, indicating a selective approach. This suggests that in VÁZQUEZ VIGO_1978P there is a greater focus on restoring banned topics like sexuality and politics than on addressing issues related to foul language.

GALÁN_2014P demonstrates variability in its approach to the ST, alternating between transfer (three instances), substitution (one instance) and omission of a fragment (one instance). Unlike previous TTs, which centred on the censoring of sensitive topics, this TT appears more focused on adapting the text to align with the target author's priorities for a specific production.

Transfer is the only translation technique observed in MIRLAS_1951R, DIÉGUEZ_2007R and ESPEJO_2019R, although in some cases, such as in MIRLAS_1951R and ESPEJO_2019R, *bastard* is replaced by the less aggressive terms *bribón* [swindler] and *sinvergüenza* [scoundrel] respectively.

Figure 31 offers a visual representation of the translation techniques used in each TT of the MENAGERIE set to deal with the translation of foul language.

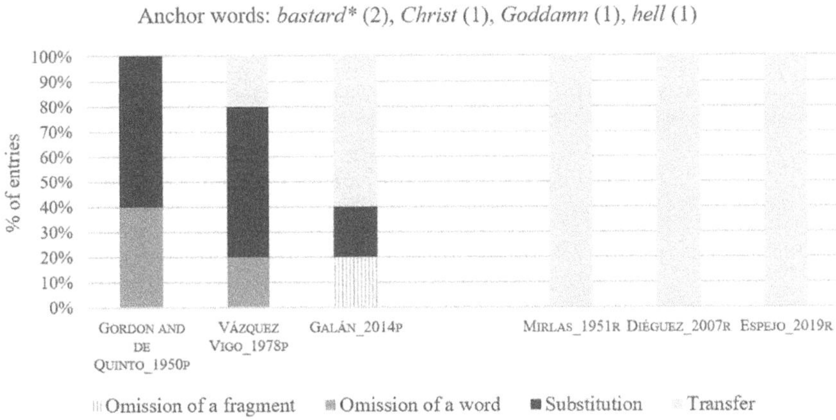

Figure 31: Translation techniques used to deal with foul language (Menagerie).

Table 25 illustrates the treatment of foul language through an example from one of Tom's utterances, where the derogatory term *goddamn* is handled differently across TTs. In the performance-oriented TTs created during the censorship period (Gordon and de Quinto_1950p and Vázquez Vigo_1978p), the term is omitted. In the post-censorship, performance-oriented TT (Galán_2014p), the entire fragment is omitted. By contrast, the reader-oriented TTs (Mirlas_1951r, Diéguez_2007r and Espejo_2019r) attempt to transfer the expression by using the adjective *maldito* [damn].

Table 25: An example of foul language in Menagerie

Williams_1948	TOM: Every time you come in yelling that Goddamn "Rise and Shine!" "Rise and Shine!"
Gordon and de Quinto_1950p	TOM: Todas las mañanas, cuando tú entras en mi habitación diciendo: "¡Despierta, despierta!" [TOM: Every morning, when you come into my bedroom saying: "Wake up, wake up!"]
Vázquez Vigo_1978p	TOM: Cada vez que entras diciendo "que vas a llegar tarde". [TOM: Every time you come in saying "you're going to be late".]

(Continued)

Table 25: Continued

GALÁN_2014P	Ø
DIÉGUEZ_2007R	TOM: Cada vez que entras con tu maldito «¡Levántate y triunfa! ¡Levántate y triunfa!» [TOM: Every time you come in with your damned "Rise and Shine! Rise and Shine!"]
ESPEJO_2019R	TOM: Cada mañana, cuando entras en la habitación con ese maldito «¡Hora de levantarse!», «¡Hora de levantarse!» [TOM: Every morning, when you come into the bedroom with that damned "Time to wake up!" "Time to wake up!"]
WILLIAMS_1945	TOM: Sure, every time you come in yelling that bloody *Rise and Shine!* Rise and Shine!!
MIRLAS_1951R	TOM: ¡Claro, cada día entras gritando ese maldito: «¡Levántate y lúcete! ¡Levántate y lúcete!» [TOM: Sure, every day you come in yelling that damned "Rise and Shine! Rise and Shine!"]

6.2. The Crucible

In the CRUCIBLE set of texts, censorship record 310–56, associated with HURTADO_1956P, indicates that no omissions were demanded by the censors in response to the first performance request. However, in a 1967 application involving the published version by Escelicer, a deletion was mandated on page 62. While the record does not specify the deleted words, the Escelicer edition contains references to adultery on that page. Two additional censorship records, 5135–60 and 2792–73, for the published version of HURTADO_1956P, show that the translation was authorized without deletions. Although the paratextual information in these censorship records provide little evidence of textual alterations in HURTADO_1956P, Chapter 5's microtexual exploration uncovers that self-censorship significantly influenced the text.

The analysis of anchor words reveals clear evidence of self-censorship in HURTADO_1956P, with a total of 168 occurrences identified in the ST that have been altered in the TT: twenty-seven related to sexual morality, fifteen to politics, 120 to religion and six to foul language. These findings confirm that controversial themes in HURTADO_1956P were deliberately softened. Notably, the CRUCIBLE set exhibits the highest overall frequency of instances of self-censorship among all the sets analysed, particularly concerning politics, religion and foul language. It ranks second only to the LOVER set in references to sexual morality, which will be discussed further in section 6.4. As with the MENAGERIE set, these changes were not imposed during the censorship scrutiny but were implemented prior to it, making HURTADO_1956P a prime example of self-censorship. The other TTs in the CRUCIBLE set show varying trends in performance and reader orientation, resembling the MENAGERIE set in their inclination towards adequacy or acceptability.

6.2.1. *Sexual morality*

In HURTADO_1956P, different techniques have been employed to self-censor sensitive content in the translation of twenty-seven anchor words from the ST related to sexuality. The most frequently observed technique is the omission of a fragment (14 instances), followed by substitution (12 instances) and the omission of a word (one instance). Most instances (20) refer to the adulterous relationship between John Proctor and Abigail Williams, which are associated with the following anchor words: *lecher** (5), *whore** (5), *harlot** (3), *adulter** (1), *bitch** (1), *fornicat** (1), *lay** (1), *lust** (1), *prostitut** (1) and *touch** (1). The significant number of self-censored cases in this area suggests that adultery was considered a sensitive topic, prompting efforts to tone it down despite its central role in the plot. HURTADO_1956P joints the list of performance-oriented TTs from the censorship period in which adultery was subjected to self-censorship (Merino-Álvarez 2000; Pérez L. de Heredia 2004; Bandín 2007). While not all the references to adultery in the ST were self-censored, their frequency was purposely reduced. Determining how many such references would be acceptable to the censors often became part of the negotiation process during censorship reviews. A notable example is Albee's *Who's Afraid of Virginia Woolf?*, record 215–65, where director José Osuna wrote to the censors seeking to retain more instances of the previously deleted word *shit* (García Escudero 1978, in Merino-Álvarez 2016a).

Among the remaining instances, two involve the anchor word *kiss** and one involves *passion**, referencing kisses shared between John Proctor and his wife, Elizabeth. These occurrences have been dealt with by means of an omission of a fragment and two substitutions, transforming a passionate kiss into a hug. The other four instances – *divorce** (2), *org** (1) and *sex** (1) – appear in the interpolations, where Miller expresses his views on the events that occurred in Salem. These sections have been omitted in HURTADO_1956P, a decision also relevant to the discussion on politics in section 6.2.2.

In GONZÁLEZ VERGEL AND ESCRIBANO_2007P, while transfer is the most frequently employed technique (12 instances), other techniques reflect the general tendency towards acceptability in this TT: omission of a fragment (10 instances), substitution (3 instances), omission of a single word (one instance) and addition (one instance). This last technique pertains to the anchor word *bitch**, which appears in the play's appendix. Here, several utterances have been introduced, including seven repetitions of the word *puta* [whore] and one instance of *adúltero* [adulterous (male)], creating what González Vergel (2007: 260, my translation), the target author and director, describes as a 'more intense and aggressive' ending to the act. This adjustment highlights the theme of adultery, which had been downplayed in the previous performance-oriented HURTADO_1956P. As seen with GALÁN_2014P in the MENAGERIE set, a theatre professional acted as both the target author and the play's producer/director, tailoring the text to align with his specific staging ideas. In such cases, the dual roles of these agents as both target authors and producers/directors significantly influenced the final text.

The reader-oriented TT MUCHNIK AND MUCHNIK_1955R, translated in Argentina, primarily employs transfer (26 instances), with a single example of substitution. In this respect, it resembles the Argentinian reader-oriented MIRLAS_1951R, from the MENAGERIE set. Like other Argentinian reader-oriented TTs of the time, it showcases a tendency towards adequacy in handling themes of sexual morality, contrasting with their contemporary performance-oriented TTs produced in Spain (Merino-Álvarez 1994b; Pérez L. de Heredia 2004). Similarly, in LÓPEZ MUÑOZ_1997R and ESPEJO_2011R, the transfer technique is consistently employed in all cases. As with the MENAGERIE set, the preference for adequate solutions in reader-oriented TTs, both during and after the censorship period, is evident in their approach to translating references to sexual mores.

Figure 32 reveals a distribution of the translation techniques activated in the TTs according to their orientation (performance or reader) and period (censorship or post-censorship), which is similar to that found in the texts in the MENAGERIE set.

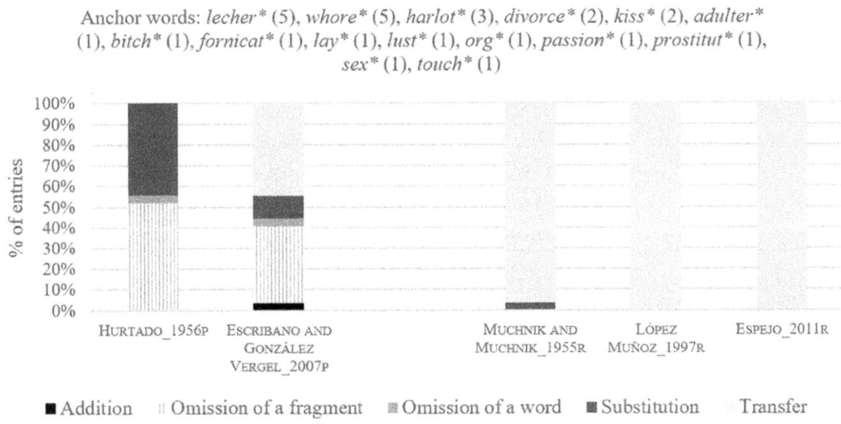

Figure 32: Translation techniques used to deal with sexual morality (Crucible).

As displayed, HURTADO_1956P, a performance-oriented TT from the censorship era, contains instances of self-censorship. In contrast, GONZÁLEZ VERGEL AND ESCRIBANO_2007P, a performance-oriented TT from the post-censorship period, employs a variety of techniques tailored to the demands of a specific theatrical production. Meanwhile, in the reader-oriented MUCHNIK AND MUCHNIK_1955R, LÓPEZ MUÑOZ_1997R and ESPEJO_2011R transfer is the predominant technique. On the whole, the CRUCIBLE set illustrates the impact of contextual factors on the translation of references to sexual morality.

Table 26, focusing on the anchor word *lecher**, highlights the contrast between the self-censored HURTADO_1956P version, where the reference has been omitted, and the other TTs, where it has been literally transferred.

Table 26: An example of a reference to sexual morality in Crucible

MILLER_1953	MARY WARREN: She'll kill me for sayin' that! *(Proctor continues toward her.)* Abby'll charge lechery on you, Mr. Proctor!
HURTADO_1956P	MARY: Si confieso ... me matará. Estoy segura que me matará. Ø [MARY: If I confess ... she'll kill me. I'm sure she'll kill me.]

(Continued)

Table 26: Continued

González Vergel and Escribano_2007p	MARY WARREN: ¡Ella me matará si lo digo! ¡Y le acusará de lujuria, señor Proctor! [MARY WARREN: She'll kill me if I say that! And she will charge you with lechery, Mr. Proctor!]
Muchnik and Muchnik_1955r	MARY: ¡Ella me matará por decir eso! *(Proctor continúa acercándose a ella.)* ¡Abby os acusará de adulterio, señor Proctor! [MARY WARREN: She'll kill me for saying that! *(Proctor continues toward her.)* Abby'll charge you with lechery, Mr. Proctor!]
López Muñoz_1997r	MARY WARREN: ¡Me matará si digo eso! *(Proctor sigue avanzando hacia ella.)* ¡Abby le acusará de lujuria, señor Proctor! [MARY WARREN: She'll kill me if I say that! *(Proctor continues toward her.)* Abby'll charge you with lechery, Mr. Proctor!]
Espejo_2011r	MARY WARREN: ¡Me matará si lo cuento! *(PROCTOR sigue avanzando hacia ella.)* ¡Abby le acusará a usted de lujuria, señor Proctor! [MARY WARREN: She'll kill me if I tell that! *(Proctor continues toward her.)* Abby'll charge you with lechery, Mr. Proctor!]

6.2.2. Politics

The analysis of Hurtado_1956p revealed fifteen cases where the political content of the ST has been neutralized. Notably, most of these anchor words appear in interpolations in the ST, where connections are made between the play and the US witch hunt against communists at the time. These references have been eliminated in Hurtado_1956p. The omission of certain fragments, mainly in the interpolations, results in the absence of the following thirteen anchor words in the TT: *law** (4), *government** (3), *politic** (3), *Communis** (2) and *ideolog** (1). Substitution is used in two instances where the authorities are depicted unfavourably, namely *King** and *torture**. In his study, Espejo (2004: 141–142, my translation) also notes the high incidence of self-censorship regarding political references, arguing that 'Hurtado also tried to stop the spectator from making a connection with what Miller describes as the political persecutions of McCarthyism.'

The documentation in the censorship record for HURTADO_1956P (record 310–56) reveals a tension between the play's political significance and the efforts to supress it. Self-censorship seems to have played a role in what Espejo (2004: 135, my translation) describes as an 'attempt at the depoliticization' of the play by the target author. However, the political dimension of the play is indisputable, given the clear parallel between the events in Salem and the anti-communist persecutions led by the House Committee on Un-American Activities – and, by extension, other repressive moments. Even though references to these connections were self-censored, critics in Spain were not blind to them (*ibid.*).

In GONZÁLEZ VERGEL AND ESCRIBANO_2007P, twelve changes involve omitted fragments, some of which occur in dialogues, though most are found in interpolations, which, surprisingly, are also excluded – similar to HURTADO_1956P. This political content is hidden not only from patrons but also from readers, as the performance-oriented TT was published in book form. However, in this publication, some chapters address the American witch hunt (Miller 2007), suggesting that the reasons for the omission of the interpolations in this TT may differ from those in HURTADO_1956P. Based on the analysis in Chapter 5, the omission of the interpolations in GONZÁLEZ VERGEL AND ESCRIBANO_2007P could reflect a broader trend of changes in stage directions, likely influenced by the director's priorities for the specific production, where these elements were deemed unnecessary. Thus, while the contexts differ, the overall effect on the TTs is similar. The remaining three occurrences involve the technique of transfer.

In contrast to the performance-oriented HURTADO_1956P, the reader-oriented MUCHNIK AND MUCHNIK_1955R uses transfer to render all the anchor words. As observed in the MENAGERIE set, there are significant differences between the Argentinian reader-oriented TT and the Spanish performance-oriented TT, both from the censorship period, particularly regarding sexual morality and politics. In LÓPEZ MUÑOZ_1997R and ESPEJO_2011R, all instances involve transfer, indicating a trend towards adequacy in the reader-oriented TTs across both the censorship period and the subsequent period, a pattern also seen in the MENAGERIE set.

Figure 33 offers a synopsis of the different translation techniques activated in the various TTs to deal with the translation of political references.

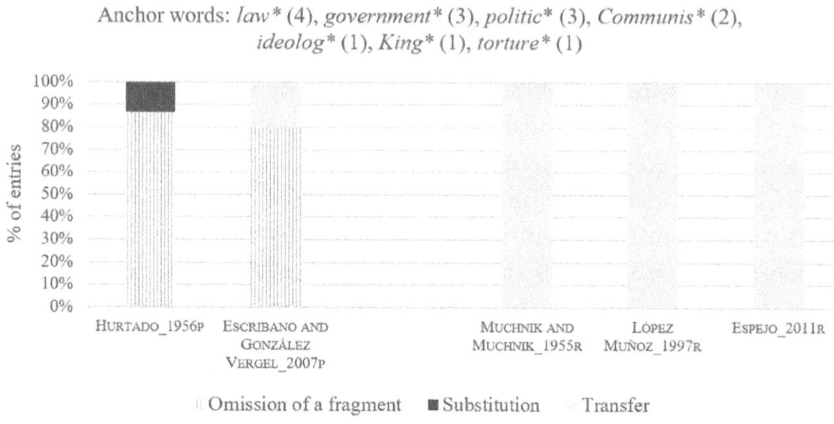

Figure 33: Translation techniques used to deal with political references (Crucible).

Table 27 shows a fragment of an interpolation containing the anchor word *politic**, which is not included in HURTADO_1956P or in GONZÁLEZ VERGEL AND ESCRIBANO_2007P, but which appears in the reader-oriented TTs.

Table 27: An example of a reference to politics in Crucible

MILLER_1953	*(A political policy is equated with moral right, and opposition to it with diabolical malevolence.)*
HURTADO_1956P	Ø
GONZÁLEZ VERGEL AND ESCRIBANO_2007P	Ø
MUCHNIK AND MUCHNIK_1955R	*(La norma política es igualada con el derecho moral, y la oposición a aquélla, con malevolencia diabólica.)* [*(The political policy is equated with moral right, and opposition to it with diabolical malevolence.)*]
LÓPEZ MUÑOZ_1997R	*(Un criterio político se identifica con el bien moral, y oponerse a él se convierte,* ipso facto, *en maldad diabólica.)* [*(A political criterium is equated with moral right, and opposing it becomes,* ipso facto, *diabolical malevolence.)*]
ESPEJO_2011R	*(Una determinada política se convierte en garante de la virtud moral y la oposición a ella en síntoma de una maldad diabólica.)* [*(A certain political policy becomes a guarantor of moral virtue and opposition to it a symptom of diabolical malevolence.)*]

6.2.3. Religion

In HURTADO_1956P, references to religion are mitigated in 120 cases using different techniques. The predominant one is the omission of entire fragments, including both interpolations and characters' utterances, accounting for ninety-four instances (78.3 per cent). It affects references to Christians, the Church, the Gospels, God, the devil, heaven and hell as well as criticism of the religious character Parris's materialistic attitudes, encompassing the following anchor words: *Devil* (16 instances), *church** (14), *Christ** (10), *sin** (9), *God* (8), *evil** (5), *holy* (4), *hell* (4), *saint** (3), *minister** (3), *Gospel* (3), **faith** (3), *spirit** (2), *sect** (2), *altar** (2), *belie** (1), *Catholic** (1), *demon** (1), *heaven* (1), *pious* (1) and *religio** (1). The second most frequent technique is substitution (24 instances, 20 per cent), which is applied to these anchor words: *Christ** (9), *God* (4), *Devil* (3), *church** (2), *minister** (2), *evil** (1), *Gospel* (1) *heaven* (1) and *saint** (1). Controversial religious content is systematically toned down, as seen in the replacement of *You are in all respects a Gospel Christian?* with *¿Sois un buen protestante?* [Are you a good Protestant?], *I see no light of God in that man* with *Yo no estoy de acuerdo con el Reverendo Parris* [I don't agree with Reverend Parris], and *God is dead* with *Dios no quiere oírme* [God does not want to hear me]. A less frequent technique, used only in two instances, is the omission of the potentially problematic word *Christ**.

The analysis of self-censorship in HURTADO_1956P reveals an intriguing pattern regarding the word *Christian*. In this TT, several references to Christianity are transformed into specific references to Protestantism. Espejo (2004: 143, my translation) notes the transformation of *Christian* into *protestante* [Protestant], *minister* into *ministro de la Iglesia reformada* [minister of the Reformed Church] and suggests that these changes are likely intended to 'avoiding the possibility that someone might interpret the play as an attack on the Catholic Church'. These types of substitutions occur repeatedly throughout the text. In addition to *protestante*, the concordances reveal other diluted translations of *Christian*, such as more general expressions like *esa pobre gente* [those poor people] or *falsos creyentes* [false believers]. Along with these substitutions, the omission of text fragments and individual words related to Christianity further underscores the intentionality of this approach.

The findings, in conjunction with the information contained in documents from the censorship record, suggest that the self-censoring applied to the TT influenced how the play was perceived during the censorship process, ultimately leading to the authorization of HURTADO_1956P for its performance. Religious content, particularly that derived from the anchor word *Christ**, was so effectively camouflaged that the ecclesiastical censor, Avelino Esteban Romero, raised no objections in his moral report. He recommended authorization for audiences over eighteen, stating that 'the play is set in a Protestant community of the Reformed Church [...]. Its religious attitude does not doctrinally endanger Catholic teachings' (record 310–56, my translation). Scholars have argued that the censors' more lenient treatment of foreign authors was part of an effort to improve the image of Spain abroad (Muñoz Cáliz 2006), resulting in a double standard between the censorship of foreign and domestic texts (Gutiérrez Lanza and Serrano 2001).

In GONZÁLEZ VERGEL AND ESCRIBANO_2007P, the most frequent technique is the omission of fragments (63 instances, 52.5 per cent), which in most cases corresponds to the deletion of the interpolations in the ST, followed by transfer (50 instances, 41.7 per cent), omission of a word (three instances, 2.5 per cent), substitution (three instances, 2.5 per cent) and addition (one instance, 0.8 per cent). The latter appears in the form of a choral utterance exclaimed by all the girls, followed by a stage indication – *¡Nooooooooo! (Un acorde sonoro subraya el final de la frase de Proctor.)* [Nooooooooo! (a loud chord underlines the end of Proctor's sentence.)] – to reply to the sentence *God is dead*.

In MUCHNIK AND MUCHNIK_1955R, transfer is the sole technique employed to translate all these references, underlining the overall strategy of adequacy. This approach to deal with content that the censors would have deemed problematic stands in stark contrasts to the considerable textual manipulation found in HURTADO_1956P, the performance-oriented TT from the censorship period. Similarly, LÓPEZ MUÑOZ_1997R and ESPEJO_2011R rely almost exclusively on transfer, reflecting their consistent adherence to adequacy. Across the reader-oriented TTs in the CRUCIBLE set, adequacy emerges as a defining feature in handling sensitive topics, paralleling the pattern observed in the MENAGERIE set.

All in all, the translation of references to these controversial topics changes across the various TTs. In her study on theatrical TTs from the censorship period, Pérez L. de Heredia (2004: 484, my translation) draws on Aaltonen's (2000: 29) notion of 'tenants' when she comments that: 'the different tenants *redecorate* each performance-oriented text with regard to their specific contextual circumstances.' Figure 34 illustrates this *redecoration* in relation to the treatment of religious content in the TTs of the CRUCIBLE set, reflecting a broader pattern in the handling of sensitive topics such as sexual morality and politics observed in both this set and the MENAGERIE one.

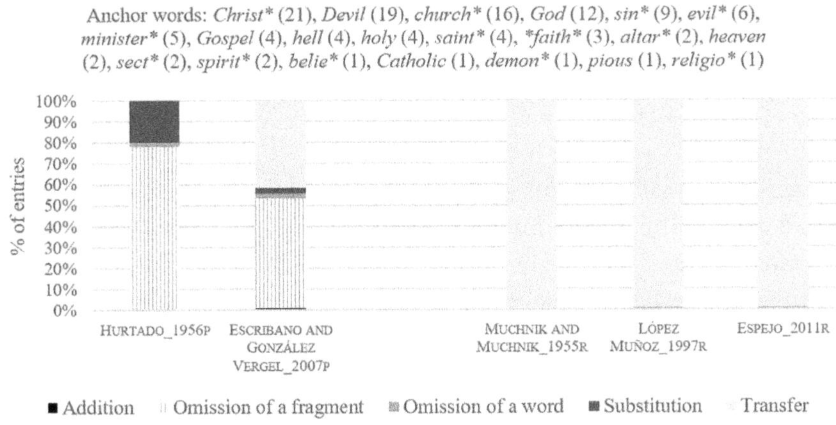

Figure 34: Translation techniques used to deal with religious references (Crucible).

Table 28 displays one of the most systematically applied changes in HURTADO_1956P, namely, the substitution of *Christian* with *protestante* [Protestant]. This manipulation is unique to this TT, as all other works in the set consistently use transfer to render the anchor word.

Table 28: An example of a reference to religion in Crucible

MILLER_1953	HALE: You would be a good Christian woman, would you not, Tituba?
HURTADO_1956P	BEVERLY: ¿Quieres volver a ser una buena protestante? [BEVERLY: Do you want to be a good Protestant again?]
GONZÁLEZ VERGEL AND ESCRIBANO_2007P	HALE: Tú quieres ser una buena cristiana, ¿verdad? *(Rotundo. TITUBA lo mira aterrada.)* [HALE: You want to be a good Christian, don't you? *(Forceful. TITUBA looks at him terrified.)*]

(Continued)

Table 28: Continued

Muchnik and Muchnik_1955r	HALE: Querrías ser una buena cristiana, ¿no es cierto, Tituba? [HALE: You would want to be a good Christian, would you not, Tituba?]
López Muñoz_1997r	HALE: Tú quieres ser una buena cristiana, ¿verdad, Tituba? [HALE: You want to be a good Christian, don't you, Tituba?]
Espejo_2011r	HALE: Tú quieres ser una buena cristiana, Tituba, ¿a que sí? [HALE: You want to be a good Christian, Tituba, right?]

6.2.4. Foul language

Hurtado_1956p contains six instances where foul language has been toned down. The affected anchor words are *damn* (3 instances), *arse** (1), *bitch** (1) and *bloody* (1), which Ávila Cabrera (2015) categorizes as cursing, body parts, animal naming and derogatory terms, respectively. The techniques employed are evenly split between omission of a fragment and substitution, with three occurrences each. Although relatively few in number, the cases hold significant qualitative weight, as Arias-Badia (2020) foregrounds the importance of taboo language for expressiveness and characterization. Indeed, these words appear in emotionally charged dialogues, delivered exclusively by two characters: Proctor and Giles, who represent opposition to authorities. The prevalence of *damn*, in particular, reflects its frequent use in English conversation (Biber *et al.* 1999), serving as a key element in conveying spontaneous orality. The omission of this type of language, along with other instances of toned-down language, strips the text of subtle nuances. As already discussed, self-censorship in Hurtado_1956p extends beyond foul language to encompass topics of sexual morality, politics and religion. Since these alterations persist in the published versions of the TT, both in the journal *Primer Acto* and the Escelicer edition, the legacy of self-censorship survives in the printed form of this TT to this day.

In the González Vergel and Escribano_2007p TT, the most commonly employed techniques for addressing foul language are omission of a word and substitution, each occurring twice. Additionally, the TT features one instance each of fragment omission and transfer. By contrast, the MUCHNIK AND MUCHNIK_1955R TT consistently relies on transfer for all cases, mirroring its approach to sexual morality, politics and religion. Likewise, LÓPEZ MUÑOZ_1997R primarily employs transfer (3 instances) but also incorporates two instances of word omission and one of substitution. Finally, ESPEJO_2011R predominantly uses transfer (5 instances) and includes one case of substitution, which retains the original meaning while seemingly enhancing fluency in the target language.

As in MENAGERIE, the dominant trends align with those observed for the other topics: self-censorship in the performance-oriented TT from the censorship period, varying techniques in the performance-oriented TT from the post-dictatorship period and the consistent use of transfer in the reader-oriented TTs. Nonetheless, a few cases of different techniques, such as omission of a word and substitution, are noted in the reader-oriented TTs (Figure 35).

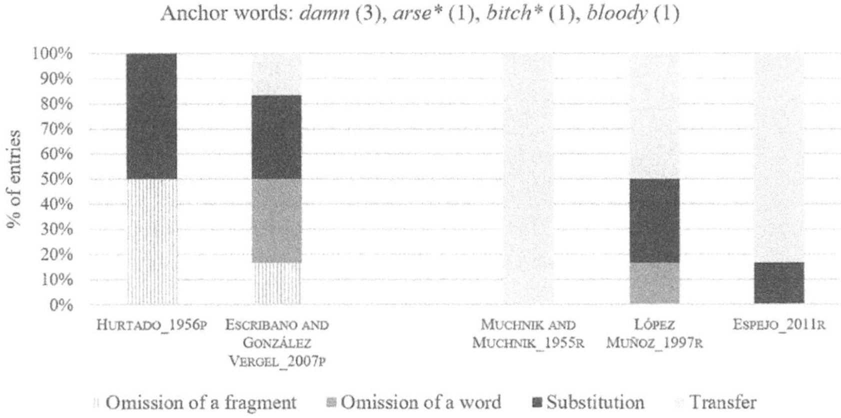

Figure 35: Translation techniques used to deal with foul language (Crucible).

Table 29 presents an example of an utterance containing *damn*, the most frequently occurring anchor word in CRUCIBLE. The translation of this word is addressed in various ways across the TTs: through omission of a fragment, substitution that conveys the meaning without retaining the foul expression and transfer that preserves the original's explicit tone.

Table 29: An example of foul language in Crucible

MILLER_1953	PROCTOR: Damn the village! I confess to God, and God has seen my name on this! It is enough!
HURTADO_1956P	PROCTOR: Ø ¡He firmado! ¡Todos me habéis visto firmar! ¡Con eso debe bastaros! [PROCTOR: I have signed! You have all seen me sign! That should be enough for you!]
GONZÁLEZ VERGEL AND ESCRIBANO_2007P	PROCTOR: *(Le corta.)* ¡No me importa este pueblo! ¡He confesado ante Dios, y Él ha visto mi nombre en el papel! Con eso basta. [PROCTOR: *(Cuts him off.)* I don't care about this village! I confess to God, and He has seen my name on the paper! That is enough!]
MUCHNIK AND MUCHNIK_1955R	PROCTOR: ¡Al diablo con el pueblo! ¡Yo confieso ante Dios, y Dios ha visto mi nombre en este papel! ¡Es bastante! [PROCTOR: To hell with the village! I confess to God, and God has seen my name on this paper! It is enough!]
LÓPEZ MUÑOZ_1997R	PROCTOR: ¡Me tiene sin cuidado el pueblo! ¡He confesado ante Dios y Dios ha visto mi nombre en este papel! ¡Es suficiente! [PROCTOR: This village doesn't matter to me! I've confessed to God, and God has seen my name on this paper! It is enough!]
ESPEJO_2011R	PROCTOR: ¡Maldito sea el pueblo! Ante quien confieso es ante Dios, y Dios ya ha visto mi nombre en este papel. ¡Es bastante! [PROCTOR: Damn the village! The one I confess to is God, and God has already seen my name on this paper! It is enough!]

6.3. Happy Days

The censorship record for MARTÍNEZ TRIVES_1963P contains a report issued during the review process, highlighting certain problematic expressions that were ultimately not considered significant. While the first censorship guide notes an omission, the specific subject of this omission cannot be determined as the relevant text is unavailable in the record, and the censor, Sebastián Bautista de la Torre, remarks that 'even a daring word is lost within the immensely dignified context' (record 47–63, my translation). When the request for the performance of this TT was submitted in 1963, eight years after the première of *Waiting for Godot* (1955), Beckett was already a prominent figure in Spanish theatrical culture and closely associated with chamber theatres (Andaluz-Pinedo and Merino-Álvarez 2020). These factors likely contributed to the performance being authorized, tailored to that specific theatrical context. However, as noted in Chapter 5, the initial analysis of the corpus has also revealed instances of self-censorship in some fragments of the TT.

In this second phase of the corpus study, a search for anchor words in MARTÍNEZ TRIVES_1963P has revealed seven instances of apparent self-censorship: four related to sexuality, two to religion and one to foul language. Among the performance-oriented TTs from the 1950s and 1960s, MARTÍNEZ TRIVES_1963P contains the fewest such interventions, which may be attributed to the plot of this work presenting fewer topics likely to be deemed problematic than other works like CRUCIBLE or LOVER. Nevertheless, even in a play with only occasional references to potentially sensitive issues, Martínez Trives, who had previously introduced several of Beckett's plays to Spain, appears to have adjusted such references to secure authorization for its performance. In fact, in Martínez Trives's 1955 TT of *Waiting for Godot*, the same topics of sexual morality, religion and foul language were flagged by censors, who excised the corresponding material (Merino-Álvarez and Andaluz-Pinedo 2020).

6.3.1. Sexual morality

In MARTÍNEZ TRIVES_1963P, four instances of problematic content related to sexual mores have been softened or eliminated. These cases include references to the human body and nudity, specifically in the anchor words *bosom** and *underneath*, each appearing twice. The techniques used in this TT consist of omission of a fragment and substitution with more general or ambiguous expressions, with two occurrences each. As noted in section 5.3., the use of expressions that deviate from the original meaning and may cause confusion in the TT is a characteristic feature of this translation.

In contrast to the variety of techniques employed in GALÁN_2014P from MENAGERIE and GONZÁLEZ VERGEL AND ESCRIBANO_2007P from CRUCIBLE, the performance-oriented MARTÍNEZ LUCIANO_2011P consistently uses transfer, adhering to its focus on adequacy. The reader-oriented RODRÍGUEZ GAGO_1989R also favours adequacy, making use of transfer to deal with all the references. Figure 36 illustrates the translation techniques activated in the various TTs of this set.

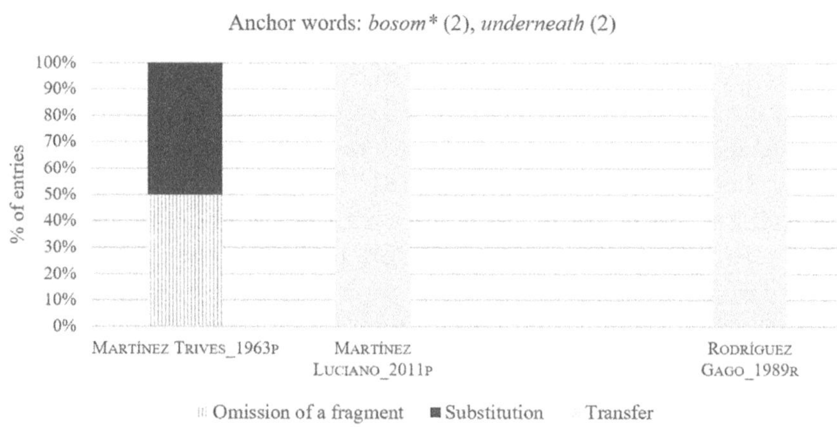

Figure 36: Translation techniques used to deal with sexual morality (Days).

Table 30 illustrates how the original sentence *Has she anything on underneath?* has been translated by the various target authors.

Table 30: An example of a reference to sexual morality in Days

BECKETT_1961	WINNIE: [...] Has she anything on underneath. *(Pause.)* Has she anything on underneath? he says.
MARTÍNEZ TRIVES_1963P	WINNIE: [...] ¿Qué le restará de lo enterrado? [WINNIE: What will be left of what is buried?]

MARTÍNEZ LUCIANO_2011P	WINNIE: [...] Si lleva puesto algo debajo. *(Pausa.)* ¿Lleva puesto algo debajo?, dice él. [WINNIE: [...] If she is wearing anything underneath. *(Pause.)* Is she wearing anything underneath? he says.]
RODRÍGUEZ GAGO_1989R	WINNIE: [...] «Si va desnuda de cintura para abajo». *(Pausa.)* «Y de cintura para abajo, ¿está desnuda?», dice. [WINNIE: [...] "If she is naked below the waist." *(Pause.)* "And below the waist is she naked?" he says.]

6.3.2. Religion

In MARTÍNEZ TRIVES_1963P, two instances of self-censorship related to religion have been identified: the substitution of the word *Almighty* with the somewhat ambiguous phrase *al máximo* [to the maximum], and the omission of a fragment containing the word *irreverent*. In the post-censorship period, both the performance-oriented MARTÍNEZ LUCIANO_2011P and the reader-oriented RODRÍGUEZ GAGO_1989R restore these references as well as those related to sexuality, demonstrating a clear trend towards adequacy.

Figure 37 offers a visual representation of the different techniques applied in the TTs of DAYS to translate references to religion, revealing a pattern similar to that seen with sexual morality.

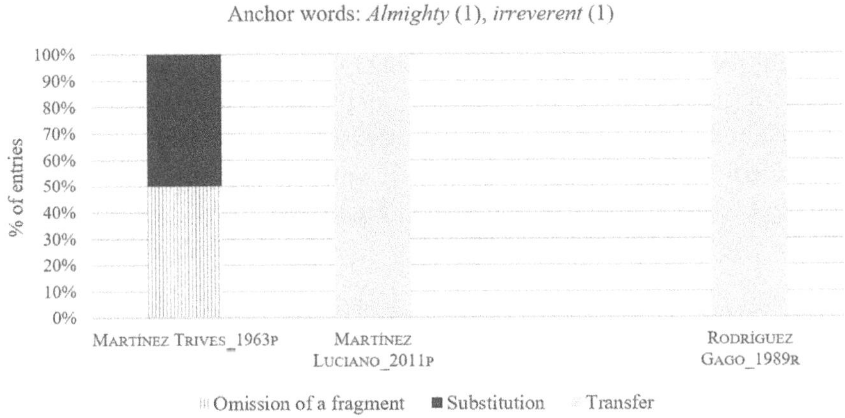

Figure 37: Translation techniques used to deal with religious references (Days).

Table 31 shows the different choices made by the target authors when faced with a potentially problematic sentence related to religion, including either the omission of a fragment of text or direct transfer of the expression.

Table 31: An example of a reference to religion in Days

Beckett_1961	WINNIE: I suppose some people might think us a trifle irreverent, but I doubt it.
Martínez Trives_1963p	Ø
Martínez Luciano_2011p	WINNIE: Supongo que algunas personas podrían considerarnos un poco irreverentes, pero no creo que lo seamos. [WINNIE: I suppose some people might think us a trifle irreverent, but I don't think we are.]
Rodríguez Gago_1989r	WINNIE: Seguro que hay quien piensa que somos un poquito irreverentes, aunque lo dudo. [WINNIE: I suppose there are some people who think we are a trifle irreverent, although I doubt it.]

6.3.3. Foul language

One instance of mitigated foul language appears in Martínez Trives_1963p, where the profane expression *for God's sake*, has been substituted. In contrast, both the performance-oriented Martínez Luciano_2011p and the reader-oriented Rodríguez Gago_1989r, from the post-censorship period, use transfer, reflecting the overall trend of adequacy in these two versions and an evident historical evolution from self-censorship to the restoration of sensitive topics in Days, as displayed in Figure 38.

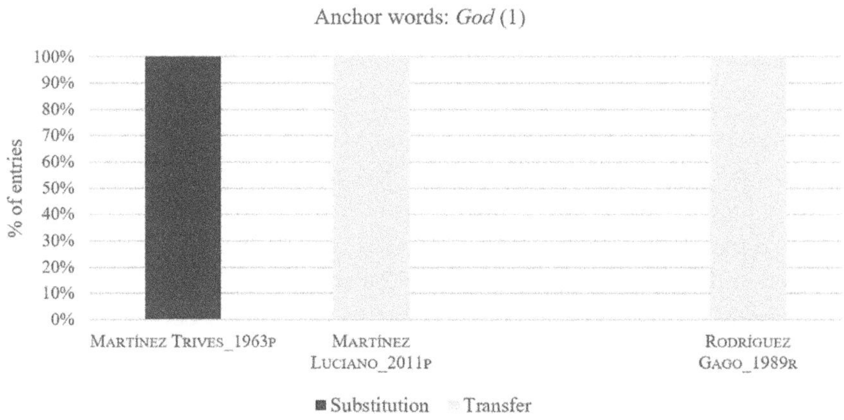

Figure 38: Translation techniques used to deal with foul language (Days).

Table 32 shows how the only example of this type of language has been handled in the three TTs.

Table 32: An example of foul language in Days

Beckett_1961	WINNIE: Let go of my hand and drop for God's sake, she says, drop!
Martínez Trives_1963p	WINNIE: Suéltame la mano y lárgate, por lo que más quieras – decía ella –, lárgate ... [WINNIE: Let go of my hand and go away, by all that's sacred, she said, go away ...]
Martínez Luciano_2011p	WINNIE: "¡Suéltame la mano y calla, por amor de Dios, cállate ya!" [WINNIE: "Let go of my hand and shut up, for God's sake, shut up now!"]
Rodríguez Gago_1989r	WINNIE: [...] ¡Suéltame y déjame en paz, por el amor de Dios, déjame, dice ella, desaparece! [WINNIE: Let go of me and leave me alone, for God's sake, leave me alone, she says, go away!]

6.4. The Lover

The first censorship record (91–66) in the AGA related to the performance of *The Lover* focuses on BOHR_1966P. The censors' reports highlight two main concerns: references to extramarital relations and stage directions deemed too suggestive. In a letter included in the censorship record, Bohr notes that the TT submitted to request authorization for performance in a commercial theatre has been adapted, thus suggesting self-censorship in the TT. The reports commend the clarification of the roles of husband and lover and the changes made to the stage directions. The second record (343–66), which pertains to ESCOBAR_1966P, refers to the prior authorization of BOHR_1966P and also grants authorization without any deletions. As with the MENAGERIE, CRUCIBLE and DAYS sets, the analysis presented in this section combines a contextual approach with textual evidence, providing a deeper exploration of instances of self-censorship.

Searches for anchor words reveal a significant number of examples related to sexual morality in BOHR_1966P and ESCOBAR_1966P, along with fewer instances of foul language. In total, 53 anchor words from the ST have been analysed, of which 49 refer to sexual morality and four to foul language. In BOHR_1966P, 41 instances of problematic content have been mitigated, 37 of which involve sexual behaviour and four relate to foul language. In ESCOBAR_1966P, self-censorship occurred in 38 cases, with 34 involving sexual morality and four foul language expressions. While some of the self-censored cases involving sexual morality overlap between the two TTs, not all of them do. Unlike the trend to acceptability observed in the MENAGERIE and CRUCIBLE sets, the performance-oriented TTs from the post-censorship period in this set reflect a trend towards adequacy, particularly in their translation of references to sexual morality and foul language. Similarly, as with MENAGERIE, CRUCIBLE and DAYS, the reader-oriented TTs show a consistent tendency to adequacy in handling these topics.

6.4.1. Sexual morality

The censors seem to have found sexuality to be the most problematic topic in the LOVER, which is unspringing given the nature of the plot. Searches for anchor words reveal 49 instances where content has been softened in the two performance-oriented TTs from the censorship period. In BOHR_1966P, 37 traces of self-censorship have been identified, while in ESCOBAR_1966P, 34 instances have been found, with some overlap. The censorship record (91–66) for BOHR_1966P reveals that the censors categorized the references into two main groups. The first group concerns extramarital relations and includes the anchor words *whore** (8 instances), *lover** (5), *mistress** (5), *lust** (4), *pleasure** (4), *affair** (2), *adulter** (1), *illegitimate* (1), *illicit* (1), *manly* (1) and *slut** (1), resulting in 25 occurrences in BOHR_1966P and 18 in ESCOBAR_1966P. The second group involves suggestive stage directions, including the anchor words *bed** (5), *leg** (3), *bod** (2), *gasp** (2), *thigh** (2), *negligee** (1) and *touch** (1), with 12 cases in BOHR_1966P and 16 in ESCOBAR_1966P. This finding confirms that sexual morality was self-censored across all the performance-oriented TTs of the censorship period, particularly in the 1950s and 1960s (GORDON AND DE QUINTO_1950P in MENAGERIE, HURTADO_1956P in CRUCIBLE, MARTÍNEZ TRIVES_1963P in DAYS and BOHR_1966P and ESCOBAR_1966P in LOVER).

In BOHR_1966P, 37 references to sexuality in the ST have been toned down by means of techniques such as substitution (18 instances), omission of a fragment (18) and omission of a word (1). The results confirm that BOHR_1966P is a clear example of self-censorship, both from a quantitative and a qualitative perspective. In a more granular analysis, the 25 references to extramarital relations have been addressed through the omission of entire fragments (14 instances) and substitution (11). In this respect, the systematic substitution of the word *whore* with *amigas* [girlfriends] is particularly striking. To deal with the 12 suggestive stage directions, the following techniques have been applied: substitution (7 instances), omission of a fragment (4) and omission of a word (1). From a qualitative viewpoint, it is worth noting that some substituted stage directions bear no relation to the ST. As noted in the censorship record 91–66, these changes were designed to clarify the roles of the lover and the husband. While the total number of cases may not appear high, the affected examples involve substantial amounts of textual material, amplifying their qualitative impact.

In ESCOBAR_1966P, the target author of the 34 occurrences under scrutiny employed the techniques of substitution (18 instances), omission of a fragment (13), and the omission of a word (3). Compared to BOHR_1966P, this other version displays a preference for more subtle substitutions, rather than the overt manipulations seen in the earlier TT, and omits fewer and shorter fragments. For the 18 references to extramarital relations, the level of self-censorship is lower than in BOHR_1966P. However, self-censorship remains evident in techniques like substitution (14 instances) and omission of a fragment (4). The relatively lower intervention in ESCOBAR_1966P may be attributed to the precedent set by the prior authorization of BOHR_1966P. Yet, one censor remarked on the restoration of a controversial reference in the play's final line: 'I find the reference with which the play finishes too harsh and I do not recall whether it matches the previous ending' (record 343–66, my translation). The line in question, *You lovely whore*, has been translated in BOHR_1966P as *mi amorosa mujercita* [my loving wifey] and in ESCOBAR_1966P as *¿Sabes lo que eres? (Pausa.) Una prostituta* [Do you know what you are? (Pause.) A prostitute]. For the 16 anchor words involving suggestive stage directions, the techniques employed are omission of a fragment (9 instances), substitution (4) and omission of a word (3). Although the authorizations to perform ESCOBAR_1966P do not formally record any deletions, a detailed comparison of the TT with its ST, based on the analysis of anchor words, paints a different picture – that of a text that exhibits clear traces of self-censorship.

The performance-oriented TTs from the post-censorship period, GÓMEZ AND CANO_2013P and ALDEGUER_2017P, are clearly adequate in their overwhelming use of transfer, mirroring the trend also observed in MARTÍNEZ LUCIANO_2011P, from the DAYS set. This contrasts with the acceptability-focused approaches seen in MENAGERIE (GALÁN_2014P) and CRUCIBLE (GONZÁLEZ VERGEL AND ESCRIBANO_2007P). Similarly, in reader-oriented TTs from the censorship period (BARBERÁ_1965R) and after (SPREGELBURD_2005R), references are maintained through transfer, a pattern that aligns with the reader-oriented TTs from MENAGERIE (MIRLAS_1951R, DIÉGUEZ_2007R and ESPEJO_2019R), CRUCIBLE (MUCHNIK AND MUCHNIK_1955R, LÓPEZ MUÑOZ_1997R and ESPEJO_2011R) and DAYS (RODRÍGUEZ GAGO_1989R). BARBERÁ_1965R offers another example of the frequent coexistence, during the censorship period, of an adequate reader-oriented TT from Argentina with a self-censored, performance-oriented TT from Spain.

Figure 39 shows how the translation of sexual innuendo has been carried out in the various TTs.

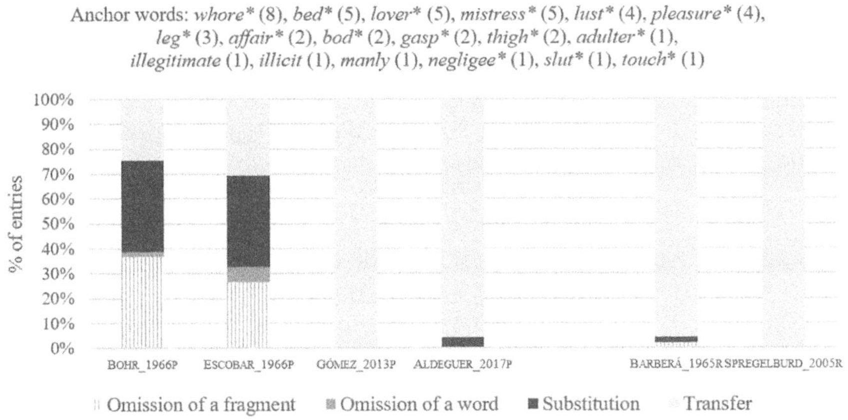

Figure 39: Translation techniques used to deal with sexual morality (Lover).

As seen in DAYS, and to a lesser extent also in MENAGERIE and CRUCIBLE, the overarching trajectory reflects a shift from self-censorship in the performance-oriented TTs produced in the 1950s and 1960s to the preservation of those references in the other performance- and reader-oriented TTs. This progression underscores the influence of the historical and cultural context in which these translations were created. As Tymoczko (2006: 453) aptly observes, 'translators and interpreters shape their words to the needs of the moment', highlighting the adaptive nature of translation in response to its environment.

To illustrate the self-censorship present in BOHR_1966P and ESCOBAR_1966P, Table 33 provides an example of a suggestive stage direction featuring the anchor word *bed**. In BOHR_1966P, the entire utterance is omitted, while in ESCOBAR_1966P, a single bed is replaced with two beds, thereby deflating the potentially contentious content. By contrast, in the subsequent TTs, the same stage direction is transferred literally.

Table 33: An example of a reference to sexual morality in Lover

PINTER_1963	RICHARD: Yes, I do agree. *(They go back into the room. They get into the bed.)*
BOHR_1966P	Ø
ESCOBAR_1966P	RICHARD: Sí. Desde luego. *(Se meten en las respectivas camas.)* [RICHARD: Yes, of course. *(They get into their respective beds.)*]
GÓMEZ AND CANO_2013P	RICHARD: Sí, estoy de acuerdo. *(Vuelven a la habitación. Se meten en la cama.)* [RICHARD: Yes, I agree. *(They go back into the room. They get into the bed.)*]
ALDEGUER_2017P	RICHARD: Sí, en eso estoy de acuerdo. *(Vuelven al dormitorio. Se meten en la cama.)* [RICHARD: Yes, I agree about that. *(They go back into the room. They get into the bed.)*]
BARBERÁ_1965R	RICHARD: Sí, estoy de acuerdo. *(Vuelven al cuarto. Van hasta la cama y se acuestan.)* [RICHARD: Yes, I agree. *(They go back into the room. They go to the bed and get into it.)*]
SPREGELBURD_2005R	RICHARD: Sí, estoy muy de acuerdo. *(Vuelven a entrar en el dormitorio. Se meten en la cama.)* [RICHARD: Yes, I very much agree. *(They go back into the room. They get into the bed.)*]

6.4.2. Foul language

In BOHR_1966P and ESCOBAR_1966P, the four cases of foul language have been mitigated. The anchor words are *bloody* (3 instances) and *damn* (1), both classified as derogatory terms according to Ávila Cabrera (2015). In BOHR_1966P, most instances appear in passages addressing extramarital relations and are handled using omission of a fragment and substitution, applied in two cases each. In ESCOBAR_1966P, all cases are dealt with through substitution. Overall, the instances of foul language in the ST serve to convey the characters' emotional states, set the tone of the scene or function as orality markers. The toning down observed in these translations diminishes expressivity, weakens character portrayal and reduces the impression of naturalness of the ensuing text. To this day, and rather surprisingly, the edition of this manipulated version is the only one available in the market in peninsular Spanish.

Figure 40 offers a graphic representation of the various translation techniques used to deal with foul language in the LOVER set.

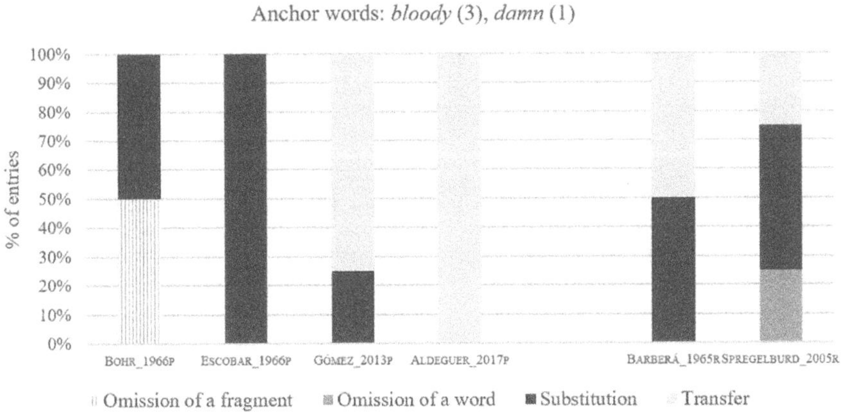

Figure 40: Translation techniques used to deal with foul language (Lover).

Table 34 shows an example of an utterance containing the anchor words *bloody* and *whore**. In BOHR_1966P, the word *bloody* is completely omitted, while the reference to *whore* is self-censored through substitution, rendering it as *amigas* [girlfriends]. A stage direction with a farcical tone is also introduced. *Bloody* is also removed in ESCOBAR_1966P, replaced with ellipsis, as is the case in SPREGELBURD_2005R. The vulgar tone of *whore* has been elevated to the more formal *prostituta* [prostitute] in some versions, while the closer equivalent *puta* [whore] is employed in others.

Table 34: An example of foul language in Lover

PINTER_1963	SARAH: What about your own bloody whore?
BOHR_1966P	SARAH: *(Corre al dormitorio, coge la bata de plumas, mientras suena la música de tono vodevil y entre risas, dice)* ¿Y qué me cuentas de todas tus amigas? [SARAH: *(She runs to the bedroom, takes a feather robe while vaudeville music plays and says, laughing)* And what about all your girlfriends?]

(Continued)

Table 34: Continued

ESCOBAR_1966P	SARAH: ¿Y qué me dices de tu… prostituta? [SARAH: And what about your… prostitute?]
GÓMEZ AND CANO_2013P	SARAH: ¿Qué me dices de tu asquerosa prostituta? [SARAH: What about your filthy prostitute?]
ALDEGUER_2017P	SARAH: ¿Y qué es de tu maldita puta? [SARAH: And what's with your bloody whore?]
BARBERÁ_1965R	SARAH: ¿Qué pasa con la cerda de tu puta? [SARAH: What about the sow of your whore?]
SPREGELBURD_2005R	SARAH: ¿Y qué me decís de tu propia puta? [SARAH: And what about your own whore?]

6.5. General trends

The analysis presented in this chapter highlights recurrent patterns in the handling of sensitive issues across the TTs included in the corpus. In all performance-oriented TTs from the dictatorship period, self-censorship was consistently employed to address references to sexual morality, politics, religion and foul language. By contrast, no evidence of self-censorship regarding these topics has been observed in the performance-oriented TTs produced after the Francoist censorship period or in the reader-oriented TTs from either period.

The censorship records of the performance-oriented TTs of the censorship period show minimal direct textual excisions. However, a detailed comparison between these TTs and their corresponding STs reveals that translation techniques such as omission of text fragments or individual words, as well as substitution, were frequently employed. These techniques appear to have been implemented to mitigate potentially problematic content and increase the likelihood of securing authorization for performance. Notable examples include the prominent self-censorship of sexual references in HURTADO_1956P (CRUCIBLE) and BOHR_1966P (LOVER), alongside significant omissions of political and religious references in HURTADO_1956P

(CRUCIBLE). Fewer instances of censored foul language have been observed, though such cases are present across all four text sets.

In the performance-oriented TTs produced after the end of Francoist censorship, a broader variety of translation techniques emerged, reflecting a tendency towards acceptability, with transfer dominating in TTs adhering to adequacy. Finally, in the reader-oriented TTs, transfer is the prevailing technique for handling references to sexuality, politics and religion, with occasional substitutions employed to address foul language.

By examining the concordances generated through TAligner, this study has demonstrated the influence of (self-)censorship on sensitive topics in TTs from the censorship period and how these issues were translated in the TTs included in the TEATRAD corpus. The final chapter provides a comprehensive summary of this research, its principal findings and conclusions and proposes avenues for future lines of research.

CHAPTER 7

Conclusions

The primary objective of this book has been to examine the translation into Spanish of English-language theatre works that were introduced during the period of Francoist censorship and have persisted in theatrical productions and publications into the twenty-first century. These works have been analysed from a variety of perspectives.

The research begins with an exploration of the authors, plays and translations that have survived from the censorship era to the present, followed by a detailed description of the TTs included in the TEATRAD corpus. The analysis then focuses on how self-censored topics – specifically sexual morality, politics, religion and foul language – have evolved over time, using the corpus tool TAligner. In this way, the book continues and expands upon the TRACE-theatre studies, by extending the scope of the research into the twenty-first century, exploring additional research questions and utilizing dedicated corpus tools for the analysis of translated plays.

The study commenced with a review of the extant literature on the unique nature of theatre translations and the TRACE-theatre project. Key sources on theatre translation shaped the focus of the analysis, particularly the distinction between performance- or reader-oriented TTs. Additionally, a review of scholarly works on prefabricated orality provided valuable insights into the discourse modes and linguistic features typical of dramatic texts. The already published TRACE-theatre studies have been instrumental in identifying the playwrights, plays and translations that formed part of the Spanish theatrical repertoire during the censorship period, which in turn proved crucial for compiling the TEATRAD catalogue. Furthermore, these studies shed light on the topics that were subject to self-censorship at the time, which have been analysed in the TEATRAD corpus, as well as the continued presence of these translated plays beyond the censorship era. Without the foundational contributions of TRACE research on translated theatre during the Franco dictatorship, this work would not have been possible.

The various stages of the study were defined through the application of key concepts from the DTS methodological framework. Consequently, the approach adopted has been descriptive, empirical, retrospective and target-oriented, with an emphasis on identifying recurrent patterns. The progression of the study moved from the creation of a catalogue to the development and analysis of a corpus. A parallel corpus of theatrical plays was specifically compiled for this purpose and subsequently analysed using the TAligner tool. The use of corpus tools to build and scrutinize this parallel corpus of theatrical plays represents a methodological advancement introduced by the present research. The TAligner tool proved particularly valuable for the application of Gómez Castro's (2009) method, which was originally developed to investigate (self-)censored translations of narrative works, to the diachronic analysis of (self-)censored references in theatre translations.

The TEATRAD catalogue and corpus were then built within the methodological framework established at the outset of the study. Before presenting the main conclusions drawn from the analysis, it is important to note that the TEATRAD catalogue and corpus have provided essential data for this research and may prove invaluable for future studies. These resources represent novel contributions to the field of theatre translation and CTS:

a) *TEATRAD catalogue*
   It comprises 307 references to translations used in theatrical productions or publications in the twenty-first century (2000–2019) and is based on the plays identified in the TRACEti catalogue (1939–1985) during the censorship period. Functioning as an extension of the TRACEti catalogue, the TEATRAD catalogue includes comprehensive details on translations, such as source and target authors and titles, as well as information about productions and publications. It also incorporates data on production dates, producers, publishers and the use of digital and accessible formats. This extensive dataset facilitates an exploration of the circulation of translated plays, in different formats, during the twenty-first century, offering a valuable lens through which to examine theatrical culture in translation, an area that remains largely underexplored.

b) *The TEATRAD corpus*
A parallel and bilingual (English-Spanish) resource specializing in theatre texts, it contains 463,012 words across twenty-five texts, including five STs and twenty TTs. These texts are organized into four sets, each corresponding to a particular play originally written in English (one of which appears in two different editions). The selection of texts was informed by the analysis of the TEATRAD catalogue, prioritizing works with frequent productions and still published in the twenty-first century. Each of the four sets of texts comprises three to six TTs, classified as either performance- or reader-oriented, spanning from the censorship period to the first two decades of the twenty-first century. The corpus is structurally annotated to include acts, scenes, utterances, speakers, stage directions and dialogues, and the TTs are meticulously aligned with their corresponding STs at utterance level. Given the relative scarcity of parallel corpora of theatre texts, the TEATRAD corpus represents a substantial advancement in the field of theatre TS.

Table 35 offers a synoptic overview of the TEATRAD catalogue and corpus, which serve as significant additions to the resources previously developed within TRACE-theatre (Section 2.2.). These contributions enrich the existing framework, offering expanded datasets and analytical tools for the study of translated theatre.

Table 35: TEATRAD catalogue and corpus

Name	Catalogue	Plays selected for the corpus
TEATRAD (TEAtro TRADucido, translated theatre)	307 entries	*The Glass Menagerie* by Tennessee Williams *The Crucible* by Arthur Miller *Happy Days* by Samuel Beckett *The Lover* by Harold Pinter

The analysis of the TEATRAD catalogue and corpus has provided answers to the three key research questions posed at the outset of this study, namely:

1) Which authors, plays and TTs from the censorship period have persisted into the twenty-first century (2000–2019)?

2) What translation strategies characterize the TTs included in the corpus?
3) How have the sensitive topics subjected to self-censorship in the TTs from the censorship period evolved in subsequent TTs?

The analysis of the TEATRAD catalogue represents the first systematic investigation into which authors, plays and TTs from the Francoist censorship period remain relevant in the twenty-first century. Approximately one third of the authors and plays introduced during Franco's dictatorship endure in twenty-first-century Spanish culture, primarily through theatrical productions. A smaller subset survives through a combination of productions and publications, while a minority exits solely in published form. These survival trajectories underscore the cultural resilience of these works, highlighting their continued relevance in contemporary Spanish culture and the significance of archival translations from the censorship era.

The corpus was selected based on authors and plays from the catalogue that remain in circulation through twenty-first-century productions and publications, reflecting their integration and sustained relevance in the target culture. The recurrence of authors and plays in the productions and publications subcatalogues served as key criteria for inclusion in the corpus. Tennessee Williams, Arthur Miller, Samuel Beckett and Harold Pinter stood out for their enduring popularity, with many of their works prominently featured in both subcatalogues. Consequently, the plays chosen for the corpus were *The Glass Menagerie* by Tennessee Williams, *The Crucible* by Arthur Miller, *Happy Days* by Samuel Beckett and *The Lover* by Harold Pinter.

The data collected on the survival of specific TTs in twenty-first-century productions and publications revealed two notable patterns. A majority of the TTs in circulation during the new millennium were signed by different target authors than those responsible for the twentieth-century TTs, indicating a discernible trend towards the use of (assumed) retranslations. A secondary trend was observed in the continued use of twentieth-century TTs in the twenty-first century, whether from the censorship era (1939–1978) or the post-censorship period (1978–1999). Nearly all these TTs are twentieth-century publications (performance- or reader-oriented) that remain in circulation in the new millennium through either productions or publications.

The predominant trend of (assumed) retranslations in the twenty-first century and the secondary trend of continued use of twentieth-century

TTs were both reflected in the TTs of the plays selected for the corpus. The corpus also included TTs from some of the most frequently represented target authors in the catalogue. For the twenty-first-century retranslations, these included Ramón Espejo, Juan Vicente Martínez Luciano and Rafael Spregelburd. For the twentieth-century TTs still in circulation, León Mirlas, José Luis López Muñoz and Antonia Rodríguez Gago were prominent contributors.

The analysis of the TEATRAD parallel corpus, composed of (re)translations of theatre texts, focused on a type of corpus rarely addressed in existing scholarship. Indeed, few studies compare (re)translations of plays from the twentieth century with those of the twenty-first century, and there is a particular scarcity of research employing corpus tools for the analysis of theatre translations. The twofold approach adopted in the present study – characterizing the TTs and examining the evolution of the self-censored textual fragments – has expanded the available data on theatre translation. In particular, the focus on the evolution of self-censored content represents a relatively underexplored line of inquiry in the field.

The research began with an in-depth description of the 20 TTs in the corpus, emphasizing their translation strategies. Following an initial contextualization, the utterances were paired at a macrotextual level in corpus 1. Subsequently, translation techniques were classified at a microtextual level in corpus 2. These results contribute to the existing body of descriptive data on theatre translations produced during the Francoist censorship period as well as those created in the post-censorship era.

The main conclusion drawn from the initial analysis of the TEATRAD corpus was the identification of two distinct types of TTs, differentiated by the degree of textual divergence from their respective STs. Clear differences were noted at both macro- and microtextual levels. At the macrotextual level, these involved the addition and omission of utterances, while at the microtextual level, they included addition, omission, reordering of utterances and substitution. These findings can be summarized as follows:

a) The textual comparison revealed a general tendency towards acceptability as the initial norm in the performance-oriented TTs of the censorship period (GORDON AND DE QUINTO_1950P and VÁZQUEZ VIGO_1978P in MENAGERIE; HURTADO_1956P in CRUCIBLE; MARTÍNEZ

TRIVES_1963P in DAYS and BOHR_1966P and ESCOBAR_1966P in LOVER). This trend also extended to some twenty-first-century performance-oriented TTs, namely, GALÁN_2014P in MENAGERIE and GONZÁLEZ VERGEL AND ESCRIBANO_2007P in CRUCIBLE. At the macrotextual level, these TTs were marked by frequent omissions and additions of utterances, while at the microtextual level, they exhibited omissions of large chunks of text as well as additions, substitutions and reordering of utterances, though the extent varied across individual TTs.

- *Performance-oriented TTs from the censorship period*
  The restrictions imposed by the official censorship played a decisive role in shaping these TTs. Traces of self-censorship were evident, particularly in the omission and alteration of potentially problematic content. The observed trend towards acceptability aligns with earlier findings by MerinoÁlvarez (1994b), Pérez L. de Heredia (2004) and Bandín (2007).
- *Performance-oriented TTs from the twenty-first century*
  While some performance-oriented TTs from the new millennium also lean towards acceptability, this phenomenon appeared qualitatively different from that observed during the censorship period. Unlike earlier TTs, these versions did not seem to stem from self-censorship but rather from practical considerations, such as performance duration and the priorities of the target authors, who often embraced greater freedom and flexibility in their translations, reflecting their professional profiles and creative objectives. For instance, in GALÁN_2014P (MENAGERIE), the focus of the play was reoriented towards the character of the mother, in line with the target author's intent as both translator and producer. In GONZÁLEZ VERGEL AND ESCRIBANO_2007P (CRUCIBLE), additional stage directions were included to enhance the mise-en-scène, reflecting the director's artistic vision. These findings suggest that the observed trends towards acceptability in twenty-first-century TTs were more aligned with the creative and performative priorities of their authors than with the external restrictions characteristic of the censorship period.

b) Linguistic evidence points towards adequate solutions in other performance-oriented TTs from the twenty-first century (MARTÍNEZ LUCIANO_2011P in DAYS; GÓMEZ AND CANO_2013P and ALDEGUER_2017P in LOVER).

This trend can be also observed in reader-oriented TTs from both the censorship period (MIRLAS_1951R in MENAGERIE; MUCHNIK AND MUCHNIK_1955R in CRUCIBLE; BARBERÁ_1965R in LOVER) and the subsequent period (DIÉGUEZ_2007R and ESPEJO_2019R in MENAGERIE; LÓPEZ MUÑOZ_1997R and ESPEJO_2011R in CRUCIBLE; RODRÍGUEZ GAGO_1989R in DAYS; SPREGELBURD_2005R in LOVER). At the macrotextual and microtextual levels, these TTs exhibit minimal divergence from their STs, if any. It appears that the target authors gave priority to creating an effect on their audience similar to that of the ST.

- *Performance-oriented TTs in the twenty-first century*
  Some performance-oriented TTs from the new millennium lean towards adequacy, in contrast with their counterparts from the censorship period. Thus, performance-oriented TTs in this century display variability between acceptability and adequacy.
- *Reader-oriented TTs from the censorship period*
  The reader-oriented TTs from the censorship period were produced in Argentina and generally exhibit syntactic expressions that are closer to the STs than their counterparts from the subsequent period.
- *Reader-oriented TTs from the post-censorship period*
  During the period following the Francoist censorship, reader-oriented TTs were often characterized by meticulous translation efforts and published in editions specifically designed for readers. These editions frequently included introductions and notes provided by the translator, further emphasizing their reader-oriented nature.

These findings illustrate a dynamic interplay between adequacy and acceptability across performance- and reader-oriented TTs, shaped by distinct historical and cultural contexts.

The theatrical and literary systems in Spain during the periods under examination exhibit distinct norms regarding translation strategies. The performance-oriented TTs from the censorship era predominantly display a tendency towards acceptability, whereas those from the subsequent period reflect a dual tendency, encompassing both acceptability and adequacy. In contrast, the reader-oriented TTs consistently lean towards adequacy across the two periods. A hallmark of the performance-oriented TTs in the

TEATRAD corpus is the diversity in their approaches to the ST, which aligns with findings from previous studies on twentieth-century theatre (Merino-Álvarez 1994b, 2007a; Espejo 2004; Pérez L. de Heredia 2004; Mateo 2010; O'Leary 2018), and appears to be part of a broader European trend. Similar patterns have been identified in other national contexts, including Finland (Aaltonen 1996), Portugal (Ramos Pinto 2008) and the United Kingdom (Brodie 2017).

In the second phase of the corpus analysis, self-censorship was examined more thoroughly. To understand how the topics that were (self-)censored during the censorship period evolved in subsequent TTs, a search was conducted for anchor words related to these topics. The translation techniques identified were then classified. This study represents one of the first to focus on the evolution of the translation of sensitive topics from the period of Francoist censorship to the twenty-first century in theatrical TTs, thereby contributing a new perspective to this line of research. The key findings from this analysis are as follows:

a) Traces of self-censorship were identified in performance-oriented TTs from the censorship period concerning themes such as sexual morality, politics, religion and foul language. These traces were observed through translation techniques like addition, omission of fragments or individual words and substitution. The extent of self-censorship varies across the TTs. HURTADO_1956P and BOHR_1966P exemplify the self-censorship of sexual references in both, as well as politics and religion in the former. These changes may have been made to secure authorization for public performance, given the strict censorship imposed during this period, which had significant implications for the control of public discourse through theatrical productions (Gutiérrez Lanza 1999). The analysis revealed that self-censorship was more common than direct deletions imposed by official censors. As a result, textual comparison emerged as a crucial tool for assessing the extent of censorship restrictions during this period. Most of the performance-oriented TTs from the censorship period (GORDON AND DE QUINTO_1950P in MENAGERIE; HURTADO_1956P in CRUCIBLE; MARTÍNEZ TRIVES_1963P in DAYS; ESCOBAR_1966P in LOVER) were also printed during that time and continue to be available today, especially in libraries. Consequently, those traces of self-censorship have survived into the twenty-first century in the form of these TTs.

b) No instances of self-censorship were observed in either the performance-oriented TTs of the post-censorship era or in the reader-oriented TTs from both periods.
   - In some performance-oriented TTs from the post-censorship period, particularly those leaning towards acceptability, various translation techniques were observed in relation to the topics under examination. This diversity in translation approaches may not be related to the ideological manipulation of these topics, as was the case in the previous period, but rather reflects accepted practices within the theatrical system (Aaltonen 2000), notably the general trend towards acceptability in accordance with the target authors' intentions for a given production. Among the techniques observed, the omission of textual fragments was especially common. Additionally, instances of intensified expressions were also found, representing the opposite mechanism to the softening of sensitive content seen during the censorship period.
   - Other performance-oriented TTs of the new millennium lean towards adequacy, particularly when it comes to the translation of the topics under investigation, where transfer was the most applied translation technique.
   - No traces of censorship or self-censorship were detected in the reader-oriented TTs from Argentina during the censorship period, consistent with their adequate approach.
   - Similarly, the reader-oriented TTs from the post-censorship era again lean towards adequacy, as they restore references that had previously been subject to manipulation.

The results underscore the fact that each TT was shaped by a specific historical context. The performance-oriented TTs from the censorship period, which are still available today, bear traces of self-censorship, especially with regard to topics like sexual morality, politics, religion or foul language. The remaining TTs tackle these topics activating a variety of techniques, either leaning towards acceptability or adequacy. Some performance-oriented TTs from the post-censorship era employ diverse techniques, while others, including both performance-oriented and reader-oriented TTs, rely predominantly on transfer. In the sets of texts examined, the (self-)censored translated plays were revitalized through retranslation.

In conclusion, this study provides a detailed description and comparison of the 20 TTs, both performance- and reader-oriented, from the censorship period and its aftermath, comprising the TEATRAD corpus. The study of the corpus initially focused on a general description of the TTs, followed by a more detailed exploration of self-censored topics. Consistencies were identified that distinguish the performance-oriented TTs of both periods from the reader-oriented TTs. The translation techniques and overarching strategy employed within the theatrical and literary systems differ, as does the treatment of topics deemed sensitive by the censors. Furthermore, the priorities and restrictions of the target authors (Zabalbeascoa 1999), operating within their particular historical context, played an essential role in shaping each TT. These influences are evident in practices such as self-censorship, which was often employed to secure official authorization for performance, as well as in decisions regarding production plans for a play or a commitment to remain faithful to the ST in order to achieve a similar effect.

Looking ahead, this study has laid the groundwork for continued exploration in the field of drama translation, particularly in the context of the impact of Francoist censorship on the English-language theatre that has survived into the twenty-first century. As we expand upon the findings presented in the TEATRAD catalogue and corpus, future research could delve deeper into the nuanced ways in which self-censorship and censorship-shaped translations continue to influence modern theatre productions and publications. The evolving relationship between translation strategies, cultural contexts and theatrical practices remains a rich area for scholarly inquiry. Additionally, the application of cutting-edge technologies to the analysis of parallel corpora, alongside the exploration of adaptations in other media such as film and television, promises to open new interdisciplinary avenues.

As the field of TS grows, it is essential to continue fostering a dialogue between historical and contemporary practices, ensuring that the legacy of censorship, along with the innovative translation trends of today, are acknowledged and understood. This book, by bridging past and present, hopes to inspire further research that will deepen our understanding of the complex dynamics of theatrical translation, while enriching the study of intercultural exchange and the role of theatre in shaping societal norms and values.

Bibliography

Primary sources

The Glass Menagerie text set

Censorship record 274–50 (*El zoo de cristal*, José Gordon and José María de Quinto trans. / Carmen Vázquez Vigo trans.). Archivo General de la Administración, IDD (03)046.

Williams, Tennessee. 1951. *Teatro: Un tranvía llamado Deseo, El zoológico de cristal, Verano y humo* (León Mirlas trans.). Losada.

Williams, Tennessee. 1975. *The Glass Menagerie*. Dramatists Play Service.

Williams, Tennessee. 2007. *El zoo de cristal; Un tranvía llamado Deseo* (Amado Diéguez trans.). Alba Editorial.

Williams, Tennessee. 2011. *The Glass Menagerie*. New Directions.

Williams, Tennessee. 2014. *El zoo de cristal* (Eduardo Galán trans.) [unpublished].

Williams, Tennessee. 2019. *El zoo de cristal; Un tranvía llamado Deseo* (Ramón Espejo trans. and ed.). Cátedra.

The Crucible text set

Censorship record 310–56 (*Las brujas de Salem*, Diego Hurtado trans.). Archivo General de la Administración, IDD (03)046.

Miller, Arthur. 1955. *Las brujas de Salem: drama en cuatro actos* (Jacobo Muchnik and Mario Muchnik trans.). Compañía General Fabril Editora.

Miller, Arthur. 1997. *Las brujas de Salem, drama y El crisol, guión cinematográfico basado en la obra de teatro* (José Luis López Muñoz trans.). Tusquets.

Miller, Arthur. 2003. *The Crucible*. Penguin Books.

Miller, Arthur. 2007. Las brujas de Salem (Alberto González Vergel and Julián Escribano Moreno trans.). Teatro Español.

Miller, Arthur. 2011. *El crisol* (Ramón Espejo trans. and ed.). Cátedra.

Happy Days text set

Beckett, Samuel. 1961. *Happy Days: A Play in Two Acts*. Faber and Faber.

Beckett, Samuel. 1963. Días felices (Trino Martínez Trives trans.). *Primer Acto*, 39, 22–35.

Beckett, Samuel. 2011. *Días felices* (Juan Vicente Martínez Luciano trans.). Unpublished.
Beckett, Samuel. 2020. *Los días felices* (Antonia Rodríguez Gago trans. and ed.). Cátedra.

The Lover text set
Censorship record 91–66 (*El amante*, Daniel Bohr trans.). Archivo General de la Administración, IDD (03)046.
Censorship record 343–66 (*El amante*, Luis Escobar trans.). Archivo General de la Administración, IDD (03)046.
Pinter, Harold. 1965. *El cuidador; El amante; El montaplatos* (Manuel Barberá trans.). Nueva Visión.
Pinter, Harold. 1996. *Harold Pinter: Plays 2*. Faber and Faber.
Pinter, Harold. 2005a. *El amante; Escuela nocturna; Sketches de revista* (Rafael Spregelburd trans.). Losada.
Pinter, Harold. 2013. *El amante* (Susana Gómez and Jorge Cano trans.). Unpublished.
Pinter, Harold. 2017. *El amante* (Nacho Aldeguer trans.). Unpublished.

Secondary sources

Aaltonen, Sirkku. 1996. *Acculturation of the Other: Irish Milieux in Finnish Drama Translation*. University of Joensuu.
Aaltonen, Sirkku. 2000. *Time-sharing on Stage: Drama Translation in Theatre and Society*. Multilingual Matters.
Aaltonen, Sirkku. 2003. Retranslation in the Finnish theatre. *Cadernos de Tradução*, 1(11), 141–159.
Abellán, Manuel L. 1980. *Censura y creación literaria en España (1939–1976)*. Península.
Academia de las Artes Escénicas. N.d.a. *Eduardo Galán*. <https://academiadelasartesescenicas.es/eduardo-galan>
Academia de las Artes Escénicas. N.d.b. *Juan Vicente Martínez Luciano*. <https://academiadelasartesescenicas.es/juan-vicente-martinez>
Álvaro, Francisco. 1963. *El espectador y la crítica. El teatro en España en 1963*. Edition of the author.
Álvaro, Francisco. 1967. *El espectador y la crítica. El teatro en España en 1967*. Edition of the author.
Andaluz-Pinedo, Olaia. 2022. Prefabricated orality in theatre translations: an overview based on an English-Spanish parallel corpus. *Across Languages and Cultures*, 23(1), 75–91. <https://doi.org/10.1556/084.2022.00090>

Andaluz-Pinedo, Olaia and Raquel Merino-Álvarez. 2020. La censura del teatro de Samuel Beckett en España (1955–1978). In José Francisco Fernández Sánchez (ed.) *Samuel Beckett en España* (pp. 91–115). Universidad de Valladolid.

Anthony, Laurence. 2013. A critical look at software tools in corpus linguistics. *Linguistic Research*, 30(2), 141–161. <https://doi.org/10.17250/khisli.30.2.201308.001>

Arias-Badia, Blanca. 2017. *Television Dialogue and Subtitling: A Corpus-driven Study of Police Procedurals*. PhD thesis. Pompeu Fabra University. <http://hdl.handle.net/10803/404733>

Arias-Badia, Blanca. 2020. *Subtitling Television Series. A Corpus-Driven Study of Police Procedurals*. Peter Lang.

Ávila Cabrera, José Javier. 2014. *The Subtitling of Offensive and Taboo Language: A Descriptive Study*. PhD thesis. Universidad Nacional de Educación a Distancia.

Ávila Cabrera, José Javier. 2015. Propuesta de modelo de análisis del lenguaje ofensivo y tabú en la subtitulación. *Verbeia. Journal of English and Spanish Studies. Revista de Estudios Filológicos*, 1(0), 8–27. <https://journals.ucjc.edu/VREF/article/view/4067>

Ávila Cabrera, José Javier. 2023. *The Challenge of Subtitling Offensive and Taboo Language into Spanish: A Theoretical and Practical Guide*. Multilingual Matters.

Ballesteros Dorado, Ana Isabel. 2021. El zoo de cristal; Un tranvía llamado Deseo. Tennessee Williams / Ramón Espejo (ed. and trans.) (Madrid: Cátedra, 2019, 382 págs.). *Signa: Revista de la Asociación Española de Semiótica*, 30, 835838. <https://doi.org/10.5944/signa.vol30.2021.29330>

Bandín, Elena. 2007. *Traducción, recepción y censura de teatro clásico inglés en la España de Franco. Estudio descriptivo-comparativo del Corpus TRACEtci (1939–1985)*. PhD thesis. University of León. <http://hdl.handle.net/10612/1885>

Baños, Rocío. 2009. *La oralidad prefabricada en la traducción para el doblaje. Estudio descriptivo-contrastivo del español de dos comedias de situación*. PhD thesis. University of Granada. <http://hera.ugr.es/tesisugr/18319312.pdf>

Baños, Rocío. 2013a. 'That is so cool': investigating the translation of adverbial intensifiers in English-Spanish dubbing through a parallel corpus of sitcoms. *Perspectives*, 21(4), 526–542. <http://dx.doi.org/10.1080/0907676X.2013.831924>

Baños, Rocío. 2013b. La compensación como estrategia para recrear la conversación espontánea en el doblaje de comedias de situación. *TRANS: revista de traductología*, 17, 71–84. <https://doi.org/10.24310/TRANS.2013.v0i17.3228>

Baños, Rocío. 2014. Orality markers in Spanish native and dubbed sitcoms: pretended spontaneity and prefabricated orality. *Meta*, 59(2), 406–435. <https://doi.org/10.7202/1027482ar>

Baños, Rocío. 2021. Creating credible and natural-sounding dialogs in dubbing: can it be taught? *The Interpreter and Translator Trainer*, 15(1), 13–33. <https://doi.org/10.1080/1750399X.2021.1880262>

Baños, Rocío. 2024. *La oralidad prefabricada en la ficción audiovisual original y doblada: Siete vidas y Friends*. Universitat Jaume I.

Baños, Rocío and Chaume, Frederic. 2009. Prefabricated orality: a challenge in audiovisual translation. *InTRAlinea. Special Issue: The Translation of Dialects in Multimedia*. <www.intralinea.org/specials/article/Prefabricated_Orality>

Bassnett, Susan. 1978. Translating spatial poetry: an examination of theatre texts in performance. In James S. Holmes, José Lambert and Raymond van den Broeck (eds) *Literature and Translation: New Perspectives in Literary Studies* (pp. 161–176). ACCO.

Bassnett, Susan. 1985. Ways through the labyrinth: strategies and methods for translating theatre texts. In Theo Hermans (ed.) *The Manipulation of Literature: Studies in Literary Translation* (pp. 87–102). Croom Helm.

Bassnett, Susan. 1991a. Translating dramatic texts. *Translation Studies* (pp. 120–132). Routledge.

Bassnett, Susan. 1991b. Translating for the theatre: the case against performability. *TTR: traduction, terminologie, rédaction*, 4(1), 99–111. <https://doi.org/10.7202/037084ar>

Bassnett, Susan. 1998. Still trapped in the labyrinth: further reflections on translation and theatre. In Susan Bassnett and André Lefevere (eds) *Constructing Cultures: Essays on Literary Translation* (pp. 90–108). Multilingual Matters.

Bednarek, Monika. 2011. Expressivity and televisual characterization. *Language and Literature*, 20(1), 3–21.

Biber, Douglas, Johansson, Stig, Leech, Geoffrey, Conrad, Susan and Finegan, Edward. 1999. *Longman Grammar of Spoken and Written English*. Longman.

Bigsby, Christopher. 2010. *The Cambridge Companion to Arthur Miller*. Cambridge University Press.

Boyle, Catherine. 1992. The mirror to nature? Latin American theatre in London. *Travesia*, 1(1), 105–117. <https://doi.org/10.1080/13569329209361776>

Braga Riera, Jorge. 2006. *La traducción al inglés en el siglo XVII: Las comedias del Siglo de Oro español*. PhD thesis. University of Oviedo.

Braga Riera, Jorge. 2011. ¿Traducción, adaptación o versión? Maremágnum terminológico en el ámbito de la traducción dramática. *Estudios de Traducción* i 1, 59–72. <https://doi.org/10.5209/rev_ESTR.2011.v1.36477>

Braga Riera, Jorge. 2024. Theatre is different: *la traducción de la experiencia dramática*. Guillermo Escolar.

Briz, Antonio. 1996. *El español coloquial: situación y uso*. Arco Libros.

Briz, Antonio. 2001. *El español coloquial en la conversación: Esbozo de pragmagramática*. Ariel.

Brodie, Geraldine. 2017. *The Translator on Stage*. Bloomsbury.

Brodie, Geraldine. 2018. Indirect translation on the London stage: terminology and (in)visibility. *Translation Studies*, 11(3), 333–348. <https://doi.org/10.1080/14781700.2018.1447990>

Brodie, Geraldine and Cole, Emma. 2017. *Adapting Translation for the Stage*. Routledge.

Brumme, Jenny. 2008. Traducir la oralidad teatral. Las traducciones al castellano, catalán, francés y euskera de *der Kontrabaß* de Patrick Süskind. In Jenny Brumme (ed.) *La oralidad fingida: descripción y traducción. Teatro, cómic y medios audiovisuales* (pp. 21–64). Iberoamericana.

Brumme, Jenny. 2012a. Traducir la oralidad teatral. Las traducciones al castellano, portugués e inglés de *Der Kontrabaß* (1980), de Patrick Süskind. In Jenny Brumme (ed.) *Traducir la voz ficticia* (pp. 117–133). De Gruyter.

Brumme, Jenny and Bernal, Elisenda. 2010. Monólogo teatral y mímesis de la oralidad. In Gemma Andújar and Jenny Brumme (eds) *Construir, deconstruir y reconstruir: mímesis y traducción de la oralidad y la afectividad* (pp. 95–119). Frank & Timme.

Bruti, Silvia. 2019. Spoken discourse and conversational interaction in audiovisual translation. In Luis Pérez González (ed.) *The Routledge Handbook of Audiovisual Translation* (pp. 192–208). Routledge.

Burton, Deirdre. 2014. *Dialogue and Discourse. A Sociolinguistic Approach to Modern Drama Dialogue and Naturally Occurring Conversation*. Routledge.

Cabanillas, Candelas. 2016. *La traducción audiovisual en ETB2: Estudio descriptivo del género western*. PhD thesis. University of the Basque Country. <http://hdl.handle.net/10810/18287>

Calzada Pérez, María and Laviosa, Sara. 2021. Twenty-five years on: time to pause for a new agenda for CTIS. *MonTI. Monografías de Traducción e Interpretación*, 13, 7–32. <https://doi.org/10.6035/MonTI.2021.13.01>

Campillo, Laura. 2005. *Estudio de los elementos culturales en las obras de Shakespeare y sus traducciones al español por Macpherson, Astrana y Valverde*. PhD thesis. University of Murcia. <https://digitum.um.es/digitum/handle/10201/178>

Campos. Prado. 2017. ¿Quién no querría un amante? Pinter y el sexo sin tabúes. *El Confidencial*, 16 March. <www.elconfidencial.com/cultura/2017-03-16/el-amante-teatro-alex-garcia-sexo-pinter_1348831>

Camus, Carmen. 2009. *Traducciones censuradas de novelas y películas del oeste en la España de Franco*. PhD thesis. University of the Basque Country.

Carrero Martín, José Fernando and L. Lapeña, Alejandro. 2020. Entre la página y la escena. ¿Dónde encuadrar la traducción teatral?. *Sendebar*, 31, 373–394. <https://doi.org/10.30827/sendebar.v31i0.11814>

Carter, Ronald and McCarthy, Michael. 1997. *Exploring Spoken English*. Cambridge University Press.

Cebrián, Helena. 2011. La traducción de la oralidad en los textos dramáticos. El caso de *Cat on a Hot Tin Roof*. *Fòrum de Recerca*, 16, 606–613. <http://hdl.handle.net/10234/77258>

Cebrián, Helena. 2015. *La traducción de la deixis en los textos dramáticos. El caso de Cat on a Hot Tin Roof de Tennessee Williams*. PhD thesis. University Jaume I. <https://core.ac.uk/download/323492368.pdf>

Censorship record 1732–65 (*El zoo de cristal*, José Gordon and José María de Quinto trans.). Archivo General de la Administración, IDD (03)050.

Censorship record 251–58 (*Un tranvía llamado Deseo*, *El zoológico de cristal*, *Verano y humo*, León Mirlas trans.). Archivo General de la Administración, IDD (03)050.

Censorship record 215–65 (*¿Quién teme a Virginia Woolf?*, José Méndez Herrera trans.). Archivo General de la Administración, IDD (03)046.

Censorship record 2792–73 (*Las brujas de Salem*, Diego Hurtado trans.). Archivo General de la Administración, IDD (03)050.

Censorship record 2982–60 (*El zoo de cristal*, José Gordon and José María de Quinto trans.). Archivo General de la Administración, IDD (03)050.

Censorship record 47–63 (*Días felices*, Trino Martínez Trives trans.). Archivo General de la Administración, IDD (03)046.

Censorship record 5135–60 (*Las brujas de Salem*, Diego Hurtado trans.). Archivo General de la Administración, IDD (03)050.

Censorship record 5862–53 (*Un tranvía llamado Deseo*, *El zoológico de cristal*, *Verano y humo*, León Mirlas trans.). Archivo General de la Administración, IDD (03)050.

Centro de Documentación de las Artes Escénicas y de la Música. 2017a. *Les bruixes de Salem; Las brujas de Salem*. <www.teatro.es/estrenos-teatro/les-bruixes-de-salem-las-brujas-de-salem-1337351/documentos-on-line/otros-documentos>

Centro de Documentación de las Artes Escénicas y de la Música. 2017b. *El amante; El montacargas*. <www.teatro.es/estrenos-teatro/el-amante-el-montacargas-7888/documentos-on-line/otros-documentos>

Centro de Documentación de las Artes Escénicas y de la Música. 2017c. *Los días felices*. <www.teatro.es/estrenos-teatro/los-dias-felices-42883/documentos-on-line/otros-documentos>

Centro de Documentación de las Artes Escénicas y de la Música. 2017d. *El amante*. <www.teatro.es/estrenos-teatro/el-amante-61983/documentos-on-line/otros-documentos>

Centro de Documentación de las Artes Escénicas y de la Música. N.d. <www.teatro.es/estrenos-teatro>

Chaume, Frederic. 2004a. *Cine y traducción*. Cátedra.

Chaume, Frederic. 2004b. Discourse markers in audiovisual translating. *Meta*, 49(4), 843–855. <https://doi.org/10.7202/009785ar>

Chaume, Frederic. 2007. Quality standards in dubbing: a proposal. *TradTerm*, 13, 71–89. <https://doi.org/10.11606/issn.2317-9511.tradterm.2007.47466>

Chaume, Frederic. 2018. The retranslation and mediated translation of audiovisual content in multilingual Spain: reasons and market trends. *Status Quaestionis*, 15, 12–27. <http://hdl.handle.net/10234/187602>

Cornellà-Detrell, Jordi. 2015. La obra de James Baldwin ante la censura franquista: El contrabando de libros, la conexión latinoamericana y la evolución del sector editorial peninsular. *Represura. Revista de Historia Contemporánea española en torno a la represión y la censura aplicadas al libro, 1*, 32–60. <www.represura.es/represura_1_nueva_epoca_2015.pdf>

Corrigan, Robert W. 1961. Translating for actors. In William Arrowsmith and Roger Shattuck (eds) *The Craft and Context of Translation* (pp. 95–106). University of Texas.

Delabastita, Dirk. 1989. Translation and mass-communication: film and TV translation as evidence of cultural dynamics. *Babel*, 35(4), 193–218. <https://doi.org/10.1075/babel.35.4.02del>

Díaz-Cintas, Jorge. 2004. In search of a theoretical framework for the study of audiovisual translation. In P. Orero (ed.) *Topics in Audiovisual Translation* (pp. 21–34). John Benjamins. <https://doi.org/10.1075/btl.56.06dia>

Díaz-Cintas, Jorge. 2019. Film censorship in Franco's Spain: the transforming power of dubbing. *Perspectives*, 27(2), 182–200. <https://doi.org/https://doi.org/10.1080/0907676X.2017.1420669>

Escribano, Julián. 2007. El abismo de los ensayos, los ensayos del abismo. In Arthur Miller, *Las brujas de Salem* (pp. 265–273). Teatro Español.

Espasa, Eva. 2000. Performability in translation: speakability? Playability? Or just saleability? In Carole-Anne Upton (ed.) *Moving Target: Theatre Translation and Cultural Relocation* (pp. 49–62). Routledge.

Espasa, Eva. 2001a. *La traducció dalt de l'escenari*. Eumo.

Espasa, Eva. 2001b. La traducció per al teatre i per al doblatge a l'aula: un laboratori de proves. In Frederic Chaume and Rosa Agost (eds) *La traducción en los medios audiovisuales* (pp. 57–64). Universitat Jaume I.

Espasa, Eva. 2009. Repensar la representabilidad. *TRANS: revista de traductología*, 13, 95–105. <https://doi.org/10.24310/TRANS.2009.v0i13.3158>

Espejo, Ramón. 1997. *Historia del zoo*, de Edward Albee, y el teatro independiente español. *Atlantis*, 19(2), 65–76.

Espejo, Ramón. 1998. *Who's Afraid of Virginia Woolf?*: Edward Albee, en España, y su posterior influencia en el teatro de Alfonso Paso. *REDEN: Revista Española de Estudios Norteamericanos*, 15(16), 111–121.

Espejo, Ramón. 2001. *Death of a Salesman*, de Arthur Miller, reestrenada y reeditada en España. *Atlantis*, 23(2), 215–220.

Espejo, Ramón. 2002. *Death of a Salesman*, de Arthur Miller, en España durante los años 50. *Atlantis*, 24(1), 85–107.

Espejo, Ramón. 2003. Traducciones al español de Arthur Miller 1950–1952. *TRANS: revista de traductología*, 7, 21–32.

Espejo, Ramón. 2004. El estreno de *The Crucible* en España y su fallido intento de despolitización. In Juan Ignacio Guijarro and Ramón Espejo (eds) *Arthur Miller: Visiones desde el nuevo milenio* (pp. 135–147). University of Valencia.

Espejo, Ramón. 2010a. Introducción. In Arthur Miller, *La muerte de un viajante* (pp. 7–169). Cátedra.

Espejo, Ramón. 2010b. *España y el teatro de Arthur Miller*. Instituto Franklin de Estudios Norteamericanos.

Espejo, Ramón. 2011. Introducción. In Arthur Miller, *El crisol* (pp. 7103). Cátedra.

Espejo, Ramón. 2012. Introducción. In Arthur Miller, *Panorama desde el puente*. Cátedra.

Espejo, Ramón. 2017. *The History of the Performance of American Drama in Spain 1912–1977: Theatre as a Weapon Against Political Authoritarianism*. Edwin Mellen Press.

Espejo, Ramón. 2018. Arte, negocio, ideología: teatro norteamericano en España y el final de la historia. *Simposio sobre traducción y teatro en los medios audiovisuales: recepción y accesibilidad*, Vitoria-Gasteiz, Spain.

Espejo, Ramón. 2019. Introducción. In Tennessee Williams, *El zoo de cristal; Un tranvía llamado Deseo* (pp. 7–108). Cátedra.

Esslin, Martin. 1990. *The Field of Drama: How the Signs of Drama Create Meaning on Stage and Screen*. Methuen.

Even-Zohar, Itamar. 1990. Polysystem Theory. *Poetics Today*, 11(1), 9–94.

Ezpeleta Piorno, Pilar. 2007. *Teatro y traducción: aproximación interdisciplinaria desde la obra de Shakespeare*. Cátedra.

Fernández López, Marisa. 2000. Comportamientos censores en literatura infantil y juvenil: traducciones del inglés en la España franquista. In Rosa Rabadán (ed.) *Traducción y censura inglés–español: 1939–1985. Estudio preliminar* (pp. 227–255). University of León.

Fernández López, Marisa. 2007. Comportamientos censores en la literatura infantil y juvenil traducida del inglés en la época franquista: Establecimiento de un corpus textual. In Raquel Merino-Álvarez (ed.) *Traducción y censura en España (1939–1985). Estudios sobre corpus TRACE: cine, narrativa, teatro* (pp. 19–48). University of the Basque Country.

Fernández Sánchez, José Francisco. 2020. La recepción de Samuel Beckett en España. Consideraciones generales. In Bernardo Santano Moreno, Concepción Hermosilla Álvarez and Severina Álvarez González (eds) *Samuel Beckett: literatura y traducción, Littérature et traduction, Literature and Translation* (pp. 15–36). Peter Lang.

Fernández-Quesada, Nuria. 2007. *Evolución de la obra teatral de Samuel Beckett en los escenarios españoles: 1955–2000. Censura, representación y crítica*. PhD thesis. University Pablo de Olavide.

Fernández-Quesada, Nuria. 2020. *Final de partida* ante la crítica teatral española del siglo XX: de íncubos, súcubos, dictadores y cloacas. In Bernardo Santano Moreno, Concepción Hermosilla Álvarez and Severina Álvarez González (eds) *Samuel Beckett: literatura y traducción, Littérature et traduction, Literature and Translation* (pp. 59–79). Peter Lang.

Fernández-Quesada, Nuria, Fernández Sánchez, José Francisco and Santano Moreno, Bernardo. 2019. *Samuel Beckett en español: bibliografía crítica de las traducciones de su obra*. Universidad de Almería.

Fischer-Lichte, Erika. 1999. *Semiótica del teatro*. Arco Libros.

Forchini, Pierfranca. 2010. "Well, uh no. I mean, you know". Discourse markers in movie conversation. In Lukasz Bogucki and Krzysztof Kredens (eds) *Perspectives on Audiovisual Translation* (pp. 45- 59). Peter Lang.

Forchini, Pierfranca. 2013. A diachronic study of familiarizers ('man', 'guys', 'buddy', 'dude') in movie language. *Perspectives*, 21(4), 504–525. <http://dx.doi.org/10.1080/0907676X.2013.831923>

Gil Fombellida, Carmen. 2002. El estreno de *Las brujas de Salem* en el Teatro Español de Madrid (1956–1957). *Revista de Literatura*, 64(127), 151–166. <https://doi.org/10.3989/revliteratura.2002.v64.i127.194>

Gómez Castro, Cristina. 2008. The Francoist censorship casts a long shadow: translations from the period of the dictatorship on sale nowadays. In Teresa Seruya and Maria Lin Moniz (eds) *Translation and Censorship in Different Times and Landscapes* (pp. 184–195). Cambridge Scholars Publishing.

Gómez Castro, Cristina. 2009. *Traducción y censura de textos narrativos inglés-español en la España franquista y de transición: TRACEni (1970–1978)*. PhD thesis. University of León. <http://hdl.handle.net/10612/1413>

Gómez García, Manuel. 1998. *Diccionario del teatro*. Akal.

Gómez, Susana. 2022. *Susana Gómez. Dirección de escena*. <www.susanagomez.com>

Goñi, Miren Edurne. 2017. *Traducción y censura, traducción de dialectos: las versiones al castellano de Pigmalión de George Bernard Shaw*. PhD thesis. University of Basque Country. <http://hdl.handle.net/10810/27646>

González Vergel, Alberto. 2007. Una versión escénica de *The Crucible*. In Arthur Miller, *Las brujas de Salem* (pp. 257–260). Teatro Español.

Gordon, José. 1960. Unas palabras. In Tennessee Williams, *El zoo de cristal* (pp. 5–6). Escelicer.

Gregory, Michael and Carroll, Susanne. 1978. *Language and Situation: Language Varieties and Their Social Context*. Routledge/Kegan Paul.

Griffiths, Malcolm. 1985. Presence and presentation: dilemmas in translating for the theatre. In Theo Hermans (ed.) *Second Hand: Papers on the Theory and Historical Study of Literary Translation* (pp. 161–182). Vlaamse Vereining voor Algemene en Vergelijkende Literatuurwetenschap.

Gutiérrez Lanza, Camino. 1999. *Traducción y censura de textos cinematográficos en la España de Franco: doblaje y subtitulado inglés-español (1951–1975)*. PhD thesis. University of León.

Gutiérrez Lanza, Camino. 2000. Proteccionismo y censura durante la etapa franquista: Cine nacional, cine traducido y control estatal. In Rosa Rabadán (ed.) *Traducción y censura inglés-español: 1939–1985. Estudio preliminar* (pp. 23–59). University of León.

Gutiérrez Lanza, Camino. 2005. La labor del equipo TRACE: metodología descriptiva de la censura en traducción. In Raquel Merino-Álvarez, José Miguel Santamaría López and Eterio Pajares Infante (eds.) *Trasvases culturales: literatura, cine, traducción 4* (pp. 55–64). University of the Basque Country.

Gutiérrez Lanza, Camino. 2015. Retranslation and counterculture in post-Francoist and modern-day Spain: Woody Guthrie's *Bound for Glory* in Star Books (1977) and Global Rhythm Press (2009). *Quaderns de Filologia: Estudis Literaris*, 20, 125–144. <https://doi.org/10.7203/qf-elit.v20i0.7533>

Gutiérrez Lanza, Camino and Serrano, Luis. 2001. Cine, traducción y censura (años cincuenta y sesenta): la recepción del adulterio en la España de la doble moralidad. In Eterio Pajares, Raquel Merino-Álvarez and José Miguel Santamaría (eds) *Trasvases culturales: literatura, cine, traducción 3* (pp. 219–228). University of the Basque Country.

Harvey, Anthony and Jordan, Glenn (directors). 2006. *El zoo de cristal; El país del dragón*. Divisa Home Video.

Herman, Vimala. 1998. Turn management in drama. In Jonathan Culpeper, Mick Short and Peter Verdonk (eds.) *Exploring the language of drama* (pp. 19–33). Routledge.

Hermans, Theo. 1985. *The Manipulation of Literature: Studies in Literary Translation*. Croom Helm.

Hermans, Theo. 1999. Translation and normativity. In Christina Schäffner (ed.) *Translation and Norms* (pp. 50–71). Multilingual Matters.

Heylen, Romy. 1993. Introduction: a cultural model of translation. In Romy Heylen (ed.) *Translation, Poetics & the Stage: Six French Hamlets* (pp. 1–25). Routledge.

Holmes, James S. 1988. The name and nature of translation studies. In James S. Holmes (ed.) *Translated! Papers on Literary Translation and Translation Studies* (pp. 67–80). Rodopi.

House, Juliane. 1981. *A Model for Translation Quality Assessment*. Gunter Narr Verlag Tübingen.

Hurtley, Jacqueline A. 2013. Lands of desire: Yeats in Catalonia, Galicia and the Basque Country, 1920–1935. In Klaus Peter Jochum (ed.) *The reception of W. B. Yeats in Europe* (pp. 76–95). Bloomsbury.

Hytner, Nicholas (director). 1996. *El crisol*. Twentieth Century Fox.

Isabel Estrada, María Antonia de. 2001. *George Bernard Shaw y John Osborne: recepción y recreación de su teatro en España durante el franquismo*. PhD thesis. Complutense University of Madrid. <https://eprints.ucm.es/id/eprint/5228>

Johnston, David. 2004. Securing the performability of the play in translation. In Sabine Coelsch-Foisner and Holger Klein (eds) *Drama Translation and Theatre Practice* (pp. 25–38). Peter Lang.

Johnston, David. 2012. Created relation: the translated play in performance. *Quaderns: revista de traducció*, 19, 43–52.

Kenny, Dorothy. 2009. Corpora. In Mona Baker and Gabriela Saldanha (eds) *Routledge Encyclopedia of Translation Studies*. 2nd ed. (pp. 59–62). Routledge.

Kowzan, Tadeusz. 1975. *Littérature et spectacle*. Mouton.

Kruger, Alet. 2004a. Shakespeare in Afrikaans: a corpus-based study of involvement in different registers of drama translation. *Language Matters*, 35(1), 275–294.

Kruger, Alet. 2004b. The role of discourse markers in an Afrikaans stage translation of *The Merchant of Venice*. *Journal of Literary Studies*, 20(3–4), 302–334.

Lambert, José and van Gorp, Hendrik. 1985. On describing translations. In Theo Hermans (ed.) *The Manipulation of Literature: Studies in Literary Translation* (pp. 42–53). Croom Helm.

Laviosa, Sara. 2002. *Corpus-based Translations Studies: Theory, Findings, Applications*. Rodopi.

Lefevere, André. 1992. *Translation, Rewriting, and the Manipulation of Literary Fame*. Routledge.

Levý, Jiří. 1968. Die Übersetzung von Theaterstücken. *Babel*, 14(2), 7782. <https://doi.org/10.1075/babel.14.2.02lev>

Ley 14/1966, de 18 de marzo, de Prensa e Imprenta (BOE 67, de 19 de marzo de 1966, pp. 3310–3315). <www.boe.es/boe/dias/1966/03/19/pdfs/A03310-03315.pdf>

Ley, de 22 de abril de 1938, de Prensa (rectificada) (BOE 550, de 24 de abril de 1938, pp. 6938–6940). <www.boe.es/buscar/doc.php?id=BOE-A-1938-4796>

Lobejón, Sergio. 2013. *Traducción y censura de textos poéticos inglés-español en España. TRACEpi (1939–1983)* PhD thesis. University of León. <http://hdl.handle.net/10612/6133>

London, John. 1997. *Reception and Renewal in Modern Spanish Theatre: 1939–1963*. W. S. Maney and Son.

López Lapeña, Alejandro. 2015. *Traducir un arte vivo. Bases para un modelo de análisis de la traducción teatral*. PhD thesis. University of Granada. <http://hdl.handle.net/10481/40530>

Marinetti, Cristina. 2020. Invisible agents in translation history: censors and actors in performed drama of eighteenth-century England. *Translation Studies*, 14(3): 263–281. <https://doi.org/10.1080/14781700.2020.1853600>

Martínez Luciano, Juan Vicente. 2006. Sobre Pinter. Notas de un traductor. *ADE Teatro: Revista de la Asociación de Directores de Escena de España*, 111, 106–111.

Martínez Trives, Trino. 1963. Mientras ensayo *Días felices*. *Primer Acto, 39*, 21.

Marzà, Anna. 2016. *La naturalitat en la traducció per al doblatge. El cas dels marcadors d'intensificació*. PhD thesis. Universitat Jaume I.

Matamala, Anna. 2008. La oralidad en la ficción televisiva: análisis de las interjecciones de un corpus de comedias de situación originales y dobladas. In Jenny Brumme

(ed.) *La oralidad fingida: descripción y traducción. Teatro, cómic y medios audiovisuales* (pp. 81–94). Vervuert/Iberoamericana.
Matamala, Anna. 2009. Interjections in original and dubbed sitcoms in Catalan: a comparison. *Meta*, 54(3), 485–502. <https://doi.org/10.7202/038310ar>
Mateo, Marta. 1995a. Constraints and possibilities of performance elements in drama translation. *Perspectives*, 3(1), 21–33. <https://doi.org/10.1080/0907676X.1995.9961246>
Mateo, Marta. 1995b. *La traducción del humor: Las comedias inglesas en español*. PhD thesis. Universidad de Oviedo.
Mateo, Marta. 2000. *Las brujas de Salem* y *El crisol*: las versiones españolas de la obra de A. Miller en teatro, TV y cine. *Quaderns. revista de traducció*, 5, 147–160. <https://raco.cat/index.php/QuadernsTraduccio/article/view/25254>
Mateo, Marta. 2010a. El juego pragmático como eje del humor de Oscar Wilde en inglés y en español. In Rosa Rabadán, Trinidad Guzmán and Marisa Fernández (eds) *Lengua, traducción, recepción: en honor de Julio César Santoyo* (pp. 323–356). University of León.
Mateo, Marta. 2010b. The reception of Wilde's works in Spain through theatre performances at the turn of the twentieth and twenty-first centuries. In Stefano Evangelista (ed.) *The Reception of Oscar Wilde in Europe* (pp. 156–172). Bloomsbury Academic.
Mattsson, Jenny. 2006. Linguistic variation in the subtitling of swearwords and discourse markers on public television, commercial television and DVD. In Mary Carroll, Heidrun Gerzymisch-Arbogast and Sara Nauert (eds) *Proceedings of the Marie Curie Euroconferences MuTra: Audiovisual Translation Scenarios*. <www.euroconferences.info/proceedings/2006_Proceedings/2006_proceedings.html>
Mattsson, Jenny. 2009. *The Subtitling of Discourse Particles. A Corpus-based Study of* well, you know, I mean, *and* like, *and Their Swedish Translations in Ten American Films*. PhD thesis. University of Gothenburg. <http://hdl.handle.net/2077/21007>
McEnery, Tony and Hardie, Andrew. 2012. *Corpus Linguistics: Method, Theory and Practice*. Cambridge University Press.
McEnery, Tony, Xiao, Richard and Tono, Yukio. 2006. *Corpus-based Language Studies: An Advanced Resource Book*. Routledge.
Merino-Álvarez, Raquel. 1992a. Profesión: adaptador. *Livius: Revista de estudios de traducción*, 1, 85–97. <http://hdl.handle.net/10810/42756>
Merino-Álvarez, Raquel. 1992b. Rewriting for the Spanish Stage. *KOINÉ. Annali Della Scuola Superiore Per Interpreti E Traduttori «San Pellegrino»*, 1–2, 283–289. <http://hdl.handle.net/10810/47781>
Merino-Álvarez, Raquel. 1993a. Panorama desde el escenario: 30 años de teatro inglés en España. *Livius: Revista de estudios de traducción*, 3, 197–207. <http://hdl.handle.net/10810/42757>

Merino-Álvarez, Raquel. 1993b. Textos originales, pecados originales (en la crítica de traducciones de obras de teatro). *Babel – AFIAL*, 2, 101–108. <http://hdl.handle.net/10810/45622>

Merino-Álvarez, Raquel. 1993c. A view from the stage: Arthur Miller in Spanish. In Catriona Picken (ed.) *XIII FIT World Congress. Proceedings* (pp. 17–25). Institute of Translation and Interpreting.

Merino-Álvarez, Raquel. 1994a. A framework for the description of drama translations. *Revista Canaria de Estudios Ingleses*, 29, 127–138. <http://hdl.handle.net/10810/47978>

Merino-Álvarez, Raquel. 1994b. *Traducción, tradición y manipulación: teatro inglés en España 1950–1990*. University of León and University of the Basque Country.

Merino-Álvarez, Raquel. 1995. La traducción del teatro inglés en España: cuarenta años de plagios. In Purificación Fernández Nistal and José María Bravo Gonzalo (eds) *Perspectivas de la traducción inglés-español* (pp. 75–89). University of Valladolid.

Merino-Álvarez, Raquel. 1999. Censura política y censura económica en el teatro traducido (inglés>español). In Alberto Álvarez Lugrís and Anxo Fernández Ocampo (eds) *Anovar-anosar, estudios de traducción e interpretación* (pp. 115–119). University of Vigo.

Merino-Álvarez, Raquel. 2000. El teatro inglés traducido desde 1960: censura, ordenación, calificación. In Rosa Rabadán (ed.) *Traducción y censura inglés-español 1939–1985* (pp. 121–151). University of León.

Merino-Álvarez, Raquel. 2001. Textos dramáticos traducidos y censurados en la España de Franco (años sesenta): el teatro y el cine, espectáculos controlados. In John D. Sanderson (ed.) *¡Doble o nada! Actas de las I y II Jornadas de doblaje y subtitulación de la Universidad de Alicante* (pp. 85–97). University of Alicante.

Merino-Álvarez, Raquel. 2003. TRAducciones CEnsuradas inglés-español. Del catálogo al corpus TRACE (teatro). In Ricardo Muñoz Martín (ed.) *Actas del I Congreso Internacional de la Asociación Ibérica de Estudios de Traducción e Interpretación* (pp. 641–670). Asociación Ibérica de Estudios de Traducción e Interpretación (AIETI).

Merino-Álvarez, Raquel. 2005. From catalogue to corpus in DTS translations censored under Franco. The TRACE project. *Revista Canaria de Estudios Ingleses*, 51, 85–104. <http://hdl.handle.net/10810/41434>

Merino-Álvarez, Raquel. 2007a. La homosexualidad censurada: estudio sobre corpus de teatro TRACEti inglés-español (desde 1960). In Raquel Merino-Álvarez (ed.) *Traducción y censura en España (1939–1985). Estudios sobre corpus TRACE: cine, narrativa, teatro* (pp. 243–313). University of the Basque Country.

Merino-Álvarez, Raquel (ed.). 2007b. *Traducción y censura en España (1939–1985). Estudios sobre corpus TRACE: cine, narrativa, teatro*. UPV/EHU.

Merino-Álvarez, Raquel. 2009. Traducciones (censuradas) de teatro inglés en la España de Franco. TRACE. una perspectiva histórica. *TRANS: revista de traductología*, 13, 19–31. <http://hdl.handle.net/10810/10578>

Merino-Álvarez, Raquel. 2010. La historia de las traducciones de teatro inglés en España en el siglo XX: perspectiva desde el proyecto TRACE. In Rosa Rabadán, Trinidad Guzmán and Marisa Fernández (eds) *Lengua, traducción, recepción: en honor de Julio César Santoyo* (pp. 357–384). University of Léon.

Merino-Álvarez, Raquel. 2016a. The censorship of theatre translations under Franco: the 1960s. *Perspectives*, 24(1), 36–47. <https://doi.org/10.1080/0907676X.2015.1051558>

Merino-Álvarez, Raquel. 2016b. Censura, traducción e integración en el teatro de la época franquista: José López Rubio, hombre de teatro y traductor. *Hispanic Research Journal. Iberian and Latin American Studies*, 17(4), 303–321. <https://doi.org/10.1080/14682737.2016.1200854>

Merino-Álvarez, Raquel. 2016c. Mapping translated theatre in Spain through censorship archives. In Catherine O'Leary, Diego Santos Sánchez and Michael Thompson (eds) *Global Insights on Theatre Censorship*. (pp. 176–190). Routledge.

Merino-Álvarez, Raquel. 2017a. Traducción y censura: investigaciones sobre la cultura traducida inglés-español (1938–1985). *Represura. Revista de Historia Contemporánea española en torno a la represión y la censura aplicadas al libro*, 2, 139163. <http://hdl.handle.net/10810/37505>

Merino-Álvarez, Raquel. 2017b. Translation and censorship under Franco and Salazar: Irish theatre on Iberian stages. In Javier Muñoz-Basols, Laura Lonsdale and Manuel Delgado (eds) *The Routledge Companion to Iberian Studies* (pp. 439–449). Routledge.

Merino-Álvarez, Raquel. 2021. *El hombre de La Mancha*: de Broadway a Madrid. *Observatorio de la Lengua Española y las Culturas Hispánicas en los Estados Unidos, Instituto Cervantes at Harvard*, Boston. <http://hdl.handle.net/10810/51713>

Merino-Álvarez, Raquel and Andaluz-Pinedo, Olaia. 2017. Peter Shaffer en la cultura española. *Creneida. Anuario de Literaturas Hispánicas*, 5, 239278. <www.creneida.com/revista/creneida-5-2017>

Merino-Álvarez, Raquel and Andaluz-Pinedo, Olaia. 2020. Sesenta años de Beckett en España: *Esperando a Godot*, de la censura a la audiodescripción. In Bernardo Santano Moreno, Concepción Hermosilla Álvarez and Severina Álvarez González (eds) *Samuel Beckett: literatura y traducción, Littérature et traduction, Literature and Translation* (pp. 37–57). Peter Lang.

Merino-Álvarez, Raquel and Rabadán, Rosa. 2002. Censored translations in Franco's Spain: The TRACE project – Theatre and fiction (English-Spanish). *TTR: traduction, terminologie, rédaction*, 15(2), 125–152. <http://hdl.handle.net/10810/43921>

Meyer, Michael. 1974. On translating plays. *20th Century Studies*, 11, 44–51.

Miguel González, Marta. 2000. El cine de Hollywood y la censura franquista en la España de los 40: un cine bajo palio. In Rosa Rabadán (ed.) *Traducción y censura inglés-español: 1939–1985. Estudio preliminar* (pp. 61–86). University of León.

Miller, Arthur. 2015. *Arthur Miller. Teatro reunido* (Victoria Alonso Blanco, Jordi Fibla Feito, José Luis López Muñoz, Eduardo Mendoza trans.). Tusquets.

Miller, Arthur. 2010. *La muerte de un viajante* (Ramón Espejo trans. and ed.). Cátedra.

Miller, Arthur. 2012. *Panorama desde el puente* (Ramón Espejo trans. and ed.). Cátedra.

Miquel, Marta. 2011. Censorship on television in Franco's Spain: the case of Estudio 1. *3rd International Conference Media For All*, Antwerp. <www.mediaforall.eu/all3/pal_3b_miquel.html>

Muñoz Cáliz, Berta. 2005. *El teatro crítico español durante el franquismo, visto por sus censores*. Fundación Universitaria Española. <www.xn--bertamuoz-r6a.es/censura/tesiscensura.pdf>

Muñoz Cáliz, Berta. 2006. Censurado por el franquismo. *El Cultural*, 30 March. <www.cervantesvirtual.com/nd/ark:/59851/bmcfx948>

Newman, Paul (director). 2015. *El zoo de cristal*. Cinema International Media.

Newmark, Peter. 1988. *A Textbook of Translation*. Prentice Hall International.

O'Leary, Catherine. 2012. El teatro de Sean O'Casey. *ADE Teatro: Revista de la Asociación de Directores de Escena de España*, 142, 109–117.

O'Leary, Catherine. 2018. Translating the armed struggle: Alfonso Sastre and Sean O'Casey in Spain. *Translation Studies*, 11(1), 47–65. <https://doi.org/10.1080/14781700.2017.1339207>

Orden de 16 de febrero de 1963 por la que se constituye una Junta de Censura de Obras Teatrales (BOE 58, de 8 de marzo de 1963, p. 3931). <www.boe.es/boe/dias/1963/03/08/pdfs/A03931-03931.pdf>

Orden de 6 de febrero de 1964 por la que se aprueba el Reglamento de Régimen Interior de la Junta de Censura de Obras Teatrales y las normas de censura (BOE 48, de 25 de febrero de 1964, pp. 2504–2506). <www.boe.es/boe/dias/1964/02/25/pdfs/A02504-02506.pdf>

Orden de 9 de febrero de 1963 por la que se aprueban las «Normas de censura cinematográfica» (BOE 58, de 8 de marzo de 1963, pp. 3929–3930). <www.boe.es/boe/dias/1963/03/08/pdfs/A03929-03930.pdf>

Pajares, Eterio. 2007. Traducción y censura: *Cumbres borrascosas* en la dictadura franquista. In Raquel Merino-Álvarez (ed.) *Traducción y censura en España (1939–1985). Estudios sobre corpus TRACE: cine, narrativa, teatro* (pp. 49–104). University of the Basque Country.

Pavesi, Maria. 2008. Spoken language in film dubbing: target language norms, interference and translational routines. In Delia Chiaro, Christine Heiss and Chiara Bucaria (eds) *Between Text and Image: Updating Research in Screen Translation* (pp. 79–99). John Benjamins.

Pavesi, Maria. 2009. Pronouns in film dubbing and the dynamics of audiovisual communication. *VIAL. Vigo International Journal of Applied Linguistics*, 6, 89–107.

Pavesi, Maria. 2014. *This* and *That* in the language of film dubbing: a corpus-based analysis. *Meta*, 58(1), 103–133. <https://doi.org/10.7202/1023812ar>

Pavis, Patrice. 1989. Problems of translation for the stage: interculturalism and post-modern theatre. In Hanna Scolnicov and Peter Holland (eds) *The Play Out of Context: Transferring Plays from Culture to Culture* (pp. 25–44). Cambridge University Press.

Pérez Álvarez, Ignacio. 2003. Historia de la censura en la narrativa inglés-español de posguerra: un breve recorrido. *Interlingüística*, 14, 855–859.

Pérez L. de Heredia, María. 2001. El traductor como (auto)censor: la traducción dramática en la España franquista. In Eterio Pajares, Raquel Merino-Álvarez and José Miguel Santamaría (eds) *Transvases culturales. Literatura, cine, traducción, 3* (pp. 311–320). University of the Basque Country.

Pérez L. de Heredia, María. 2003. Las reescrituras españolas del teatro norteamericano. textos, paratextos, metatextos. In Ricardo Muñoz Martín (ed.) *Actas del I Congreso Internacional de la Asociación Ibérica de Estudios de Traducción e Interpretación* (pp. 469–493). AIETI.

Pérez L. de Heredia, María. 2004. *Traducciones censuradas de teatro norteamericano en la España de Franco (1939–1963)*. PhD thesis. University of the Basque Country.

Perteghella, Manuela. 2004. *A Descriptive Framework for Collaboration in Theatre Translation*. PhD thesis. University of East Anglia.

Perteghella, Manuela. 2008. Adaptation: 'bastard child' or critique? Putting terminology centre stage. *Journal of Romance Studies*, 8(3), 51–65. <https://doi.org/10.3828/jrs.8.3.51>

Pfister, Manfred. 1988. *The Theory and Analysis of Drama*. Cambridge University Press.

Pinter, Harold. 1967. *El amante* (L. Escobar trans.). *Primer Acto, 83*, 23–32.

Pinter, Harold. 2005b. *La fiesta de cumpleaños; La habitación; Un leve dolor; El Blanco y Negro; El examen* (R. Spregelburd trans.). Losada.

Pinter, Harold. 2006. *El montaplatos; El invernadero; Una noche de juerga* (R. Spregelburd trans.). Losada.

Pinter, Harold. 2008. *Viejos tiempos; Traición* (R. Spregelburd trans.). Losada.

Rabadán, Rosa. 1991. *Equivalencia y traducción: problemática de la equivalencia translémica inglés-español*. University of León.

Rabadán, Rosa. 2001. Las cadenas intertextuales inglés-español: traducciones y otras transferencias (inter)semióticas. In Eterio Pajares, Raquel Merino-Álvarez and José Miguel Santamaría (eds) *Trasvases culturales: Literatura, cine, traducción 3* (pp. 29–41). University of the Basque Country.

Rabadán, Rosa. 2022. Equivalence. *Enciclopedia de Traducción e Interpretación*. <www.aieti.eu/enciclopedia>

Rabadán, Rosa. 2000a. Con orden y concierto: la censura franquista y las traducciones inglés-español 1939–1985. In Rosa Rabadán (ed.) *Traducción y censura, inglés-español 1939–1985: estudio preliminar* (pp. 13–22). University of León.

Rabadán, Rosa (ed.). 2000b. *Traducción y censura, inglés-español 1939–1985: estudio preliminar*. University of León.

Rabadán, Rosa and Merino-Álvarez, Raquel. 2004. Introducción a la edición española. In Rosa Rabadán and Raquel Merino-Álvarez (trans.) *Los Estudios Descriptivos de Traducción y más allá: Metodología de la investigación en Estudios de Traducción* (pp. 17–33). Cátedra.

Ramos Pinto, Sara. 2008. Texto dramático vs texto teatral. As traduções portuguesas de *Pygmalion* de G. B. Shaw. In Maria João Brilhante and Manuela Carvalho (eds) *Theatre and Translation: Contact Stage* (pp. 189–208). Campo das Letras.

Ramos Pinto, Sara. 2012. Quando o palco e a página se encontram na tradução. In Daniela Di Pasquale and Manuela Carvalho (eds) *Depois do labirinto: teatro e tradução* (pp. 213–250). Nova Vega.

Real Decreto 262/1978, de 27 de enero, sobre libertad de representación de espectáculos teatrales (BOE 53, de 3 de marzo de 1978, pp. 5153–5154). <www.boe.es/boe/dias/1978/03/03/pdfs/A05153-05154.pdf>

Real Decreto-ley 24/1977, de 1 de abril, sobre libertad de expresión (BOE 87, de 12 de abril de 1977, pp. 7928–7929). <www.boe.es/boe/dias/1977/04/12/pdfs/A07928-07929.pdf>

Rioja Barrocal, Marta. 2008. *Traducción inglés-español y censura de textos narrativos en la España de Franco: TRACEni (1962–1969)*. PhD thesis. University of León.

Rodríguez Gago, Antonia. 2010. Staging Beckett in Spain: theatre and politics. In S. E. Gontarski (ed.) *A Companion to Samuel Beckett* (pp. 403–412). Wiley-Blackwell.

Rodríguez-Gago, Antonia. 2020a. Beckett transcultural y los "clásicos" españoles de Winnie. In José Francisco Fernández Sánchez (ed.) *Samuel Beckett en España* (pp. 15–30). University of Valladolid.

Rodríguez-Gago, Antonia. 2020b. Introducción. In Samuel Beckett, *Los días felices* (pp. 25–108). Cátedra.

Romero-Fresco, Pablo. 2009a. *A Corpus-based Study on the Naturalness of the Spanish Dubbing Language: The Analysis of Discourse Markers in the Dubbed Translation of* Friends. PhD thesis. University of Edinburgh. <http://hdl.handle.net/10399/2237>

Romero-Fresco, Pablo. 2009b. Naturalness in the Spanish dubbing language: a case of not-so-close *Friends*. *Meta*, 54(1), 49–72. <https://doi.org/10.7202/029793ar>

Romero-Fresco, Pablo. 2012. Dubbing dialogues ... Naturally: a pragmatic approach to the translation of transition markers in dubbing. *MonTI: Monografías de Traducción e Interpretación*, 4, 181–205. <http://dx.doi.org/10.6035/MonTI.2012.4.8>

RTVE. 2022. *Las brujas de Salem.* <www.rtve.es/alacarta/videos/estudio-1/estudio-1-brujas-salem/871609>

Sainz de Robles, Federico Carlos. 1950. *Teatro español 1949–1950*. Aguilar.

Sanderson, John. 2002. *Traducir el teatro de Shakespeare: figuras retóricas iterativas en Ricardo III.* University of Valencia.

Sanjurjo-González, Hugo. 2018. *Creación de un framework para el tratamiento de corpus lingüísticos.* University of León.

Santamaría, José Miguel. 2000. La traducción de obras narrativas en la España franquista: panorama preliminar. In Rosa Rabadán (ed.) *Traducción y censura inglés-español: 1939–1985. Estudio preliminar* (pp. 207–225). University of León.

Santamaría, José Miguel. 2007. Censura y género 'Western' en la época de Franco: traducciones genuinas y pseudotraducciones. In Raquel Merino-Álvarez (ed.) *Traducción y censura en España (1939–1985). Estudios sobre corpus TRACE: cine, narrativa, teatro* (pp. 105–152). University of the Basque Country.

Santoyo, Julio César. 1980. Propuesta para una sistematización del análisis diferencial de traducciones inglés-español. *Revista Española de Lingüística*, 10(1), 240–241.

Santoyo, Julio César. 1989. Traducciones y adaptaciones teatrales: Ensayo de tipología. *Cuadernos de Teatro Clásico*, 4, 95–112.

Santoyo, Julio César. 1995. Reflexiones, teoría y crítica de la traducción dramática. Panorama desde el páramo español. In Francisco Lafarga and Roberto Dengler Gassin (eds) *Teatro y traducción* (pp. 13–24). University Pompeu Fabra.

Sanz-Villar, Zuriñe and Andaluz-Pinedo, Olaia. 2021. TAligner 3.0: a tool to create parallel and multilingual corpora. In Julia Lavid-López, Carmen Maíz-Arévalo and Juan Rafael Zamorano-Mansilla (eds) *Corpora in Translation and Contrastive Research in the Digital Age: Recent Advances and Explorations* (pp. 126–146). John Benjamins.

Savirón, Estrella. 2014. *EL ZOO DE CRISTAL de Tennessee Williams.* <www.agolpedeefecto.com/teatro_2014/teatro_zoo_cristal_marso.html>

Schultze, Brigitte. 1998. Highways, byways, and blind alleys in translating drama. Historical and systematic aspects of a cultural technique. In Kurt Mueller-Vollmer and Michael Irmscher (eds) *Translating Literatures Translating Cultures New Vistas and Approaches in Literary Studies* (pp. 177–196). Stanford University Press.

Serra Porteiro, Elisa. 2015. *Performing Irishness: Translations of Irish Drama for the Galician Stage (1921–2011).* PhD thesis. University College Cork. <http://hdl.handle.net/10468/2887>

Serrano Fernández, Luis. 2003. *Traducción y censura de textos cinematográficos inglés-español 1970–1985*. PhD thesis. University of León.

Spregelburd, Rafael. 2005. Nota del traductor. In Harold Pinter, *El amante; Escuela nocturna; Sketches de revista* (pp. 7–17). Losada.

Stavinschi, Alexandra Corina. 2012. Deixis and dramatic dialogue. In Jenny Brumme and Anna Espunya (eds) *The Translation of Fictive Dialogue* (pp. 233–249). Rodopi.

Tahir-Gürçağlar, Şehnaz. 2002. What texts don't tell: the uses of paratexts in translation research. In Theo Hermans (ed.) *Crosscultural Transgressions. Research Models in Translation Studies II: Historical and Ideological Issues* (pp. 44–60). St. Jerome.

TEI Consortium. 2021. Performance Texts. *TEI P5: Guidelines for Electronic Text Encoding and Interchange* (pp. 246–271). <https://tei-c.org/release/doc/tei-p5-doc/en/Guidelines.pdf>

Teruel, Miguel, Montalt, Vincent and Ezpeleta Piorno, Pilar. 2009. Traducir a Shakespeare. La palabra del actor. *TRANS: revista de traductología*, 13, 43–55. <https://doi.org/10.24310/TRANS.2009.v0i13.3154>

Törnqvist, Egil. 2002. *El teatro en otra lengua y otro medio: estudios sobre la representación* (Marta Mateo trans.). Arco Libros.

Toury, Gideon. 1995. *Descriptive Translation Studies*. John Benjamins.

Toury, Gideon. 1997. What lies beyond descriptive translation studies? In Miguel Ángel Vega and Rafael Martín-Gaitero (eds) *La palabra vertida: investigaciones en torno a la traducción* (pp. 69–80). Editorial Complutense.

Toury, Gideon. 2004. *Los Estudios Descriptivos de Traducción y más allá: metodología de la investigación en Estudios de Traducción* (Rosa Rabadán and Raquel Merino-Álvarez trans.). Cátedra.

Toury, Gideon. 2012. *Descriptive Translation Studies – and beyond*. 2nd ed. John Benjamins.

Tymoczko, Maria. 2006. Translation: ethics, ideology, action. *The Massachusetts Review*, 47(3), 442–461.

Van den Broeck, Raymond. 1986. Translating for the theatre. *Linguistica Antwerpiensia*, 20, 96–110.

Vigara, Ana María. 1992. *Morfosintaxis del español coloquial: esbozo estilístico*. Gredos.

Vilaró, Jordi. 2017. *La recepció del teatre de Tennessee Williams a Barcelona durant el franquisme*. PhD thesis. University Autònoma of Barcelona. <http://hdl.handle.net/10803/457758>

Wellwarth, George E. 1981. Special considerations in drama translation. In Marilyn Gaddis Rose (ed.) *Translation Spectrum: Essays in Theory & Practice* (pp. 140–146). State University of New York Press.

Xiao, Richard and Yue, Ming. 2009. Using corpora in translation studies: the state of the art. In Paul Baker (ed.) *Contemporary Corpus Linguistics* (pp. 237–261). Continuum.

Zabalbeascoa, Patrick. 1999. Priorities and restrictions in translation. In Jeroen Vandaele (ed.) *Translation and the (Re)Location of Meaning* (pp. 159–167). CETRA.

Zabalbeascoa, Patrick. 2012. Translating dialogues in audiovisual fiction. In Jenny Brumme and Anna Espunya (eds) *The Translation of Fictive Dialogue* (pp. 63–78). Rodopi.

Zago, Raffaele. 2015. "That's none of your business, Sy": the pragmatics of vocatives in film dialogue. In Marta Dynel and Jan Chovanec (eds) *Participation in Public and Social Media Interactions* (pp. 183–210). John Benjamins.

Zamora, Pablo and Pavesi, Maria. 2021. El lenguaje malsonante y su traducción: comparación entre los doblajes de filmes anglófonos al italiano y al español. *Quaderns: revista de traducció*, 28, 175–195. <https://doi.org/10.5565/rev/quaderns.40>

Zuber-Skerritt, Ortrun. 1980. *The Languages of Theatre: Problems in the Translation and Transposition of Drama*. Pergamon Press.

Zuber-Skerritt, Ortrun. 1984. *Page to Stage: Theatre as Translation*. Rodopi.

Zubillaga, Naroa, Sanz-Villar, Zuriñe and Uribarri, Ibon. 2015. Building a trilingual parallel corpus to analyse literary translations from German into Basque. In Claudio Fantinuoli and Federico Zanettin (eds) *New Directions in Corpus-based Translation Studies* (pp. 71–92). Language Science Press.

Index

New Trends in Translation Studies

In today's globalised society, translation and interpreting are gaining visibility and relevance as a means to foster communication and dialogue in increasingly multicultural and multilingual environments. Practised since time immemorial, both activities have become more complex and multifaceted in recent decades, intersecting with many other disciplines. *New Trends in Translation Studies* is an international series with the main objectives of promoting the scholarly study of translation and interpreting and of functioning as a forum for the translation and interpreting research community.

This series publishes research on subjects related to multimedia translation and interpreting, in their various social roles. It is primarily intended to engage with contemporary issues surrounding the new multidimensional environments in which translation is flourishing, such as audiovisual media, the internet and emerging new media and technologies. It sets out to reflect new trends in research and in the profession, to encourage flexible methodologies and to promote interdisciplinary research ranging from the theoretical to the practical and from the applied to the pedagogical.

New Trends in Translation Studies publishes translation- and interpreting-oriented books that present high-quality scholarship in an accessible, reader-friendly manner. The series embraces a wide range of publications – monographs, edited volumes, conference proceedings and translations of works in translation studies which do not exist in English. The editor, Professor Jorge Díaz Cintas, welcomes proposals from all those interested in being involved with the series. The working language of the series is English, although in exceptional circumstances works in other languages can be considered for publication. Proposals dealing with specialised translation, translation tools and technology, audiovisual translation and the field of accessibility to the media are particularly welcomed.

Vol. 1 Meng Ji: Phraseology in Corpus-Based Translation Studies
251 pages. 2010. ISBN 978-3-03911-550-1

Vol. 2 Josu Barambones Zubiria: Mapping the Dubbing Scene: Audiovisual Translation in Basque Television
191 pages. 2012. ISBN 978-3-0343-0281-4

Vol. 3 Elisa Ghia: Subtitling Matters: New Perspectives on Subtitling and Foreign Language Learning
234 pages. 2012. ISBN 978-3-0343-0843-4

Vol. 4 Anabel Borja Albi and Fernando Prieto Ramos (eds): Legal Translation in Context: Professional Issues and Prospects
325 pages. 2013. ISBN 978-3-0343-0284-5

Vol. 5 Kieran O'Driscoll: Retranslation through the Centuries: Jules Verne in English
302 pages. 2011. ISBN 978-3-0343-0236-4

Vol. 6 Federico M. Federici (ed.): Translating Dialects and Languages of Minorities: Challenges and Solutions
245 pages. 2011. ISBN 978-3-0343-0178-7

Vol. 7 Silvia Bruti and Elena Di Giovanni (eds): Audiovisual Translation across Europe: An Ever-changing Landscape
289 pages. 2012. ISBN 978-3-0343-0953-0

Vol. 8 Tong-King Lee: Translating the Multilingual City: Cross-lingual Practices and Language Ideology
176 pages. 2013. ISBN 978-3-0343-0850-2

Vol. 9 Laura Incalcaterra McLoughlin, Marie Biscio and Máire Áine Ní Mhainnín (eds): Audiovisual Translation. Subtitles and Subtitling: Theory and Practice
301 pages. 2011. ISBN 978-3-0343-0299-9

Vol. 10 Xiaohui Yuan: Politeness and Audience Response in Chinese–English Subtitling
250 pages. 2012. ISBN 978-3-0343-0732-1

Vol. 11 Isabel García-Izquierdo and Esther Monzó (eds): Iberian Studies on Translation and Interpreting
401 pages. 2012. ISBN 978-3-0343-0815-1

Vol. 12 Claire Ellender: Preserving Polyphonies: Translating the Writings of Claude Sarraute
250 pages. 2013. ISBN 978-3-0343-0940-0

Vol. 13 Pilar Sánchez-Gijón, Olga Torres-Hostench and Bartolomé Mesa-Lao (eds): Conducting Research in Translation Technologies
329 pages. 2015. ISBN 978-3-0343-0994-3

Vol. 14 Claire Ellender: Dealing with Difference in Audiovisual Translation: Subtitling Linguistic Variation in Films
221 pages. 2015. ISBN 978-3-0343-1816-7

Vol. 15 Anna Jankowska and Agnieszka Szarkowska (eds): New Points of View on Audiovisual Translation and Media Accessibility
316 pages. 2015. ISBN 978-3-0343-1842-6

Vol. 16 Charlotte Bosseaux: Dubbing, Film and Performance: Uncanny Encounters
251 pages. 2015. ISBN 978-3-0343-0235-7

Vol. 17 Guadalupe Soriano-Barabino: Comparative Law for Legal Translators
220 pages. 2016. ISBN 978-3-0343-1725-2

Vol. 18 Şebnem Susam-Saraeva: Translation and Popular Music: Transcultural Intimacy in Turkish–Greek Relations
184 pages. 2015. ISBN 978-3-03911-887-8

Vol. 19 Celia Martín de León and Víctor González-Ruiz (eds): From the Lab to the Classroom and Back Again: Perspectives on Translation and Interpreting Training
371 pages. 2016. ISBN 978-3-0343-1985-0

Vol. 20 Carla Mereu Keating: The Politics of Dubbing: Film Censorship and State Intervention in the Translation of Foreign Cinema in Fascist Italy
191 pages. 2016. ISBN 978-3-0343-1838-9

Vol. 21 Susanne M. Cadera and Andrew Samuel Walsh (eds): Literary Retranslation in Context
252 pages. 2017. ISBN 978-3-0343-1996-6

Vol. 22 Kayoko Nohara: Translating Popular Fiction: Embracing Otherness in Japanese Translations
248 pages. 2018. ISBN 978-3-0343-1963-8

Vol. 23 Pierre-Alexis Mével: Subtitling African American English into French: Can We *Do the Right Thing*?
256 pages. 2017. ISBN 978-3-0343-1897-6

Vol. 24 Micòl Beseghi: Multilingual Films in Translation: A Sociolinguistic and Intercultural Study of Diasporic Films
256 pages. 2017. ISBN 978-1-78707-159-9

Vol. 25 Michal Borodo: Translation, Globalization and Younger Audiences: The Situation in Poland
248 pages. 2017. ISBN 978-1-78707-473-6

Vol. 26 Eugenia Dal Fovo and Paola Gentile (eds): Translation and Interpreting: Convergence, Contact and Interaction
308 pages. 2019. ISBN 978-1-78707-750-8

Vol. 27 Nana Sato-Rossberg and Akiko Uchiyama (eds): Diverse Voices in Translation Studies in East Asia
224 pages. 2019. ISBN 978-178874-022-7

Vol. 28 Sarah M. A. Reed: Translating Cultural Identity: French Translations of Australian Crime Fiction
260 pages. 2019. ISBN 978-1-78874-007-4

Vol. 29 Blanca Arias-Badia: Subtitling Television Series: A Corpus-Driven Study of Police Procedurals
274 pages. 2020. ISBN 978-1-78707-796-6

Vol. 30 Károly Polcz: Speech Acts, Directness and Politeness in Dubbing: American Television Series in Hungary
270 pages. 2020. ISBN 978-1-78874-232-0

Vol. 31 María Dolores Rodríguez Melchor, Ildikó Horváth and Kate Ferguson (eds): The Role of Technology in Conference Interpreter Training
262 pages. 2020. ISBN 978-1-78874-407-2

Vol. 32 Ali Almanna and Juan Jose Martinez Sierra (eds): Reframing Realities through Translation
300 pages. 2020. ISBN 978-1-78997-228-3

Vol. 33 Alícia Moreno Giménez: The Translation of Irony: Examining its Translatability into Narratives
262 pages. 2022. ISBN 978-1-78997-984-8

Vol. 34 Esther de Boe: Remote Interpreting in Healthcare Settings 290 pages. 2023. ISBN 978-1-80079-373-6

Vol. 35 Ali Almanna and Juliane House (eds): Translation Politicised and Politics Translated
268 pages. 2023. ISBN 978-1-80079-446-7

Vol. 36 Carmen Pena-Díaz (ed.): The Making of Accessible Audiovisual Translation
202 pages. 2023. ISBN 978-1-80079-677-5

Vol. 37 Michela Canepari: Specialized Languages and Graphic Art: Translating Specialized Discourse Intralingually and Intersemiotically
288 pages. 2023. ISBN 978-1-80079-858-8

Vol. 38 Almudena Nevado Llopis and Ana Isabel Foulquié Rubio (eds): Medical Interpreting: Training the Professionals
266 pages. 2024. ISBN 978-1-80079-321-7

Vol. 39 Martyn Gray: Making the 'Invisible' Visible?: Reviewing Translated Works
228 pages. 2024. ISBN 978-1-80374-030-0

Vol. 40 Alessandro Amenta, Natascia Barrale and Chiara Sinatra (eds): Retranslation and Socio-Cultural Changes
244 pages. 2025. ISBN 978-1-80374-306-6

Vol. 41 Arista Szu-Yu Kuo: Singlish on Screen: Subtitling Challenges and Identity Encoding in Multilingual Singapore
Forthcoming. ISBN 978-1-80079-253-1

Vol. 42 Olaia Andaluz-Pinedo: Translating English-Language Theatre into Spanish (1939–2019)
214 pages. 2025. ISBN 978-1-80079-963-9

www.ingramcontent.com/pod-product-compliance
Ingram Content Group UK Ltd.
Pitfield, Milton Keynes, MK11 3LW, UK
UKHW020159290926
15471UKWH00005B/970

9 781800 799639